Advances in Contemporary Educational Thought Series
Jonas F. Soltis, Editor

DEWEY
AND
EROS

Wisdom and Desire in the Art of Teaching

JIM GARRISON

Teachers College, Columbia University
New York and London

Published by Teachers College Press, 1234 Amsterdam Avenue, New York, NY 10027

Library of Congress Cataloging-in-Publication Data

Garrison, James W., 1949–
    Dewey and eros : wisdom and desire in the art of teaching / James W. Garrison.
        p.   cm. — (Advances in contemporary educational thought series ; v. 19)
    Includes bibliographical references (p.   ) and index.
    ISBN 0-8077-3625-2 (cloth). — ISBN 0-8077-3624-4 (pbk.)
    1. Teaching—Philosophy.   2. Reasoning.   3. Moral education.
    4. Dewey, John, 1859–1952.   5. Education—Philosophy.   I. Title.
    II. Series.
    LB1025.3.G378   1997
    371.102'09—dc21   96-48450

ISBN 0-8077-3624-4 (paper)
ISBN 0-8077-3625-2 (cloth)

Printed on acid-free paper
Manufactured in the United States of America

04 03 02 01 00 99 98 97   8 7 6 5 4 3 2 1

To KSL, whose elusiveness taught me that though love is for our growth it must also be for our pruning.

Contents

Foreword

In recent years, there has been a growing renewal of interest in John Dewey's philosophy. Although many educational researchers and scholars today quote Dewey with favor, some still make him out to be the cause of all evil in education, and few—if any—seem to connect Dewey's philosophy with the growing interest in the qualitative study of teaching and teachers' reflections on their own practice. In this book, Jim Garrison boldly makes the connection and brings a passionate and perceptive interpretation of Dewey's philosophy of education to bear upon the ways teachers feel, think, and act in the everyday world of practice.

The guiding force of good teaching, Garrison tells us, is erōs, the passionate desire to attain or do good. He takes us back to the ancient Greeks, to recover their language and understanding of erōs, technē, and poiesis; of passion, of skillful art, and creative imagination. He uses this language to display what wisdom in teaching and in every day life is all about. Qualitative researchers and teacher researchers would do well to learn this language. It provides wonderful insights into wise practice.

Garrison also uses this language to bring us a new and deeper understanding of Dewey's concepts of growth, reflective thinking, practical reasoning, aesthetic experience, moral perception, and practical inquiry. Unlike the more frequently found mechanical accounts, Garrison emphasizes the aesthetic and moral dimensions of Dewey's instrumental philosophy as he explicates the means–ends, practical reasoning, and logic-in-use of passionate and engaged practitioners. He argues that the best way to improve teaching is to cultivate wisdom in practice. To this end, he urges teachers to be sympathetic and caring, imaginative and creative, and morally perceptive.

In Garrison's reconstruction of Dewey's philosophy of education, Dewey's moral theory and aesthetics get recast into a foundational role. Dewey's aesthetics become the groundwork for understanding living examples of practical inquiry. One dominant version of Dewey's description of intelligent inquiry is the cool, scientific, logical one: of five linear steps—from doubt, problem, data, hypothesis, test—to solution. Garrison gives us a different and warmer interpretation of feeling, desire, and the human need to deal with one's perceived disequilibrium by engaging imaginatively and creatively to resolve the situation, thereby restoring one's sense of equilibrium and finding satisfaction.

This is a poetic, and not a scientific, view of problem solving that should speak intimately to both the teacher and the qualitative researcher. Garrison further explores and explicates this version of practical inquiry by using the ideas of narrative, cultural scripts, and the social construction of reality. He also uses apt examples from literature and extended case studies of teachers and students in classrooms to display in practice the key ideas of imagination, creativity, sensitivity, moral perception, and wisdom.

This is a book that recasts and unveils new insights into Dewey's philosophy and speaks to the high purposes of teaching and educating. It is truly an advance in contemporary educational thought and builds on the rich and sometimes hidden and overlooked ideas of America's greatest philosopher of education, John Dewey.

Jonas F. Soltis
Series Editor

Acknowledgments

I would like gratefully to acknowledge the many people who have read parts of this manuscript and have offered many helpful suggestions. They include Lynn Bustle, Michelle Griffith, Gary Haynes, Ethyl Houghton, Stephanie Kimball, Tim Lensmire, Rob Lockhart, Julie Meltzer, Leslie Murrill, Kim Oliver, Suzanne Reid, Liz Roth, Delia Shargel, Manny Shargel, Mia Shargel, and Tammie Smith. Special thanks to Linda Pacifici and Pam Simpson for allowing me to use their ideas, their stories, and the papers we published and presented. Their influence can be found throughout. Thanks also to Bev Strager for allowing me into her class and for providing many examples of the everyday practical wisdom of teaching. I am grateful to Ray E. Van Dyke for demonstrating to me what a devoted principal can do to help students and teachers.

I would also like to acknowledge the following students in my philosophy of education course in the spring of 1996 who read a preliminary draft of this manuscript and offered many valuable criticisms: John E. Adams, Liz Altieri, Debbie Colley, Dan Dunlap, Inez Giles, Monique Granville, Jutta Green, Yolanda Hegngi, Barry Keith, Lisa Nienkark, Paul Okafor, Cathy Stower, Archie Tinelli, Carmel Vaccare, David Warner, and David Wiley Williams. I am grateful to Judi M. Lynch, Elaine I. O'Quinn, Stacy Zell, and Barbara J. Reeves for providing much needed proofreading on several preliminary drafts. Elaine provided several useful examples and Barbara provided detailed scholarly critique.

I thank the following journals for permitting me to make substantial use of papers previously published: *The Alan Review, The American Journal of Education, Qualitative Studies in Education,* and *Teachers College Record.* The many anonymous reviewers of these journals indirectly contributed a great deal to improving this book. I would also like to acknowledge Atheneum Publishers for allowing me to cite long passages from Cynthia Voigt's lovely book, *Jackaroo.* Similarly, I thank Southern Illinois University Press for allowing such extensive citations from the works of John Dewey. The reviewers of the manuscript for Teachers College Press provided thoughtful commentary. I would like to express special appreciation to Jonas F. Soltis, editorial consultant, Teachers College Press, for many helpful comments.

Introduction

For in its ethical sense, love signifies completeness of devotion to objects esteemed good.
—Dewey, 1932/1985b, p. 259

We become what we love. Our destiny is in our desires, yet what we seek to possess soon comes to possess us in thought, feeling, and action. That is why the ancient Greeks made the education of *erōs,* or passionate desire, the supreme aim of education. They thought it necessary to educate erōs to desire the good. The result of such an education is practical wisdom, the ability to distinguish between what we immediately desire and what proves truly desirable after reflection. Values are objects of desire. The education of erōs *is* values education. Wisdom allows us to recognize what is authentically good or valuable for ourselves and others.

I would like to renew the ancient conversation about educating erōs to desire the good. The modern age has almost lost the ability to talk passionately about the passions, about beauty, or about the good. Our bureaucratic world desperately needs reenchantment, and our technocratically controlled schools are no exception. When the Greek philosopher Plato discussed the education of erōs, he spoke of prophecy, poetry, and *daimōns* (the guardians of our destiny), among many other marvelous things. Unfortunately, he gave them an elitist sense by connecting them with the idea of philosopher kings. I want to recover this remarkable way of talking about education and then modify it for use in a modern democratic society. The first chapter is devoted to recovering and reconstructing Platonic wisdom regarding the education of erōs. My ultimate goal in this book, however, is to use this reconstruction to help us better understand teaching for the loving, vigorous, and logical vocation that it is.

I believe that the education of erōs should be the supreme aim of teacher education, whether it be preservice, in-service, or, most importantly, the wisdom that arises from reflecting on the daily activities of classroom teaching. Good teachers passionately desire the good for their students. Practical wisdom, or what the Greeks called *phronesis*, allows teachers to recognize what is authentically good for their students and themselves. The ancient Greeks, though, do not seem to have recognized the double difficulty of educating the erōs of teachers. The greatest good of teaching is self-transcending, because good teachers desire what is best for their students. Teachers desire to educate the erōs of their students to passionately desire what is truly good. That is the double difficulty. There is a way out of this difficulty, but it lies beyond love understood as erōs alone. What is wrong with erōs is that it is a possessive form of love. Teaching involves *bestowing* value on others. Loving bestowal is what is missing from the ancient Greek ideal of education.

Good teachers passionately desire to bestow enduring value on their students. Recognizing this leads us out of the double difficulty, although it is a narrow road to travel. There are rocky shoals on either side. We must neither slip into self-deception by believing that what is good for ourselves is good for everyone nor fall into destructive self-sacrifice. Emotions such as sympathy involve seeing the thoughts, needs, and desires of others as similar to our own; yet, in many ways that are significant to teaching, sympathy can suppress substantial differences. Sometimes sympathy is condescension or domination cloaked as an offer to help. Conversely, many expect teachers to be self-sacrificing and to ignore their own needs, desires, and dreams. Self-transcending, expansive growth through sympathy, care, and community allows us to stay safely in the center. Mapping the middle passage is the task of the second chapter.

Teachers need to be needed. In Chapter 2 I suggest that this is true of all those seeking growth through expansive relationships. This stance allows us to identify a number of other paradoxes involved in navigating the main channel. For instance, I feel that to care for others we must learn to care for ourselves and to care for ourselves we must learn to care for others. This includes letting others care for us. Further, I believe that to bestow enduring value on their students, teachers must bestow value on themselves and to bestow value on themselves, teachers must bestow enduring value on their students. This includes allowing students or colleagues, directly, and the virtues of good practice, indirectly, to bestow value on us. I think that teaching is a caring profession and that the ethics of care, as opposed to the ethics of rules and justice, is full of such paradoxes, all of which stem from a common root. Everyone is a mixture of the actual and the potential. Who we actually already are actualizes the potential of others, and who they actually already are actualizes our potential. Understanding these elusive transactions allows us to appreciate the paradoxical structure of the teacher–student relationship. In Chapter 3 I illustrate this idea, as I have done for many years in my own teacher education classes, by playing with Play-Doh, a modeling compound that many are familiar with. The transactions between the student artist and the modeling compound they are attempting to mold resemble the transactions between teacher and student in many surprising ways. Teaching is a creative calling; it is poetry in the archaic Greek sense of *poiēsis*, that is, "calling something into existence." This sense of poetry allows us to better understand the aesthetic dimensions of teaching.

Bestowing value on our students, I argue, is a creative activity that involves helping them actualize their best possibilities. Sometimes it requires creating things that have never appeared before. Following the philosopher John Dewey, I call these "ethereal things." I want to show that such original creativity is a commonplace of good teaching. Perhaps the two most prominent goals held by those who answer the call to teach are (1) creative self-expression and (2) connecting with students and helping them learn. In Chapter 3 I build on the insights of the first two chapters to show why this is so. There we begin to see the intimate relation between creative imagination, passion, and logic. The ancients knew this relation well—that is one reason why the education of erōs was so significant to them—but we moderns have long since lost sight of it.

One reason so many overlook the aesthetic dimension of logic is that it lies hidden in the background of inquiry. Most people assume that there is a chasm between creative and rational thinking that cannot be bridged. Chapter 4 shows that this is false. All thinking occurs in problematic contexts where something is not right and we are, therefore, in a state of need. If we can imagine what is missing, then we can frame a hypothesis about what we require. This hypothesis then becomes an object of desire. Next there is inquiry, the goal of which is to secure the object of our desire, satisfy our need, and resolve the conflict. Need, desire, and selective interest are part of the background of any inquiry; so, too, is creative imagination.

Inquiry, I will show, is the creative activity of transforming needful situations into more desirable circumstances. Examining the teachable moment will help illustrate this claim. The teachable moment occurs when teachers and students engage in meaningful inquiry regarding some problematic situation involving themselves and the subject matter being taught. It is here that teaching, loving, and logic clearly begin to come together. On such occasions teacher and students share needs, desires, and interests, as well as imaginatively engage in shared creative inquiry. I will discuss one such moment, related to me by Linda Pacifici, that occurred when she was teaching Susan Cooper's (1973) *The Dark Is Rising*. The moment involves this paradoxical passage: "The snow lay thin and apologetic over the world" (p. 3). How can snow lay apologetically over the world? Why would a writer use such a combination of words? What images does it create? Such questions initiate the foreground of inquiry for those who feel the background need and desire to understand what things mean. Answering such questions requires imagination and creativity, and there is no one right answer. I think that the teachable moment arises when everyone in the class desires to explore possibilities together.

Not all possibilities are equally desirable. Determining the difference between possibilities that one immediately desires and those that are genuinely desirable is the very essence of educating erōs. Values education understood as the education of erōs is the topic of Chapter 5. Part of the answer to the enigma of how to educate erōs is that teachers must teach students the techniques of rational deliberation. Rational *criticism* is the modern answer to the question: How should we educate the passions? Paradoxically, it assumes a dispassionate logic free from the influence of adventitious imagination. Once it is recognized that inquiry is contextual and involves needs, desires, and imagination, it becomes clear that the foreground of inquiry cannot be separated from the background. The moderns cannot be entirely correct.

Overcoming the modern prejudice against emotion and imagination in value inquiry is only part of the answer to the problem of values education. It allows us to choose intelligently among existing value alternatives. But what if those things that are most truly desirable, given our needs and potentials, are not among the specified set of alternatives? Oppression often consists in being assigned false choices, that is, choices among alternatives specified by others that do not necessarily have our best interests at heart. The curriculum for the complete education of erōs involves teaching how to *create* value alternatives. The education of erōs should be both critical and creative. More than that, it means teachers must be prophetic and poetic.

By prophecy I mean naming the values needed in needful times. It involves poetry because we must imagine what is absent yet present in our need. Poetry is also required to call what is needed into existence. I will rely on Cynthia Voigt's (1985) romance *Jackaroo* to illustrate the importance of poetry and prophecy to the education of erōs. On first picking up this novel, one might expect a typical young women's romance, and in a sense one would be right. In another sense, however, the novel is a defiant challenge to conventional social constructions of gender and social class. The young heroine, Gwyn, challenges these constructions by assuming the mantle of the outlaw Jackaroo, a Robin Hood–like character. Role models educate erōs by presenting personas of persons that students might desire to become. Outlaws represent possibilities beyond the bounds, and perhaps the bondage, of the actual. I conclude Chapter 5 by suggesting that where oppressors write the laws, educating erōs for freedom may mean going beyond conventional good and evil. Teachers, too, must sometimes act like outlaws. They sometimes choose to break rules rather than students. That is another one of the paradoxes of pursuing the ethics of care rather than that of justice and rules.

To fulfill the obligations of a caring profession, to bestow value on students by educating erōs, teachers must recognize their students' unique, individual needs, desires, interests, dreams, and best future possibilities. I call such recognition "moral perception." Moral perception, which is the topic of Chapter 6, involves sympathy and imagination. I illustrate moral perception by reflecting on some of the predicaments that arose in a special education placement shared with me by Pam Simpson, a participant researcher who may, perhaps, have broken the rules of good research. The tension lies between Pam's perception of Tony Mitchell's ability based on what he could do in various practical contexts and the result of a battery of pencil-and-paper tests that labeled him as needing special education placement.

Throughout this book I argue for an intimate connection among teaching, loving, and logic. There is a concealed connection between loving and logic that guides practical reasoning of all kinds, including the kind of reasoning teachers engage in to intelligently guide their practice. Many distinguish pure reasoning from practical reasoning. My concern is with practical reasoning. Pure reasoning, such as mathematical proof, is supposedly deductive and self-enclosed. Rather than creating things, pure reasoning strives to discover what already exists. Presumably it describes purely abstract and formal relations apart from whether anything really participates in them. There is nothing in the conclusion that is not already in the premises. If no mistakes are made in constructing inferences from the premises, the conclusion must be true if the premises are true. Pure rationality secures its claims to certainty at the cost of all material content. It is lifeless—and useless to teachers.

Practical reasoning, by contrast, concerns itself with the material conditions of daily life, and it therefore abandons the quest for certainty. While in pure reasoning we concern ourselves with inferences from premises to conclusion, practical reasoning is means–ends reasoning. We seek means for securing the ends we desire to obtain. The means may constitute the end upon completion, just as the wood, nails, and bricks that are the means of building a house come to constitute the finished construction. Unlike pure reasoning, practical reasoning can be productive, creative, and full of life.

I want to disclose the mysteries of practical reasoning. The eventual goal is an understanding of the practical wisdom, or what the Greeks called phrōnesis, inherent in good teaching. It will be a difficult journey. Practical reasoning has an intelligent logical pattern, though. We may use this pattern to chart our course. Aristotle first expressed the general structure of this pattern over 2,300 years ago. The formal skeleton of practical reasoning, or practical deliberation as Aristotle called it, is introduced below, but it will take this entire book to give it body, breath, and passion (including compassion). The formal schema of practical reason is shown in Figure I.1.

Please begin by noting the ideas in the left-hand column. Everyday intuitions about desire, deliberation, perception, choice, and action say that you already know a great deal about practical means–ends reasoning. That should come as no surprise. Obtaining the valuable things one desires requires engaging in well-formulated practical reasoning every day. Trust your intuitions as you read this book and the right-hand column will eventually clarify itself.

To fully disclose the hidden connection between love and logic, it is necessary to eventually comprehend this formal abstract symbolism. The major premise of practical reasoning declares that there is some good, some value, that the practical reasoner seeks to secure. Formally the major premise of practical reasoning reads: ''I desire V.'' Here ''I''

FIGURE I.1. *The schema of practical reasoning (adapted from Ross, 1971, p. 199).*

Desire	I desire V.
Deliberation	U is the means to V. T is the means to U. N is the means to O.
Perception *Choice* *Action*	N is something I can do here and now. I choose N. I do N.

refers to a flesh-and-blood person, the practitioner, you or me, while "V" is something the practitioner values, the object of passionate desire. Now look carefully, because it is hidden in the middle of the major premise of practical deliberation. Patiently, it has waited over 2,300 years for us to notice it. What is this thing that every teacher intuitively understands lies in the middle of everyday practice yet is missing from almost all theory and research on teaching? It is loving, life-affirming passionate "desire," or erōs. Erōs is the most basic type of love. All practical reasoning is about obtaining values we desire. It is the kind of reasoning that practitioners such as teachers use every day to obtain the results they value. It is the kindling that fires their other professional passions.

There is a strange and unnatural silence in theory and research on teaching. The vocabulary of practical reasoning is largely missing. There is not much moral and even less aesthetic conversation about teaching because it is difficult to research feelings. Researchers say little about deliberation, choice, and action. They say nothing about moral perception or desire. Theorists and researchers rarely talk about teaching in the vocabulary teachers themselves use to describe their practice. This may help explain the difficulty of translating theory into practice. There is one modern philosopher of education who rejected the dualism of theory and practice, insisting instead that all reasoning is practical reasoning. Fortunately, we will not have to rely solely on ancient wisdom.

John Dewey, the most prominent philosopher of education in the twentieth century, has already done an immense amount of work on the topics of practical wisdom, practical reasoning, and the education of erōs. Most educators, philosophers of education included, think the field has closed the book on Dewey's pragmatic philosophy. Occasionally they pull *Democracy and Education* off the shelf to reference Dewey's work as a prototypical instance of liberal progressivism, someone to praise or condemn depending on their political preference. Few want to employ Dewey's philosophy to clear new trails for educational inquiry, but that is my intention. Educators have ignored the extensive body of new scholarship on Dewey that has emerged in recent years.[1]

The new scholarship has opened two novel avenues of inquiry into Deweyan thought. Many of the new scholars have called attention to Dewey's aesthetics. Some even suggest that it is the unifying theme of his entire philosophy.[2] Meanwhile, growing numbers of neopragmatist feminists have written approvingly about Dewey, even as they reconstruct him to fit their various feminist projects.[3] Their work helps make Dewey's philosophy more relevant for our times. Dewey advocated the continuous reconstruction of ideas to meet the needs and purposes of an ever-changing world and would have commended the same attitude toward his own thought.

This book investigates practical wisdom, practical reasoning, and the education at the crossroads where the two new avenues of scholarship on Dewey meet. I want to reveal something thus far overlooked by Deweyan scholars old and new. Dewey held a consistent, although constrained, philosophy of love that laced together the threads of his educational thinking. It is not possible to comprehend his philosophy of education without appreciating his hidden philosophy of love.

Practical wisdom was the warp upon which Dewey strung the woof of love and logic. It is imperative to perceive with compassion, creative imagination, and discerning deliberation. Only then will the ethical, aesthetic, and cognitive threads of vital experience draw tightly together to yield the whole fabric of life, not just shreds. As with the ancient Greeks, Dewey understood the intimate relations among practical wisdom, loving, and logic. Modernity has lost the weave, and we must now strive to rethread the tapestry.

Good teaching requires a complete philosophy because it involves the three great questions of life: What is life (or teaching)? How should we live (or teach)? What does life (or teaching) mean? By obtaining practical wisdom about teaching, it becomes possible to understand why Dewey (1916/1980a) would write, "If we are willing to conceive education as the process of forming fundamental dispositions, intellectual and emotional, toward nature and fellow-men, philosophy may even be defined *as the general theory of education*" (p. 338). Dewey developed philosophy *as* education rather than just a philosophy of education. Recalling the etymology of the word *philosophy* allows us to feel the full impact of this claim. *Philosophy* derives from the ancient Greek *philein* ("to love") and *sophia* ("wisdom"). Philosophers are lovers of wisdom; that is what they passionately desire. This means that they love to learn well and teach logically, and they realize that the two activities must occur together. I believe that restoring the ancient vocabulary can liberate meanings overgrown and hidden from the modern, or so-called postmodern, mind. In seeking wisdom I use ancient implements to clear a path.

DEWEY
AND
EROS

Wisdom and Desire
in the Art of Teaching

CHAPTER 1

Plato's Symposium: Erōs, the Beautiful, and the Good

A self changes its structure and its value according to the kind of object which it desires and seeks; according, that is, to the different kinds of objects in which active interests is taken.

—*Dewey, 1932/1985b, p. 296*

Love begins in need and lack. Everyone passionately desires to possess what is good, or at least what they perceive as good, and to live a life of ever-expanding meaning and value. The Deweyan philosopher Thomas M. Alexander (1993) calls this the "human erōs." Sound practice translates desire into satisfaction. It is for the sake of the perceived good that practitioners strive to perfect their practice. What they seek, however, soon comes to possess them and eventually becomes the content of their character.

The teaching erōs is an overflowing love that is giving and caring. That teachers desire to serve, to make the good of others their good and the object of their practice, complicates the usual understanding of erōs as passionate desire for possession of what it values. It bestows value on those to whom it attends. Bestowing value on others is the greatest good of a caring vocation such as teaching. Those that strive to love wisely, and persist in the pursuit, may become wise. In teaching such wisdom is practical wisdom (phrōnesis), and those possessed of it excel at practical logic.

Teaching success depends on our wisdom about the ways of love. Wisdom, though, is beyond knowledge. For even if someone had complete knowledge of the world as it actually is, even if that person could complete the mistaken quest for absolute certainty, the moral questions would remain: What should I do? How ought I respond to this student's aggressive need for attention? Should schools mainstream special-needs children? Should teachers teach for the test using worksheets or trust reading and writing workshops? Suppose a teacher is using reflective journals in a fourth-grade class and one of the students explicitly and in detail describes sexual abuse (see McCarthy, 1994)? She is reasonably sure about what she sees. Years of teaching tell her that children at this age are not ordinarily able to describe such things. She knows the way it is, but what should she do? Answering such questions requires practical wisdom.

A good education brings out the best in us. It holistically unifies our character in judgment, compassion, and practice. It disciplines our desires to serve the greatest good, that is, those persons, things, and ideals that are of most value. Traditionally philosophers, the lovers of wisdom, have received the education beyond knowledge. Looking at contemporary educational curricula, however, it appears that almost all the subjects and objectives are cognitive and intellectual. Moral education is restricted to precepts and rules, while values education, if it has an explicit place in the school at all, probably just teaches students how to calculate their utilities. Aesthetic education is almost unheard of, and passionate desire is entirely ignored.

I want to reclaim the ancient wisdom that emphasized aesthetics and morality in the education of erōs. I also want to efface the remote, abstract, and elitist sense given to philosophy by Plato when he spoke of "philosopher kings." With Dewey, I insist that there is no theory-versus-practice dualism, all reasoning is practical reasoning, and everyone should be a lover of wisdom. Regrettably, the elite rule of philosopher kings continues today in many quarters in the guise of detached theoretical and technocratic experts. These influential few frequently regard themselves as potentates of prescribed practice and consider teachers lowly practitioners appropriately subservient to their will.

It is time to reawaken the ancient conversation about teaching our passions to desire the good. To see the false dichotomy between theory and practice requires talking about the education of erōs, or passionate desire. It is crucial to recover erōs as a creative, poetic force that eventually provides the content of our character. Fully comprehending teaching requires grasping the role of prophecy in educating erōs. Sadly, the ancient conversation about poetry, prophecy, and the education of erōs has been almost totally forgotten. It is time to break the silence and recover the relationship between love and logic. These meditations may seem untimely, but they are essential to a richer understanding of teaching. I want to call the past into a present that promises a better future.

PLATO'S *SYMPOSIUM*: DIOTIMA THE
MANTINEAN AND DAIMŌNS

One of Plato's most influential dialogues is the *Symposium*. It is the origin of refined thinking about love in the Western philosophical tradition, and its themes have persisted in the West for more than 2,300 years. Dewey's philosophy of erōs and education disagrees with Plato's in almost every detail. Still, they both discussed topics essential to an expanded understanding of teaching. I accept Plato's themes and topics; later I provide a Deweyan critique and reconstruction.

Plato's task in the *Symposium* was to explain the significance of erōs to the lover of wisdom. There are six speakers who offer various accounts of love. Socrates follows Agathon, the dramatic poet whose name means "the good." Agathon gives "a lovely speech" but fails because he describes the object of love, the lovable, but not love. Agathon seeks only to give a beautiful speech. He does not sincerely care to contemplate the true or the good. Plato felt such failures typical of artists, even those concerned with the good, because at best they could merely imitate reality; only philosophers could know it. This attitude led Plato in the *Republic* to recommend censoring artists.

Plato believed that the arts, including the arts of public speaking, should be edifying. They should be aesthetically beautiful and morally good, yet truth is beyond them. Truth is the province of the philosopher kings. Plato's politics were not democratic. Socrates leads Agathon to understand first that erōs "is always the love of something, and second, that something is what he lacks" (*Symposium*, 201e). Socrates then states that he will leave Agathon "in peace, because I want to talk about some lessons I was given . . . by a Mantinean woman called Diotima" (201d).

Diotima begins by teaching Socrates that erōs is one of the daimōns. In ancient Greek religion daimōns were a kind of personality midway between humankind and the gods. They acted as intermediaries between heaven and earth, taking prayers up and bringing down rewards and commands. The Greeks also believed that at birth a daimōn seizes each of us, determining our unique individual potential and mediating between us and our best possible destiny. Plato gave the idea of daimōns philosophical meaning; but though concealed, the religious sense remained.

Let us pause to note something important about Diotima herself. As her name suggests (it means "cherished by God"), she was a prophet. For Plato, the gods called prophets to do their bidding. Diotima was herself, therefore, among the mediating daimōns. Rosen (1968/1987) describes the connection:

> Philosophy, as the pursuit or love of knowledge, is ignorance [i.e., a *lack* of knowledge]. . . . Prophecy is that aspect of the divine madness which allows us to surmise what we seek to know. The disjunction between intuition and discursive reason is bridged by the mantic [prophetic] art. (p. 207)

Prophecy provides the intuitions (e.g., hypotheses) necessary to initiate inquiry of all kinds. Prophetic art provides a vision of values in needful times. When Martin Luther King, Jr., said he had a dream of a racially integrated and harmonious society, he obviously was not making a statement of known fact. He was naming a need, a wound in the body politic. He was addressing a possible value into which the people should inquire and perhaps engage in practical reasoning to actualize. Prophecy is that part of poetry that provides a vision of possibilities worthy of our creative efforts. It mediates between vague intuitions and the analytic rigor of discursive either/or reasoning.

Rosen (1968/1987) suggests that for Plato erōs served as a "harmony of opposites" (p. 199). Plato comprehended erōs as an intermediary between emotional intuition and its presumed opposite, reason. I want to explore Diotima's teaching further since she helps us to understand the role of erōs in the logic of contraries and the mediation of apparent opposites. Diotima the prophet taught Socrates that "there is a mean between wisdom and ignorance" (*Symposium*, 202a). It is impossible for inquiry to pass between these two opposites without mediation.

THE MENO PARADOX AND PLATONIC
METAPHYSICS: BEYOND THE LOGIC OF EITHER/OR

Diotima sees that Socrates is ignorant of intermediaries. As with most of us, the excessively simplistic logic of either/or has captivated him. Statements such as "Tony is *or* is not learning disabled" are instances of the "law of the excluded middle" (formally, A *or* not A). Such abstract, purely logical statements are supposedly necessarily and eternally true prior to any experience. Similarly, "Tony is *and* is not learning disabled" is an instance of the "principle of noncontradiction" (formally, A *and* not A). Such statements are supposedly necessarily and eternally false prior to any experience. Such abstract, analytic, and theoretical logic leaves no room for the vague, indeterminate, or changeable. It does not accommodate growth, becoming, development, or most of the facts of our daily lives. It is the wrong logic for the practice of teaching.

The context of teaching is always vague, inexact, and changing. The classroom is not the same in the fall as it is in the spring, or in the morning as it is in the afternoon. Students' and teachers' moods change throughout the day. Students become and cease being discipline problems, but exactly when it is sometimes difficult to say. The effect of our teaching frequently cannot be determined. We may have taught well, but the results will not reveal themselves until next year in Mr. Robb's class. Above all, students grow. If they did not, then there would be no reason to teach.

Many bureaucratic mandates are cookie-cutter rules. Students either are *or* are not in some category such as gifted, average, or special-needs. That is the Platonic legacy for our times. Perfectly precise, this cookie-cutter logic can block our ability to perceive our students' unique needs as well as to respond appropriately for the sake of their future. Teachers may act like daimōns mediating between students' present needs and their future good, but technocratic either/or logic sometimes interferes.

Learning is a process of growth and change. Some learning, such as learning through self-initiated inquiry, caused Plato special problems in the dialogue called the *Meno*. There he set out the Meno paradox: It is impossible to learn anything through inquiry. Why? Because either you already know the thing sought, so there is no need to inquire, *or* you have no knowledge whatsoever and therefore would never recognize it. This paradox results from either/or thinking. It does not allow for coming to know. Plato took it very seriously. His solution was metaphysical and epistemological: He asserted a theory of recollection. This theory presumed that before birth everyone caught a brief glimpse of what he called the immutable and eternal Forms. For him learning just meant recollecting the Forms.

Plato believed that theoretical wisdom (thēoria) is knowledge about these metaphysical verities that he called Forms. The Forms are abstract and indubitable supernatural entities, existing outside space and time and therefore unchangeable. For Plato, everyday things located in space and time, hence subject to the vicissitudes of change and fortune, are but contingent and imperfect copies of the perfect Forms of true reality. For example, a circle drawn freehand on the chalkboard, or even a protractor, is only an imperfect copy of the abstract perfect circle represented mathematically by $x^2 + y^2 = r^2$. The line of this ideal circle, unlike the drawn material circle, has no width, breadth, or depth. The perfect circle is a rational Form, Idea, or Ideal that is unknowable empirically. For Plato all knowledge is of the entirely abstract, immutable, indubitable, and eternally fixed Forms. All the rest is just opinions about things in the empirical world of space and time copied from the Forms. Plato placed a supreme harmonizing principle—the Good—above the Forms. By harmoniously structuring the Forms, "the Good" not only guarantees that reality is rational, it also assures that reality is an aesthetic and moral order. For Plato, indubitable knowledge of the Forms (and above all "the Good") is the source of timeless wisdom. Through a variety of expressions, the metaphysic of Platonic supernaturalism exercises an immense influence on Western thought.

There is, however, a natural alternative to Platonism for those who prefer to live in this imperfect world of becoming rather than the perfect world of Being. Instead of appealing to supernatural Forms, let us simply use our mortal imagination to construct hypotheses from our background knowledge and use them to initiate and continue the inquiry. Hypotheses are testable and may be refined in everyday practice. Imagination is another daimōn. Inquiry mediates between our ignorance and our coming to know. Thus knowledge is born into the world. Moral inquiry can carry us beyond knowledge of some actual state of affairs and aid us in securing others that *ought* to exist. Such inquiry requires moral vision of possible values. Moral vision is, therefore, a product of moral imagination. The either/or logic of Plato and his modern-day descendants, however, does not allow for becoming or being born. Indeed, Plato claimed that becoming or change is illusory. The dream of a perfect realm apart from the messy changeable world of everyday practice has been the persistent illusion of those would-be theoretical kings who seek to complete the quest for the certain, fixed, and final knowledge.

Plato's idea of erōs as a daimōn is a valuable one, though. The desire for a better world drives us from where we are to where we ought to be. Eventually, I want to take Diotima's specific supernaturalistic teaching less literally and the idea of daimōns, genesis, and becoming more seriously and naturalistically. To practitioners the logic of mediating contraries is often more useful than the logic of either/or. Teachers know that children are constantly changing and growing.

THE MYTH OF ERŌS' BIRTH: GENESIS AND COMING TO BE

Erōs is a mediating daimōn existing midway between being and not being. It defies the law of noncontradiction. Erōs is a principle of genesis, birth, and becoming. Becoming and development are intermediate between being and not being. I will return to further discussion of Diotima's teaching about creation, genesis, and coming into existence. First, though, I want to consider her mythological account of the birth of erōs.

As with any myth, Plato meant Diotima's story to be good for us, beautiful to listen to, and conducive to right opinion. When Plato censored myths (poetry, prophecy, and art) in the *Republic*, he did so if they violated any of these three criteria. Only philosopher kings can censor, for only they know *the* truth.

According to the myth Diotima tells, erōs is the son of Poros and Penia. *Poros* means "plenty," "way," "method," "craft," or "skill." The myth associates the minor Olympian deity Poros with the virtues of practical ability. Penia was unattractive, poor, and homeless. When Aphrodite, goddess of beauty, was born, the Olympian Gods feasted. Drunk from too much nectar, Poros falls asleep in the garden of Zeus. In a scheme to overcome her poverty, Penia contrived to lie down beside Poros, and together they conceive erōs (*Symposium*, 203b–c). Erōs' conception occurred in the excesses of intoxication, a kind of madness. If Diotima is right, conception and birth require the mediation of passionate desire. Erōs, the product of the union of Poros and Penia, helps unite opposites. For all his energy, power, and force, he is needful, homeless, and lacking all beauty—but he is very resourceful, crafty, and clever. Foolish, he is nonetheless full of practical skill. If the values that sustain his conduct were good, he would be wise. Erōs needs educating. By nature he is neither moral *nor* immoral, wise *nor* ignorant. He quickly wastes what he acquires, but he swiftly regains what he needs. He is thus neither rich *nor* poor. It is impossible to fully explain his nature using analytic either/or logic. Erōs is a powerful and paradoxical passion that mediates a multitude of opposites and brings people together.

ERŌS, THE BEAUTIFUL, AND THE GOOD: THE TRUE SENSE OF POETRY

Socrates wonders, "What good can Love [erōs] be to humanity?" Diotima teaches him that although individuals desire to possess the beautiful, it is what the beautiful brings that they really want; what they truly desire is the happiness that possessing the good brings. Diotima concludes, "For Love, that renowned and all beguiling power, includes every kind of longing for happiness and for the good" (*Symposium*, 205d). Humanity loves beauty because it helps bring them the good, or at least what they perceive as the good. Diotima teaches that erōs is itself formless and without order or logic. Beauty, or at least what is taken for beauty, shapes and guides erōs. In many ways the beautiful for Plato is identical with aesthetic harmony.

Beauty unifies and structures the practical context in such a way as to secure the desired good. For example, a good scheme of classroom discipline that restores and maintains order without stifling student creativity is "beautiful" to a teacher exhausted by a particularly unruly class. Earlier Diotima taught Socrates that erōs "is the mediator who spans the chasm which divides . . . therefore by him the universe is bound together" (*Symposium*, 202d). If Diotima is correct, erōs is the principle that unifies opposites, such as need and fulfillment, throughout the cosmos. Chaotic, formless erōs requires containment. The beautiful harmonizes erōs and conducts it intelligently toward the good. Desiring better classroom conditions is not enough. Overcoming chaos requires a vision of a value that resolves the dilemma. It also requires sound practical reasoning to secure the desired value. Passionate desire, though, mediates between the initial actual situation and the outcome that is sought.

What comes next in the conversation between Socrates and Diotima is stunning. Everyone desires what they take (or mistake) for the good. Diotima wants to show that all kinds of love are a desire for the good. Diotima concludes that "all desire of good and happiness is only the great and subtle power of love; but they who are drawn towards him by any other path, whether the path of money-making or gymnastics or philosophy are called lovers—the name of the whole is appropriated to those whose desires take one form only" (*Symposium*, 205c–d). People misunderstand love because they confuse a part for the whole. They take the name of a part—say, the love of persons—for the whole: persons, things, situations, ideas, and ideals. Diotima leads Socrates to this insight by way of a remarkable analogy that exposes the "true sense" of poetry. This true sense of poetry will become very important in our quest to understand the hidden relations among teaching, loving, and logic.

In a dazzling revelation Diotima the prophet connects poetry, practical reasoning, art, and creativity. She declares "there is more than one kind of poetry in the true sense of the word—that is to say, calling something into existence that was not there before, so that every kind of artistic creation [poiēsis] is poetry, and every artist is a poet" (*Symposium*, 205b). This is the most significant moment in the *Symposium* for us. Eventually it will allow us to see why every teacher is a poet. Poiēsis for the ancient Greeks meant productive science, art, or making. Creation, "calling something into existence," or simply making meaning *is* poetry. Words written or recited with meter are but a small part of poetry in its fullest sense, which includes any skillful poetic production. It is necessary to understand what Diotima meant by poetry.

Technē for the ancient Greeks meant craft, skill, art; it is the knowledge of poiēsis, involving knowing how to create what the craftsperson desires. By contrast, *thēoria*, from which the word *theory* is derived, meant speculation, contemplation, or "a spectator above." Thēoria assumes an attitude of detachment and distance from everyday life and practice. The form of knowledge associated with thēoria was *epistēmē*, which meant certain knowledge of perfectly clear, immutable, and timeless truths. Epistēmē opposes technē because technē is knowledge of how to do things in this vague, changeable, and ephemeral world. The Greeks put thēoria and epistēmē at the top of the hierarchy of knowledge. Poiēsis and technē were at the bottom. Nothing has changed over the millennia. Today educators research teaching as they should, but too much of it is done *on* teachers rather than *with* them. Theoreticians and technocrats sometimes assume their wisdom is at the top of the knowledge hierarchy and that of teachers at the bottom.

ERŌS, GENESIS, AND IMMORTALITY

Diotima quickly connects love, poiēsis, and creativity to genesis by further confounding Socrates. If the aim of erōs is to possess the beautiful and good forever, Diotima asks, "in what way and by what activity is it to be pursued if the eagerness and intensity of the pursuit is to be called love?" (*Symposium*, 205b). The answer is startling. The actions most appropriate to the passion of erōs are procreation, creation, and acts of conception. Socrates learns that "Love is not exactly a longing for the beautiful," but rather "for the conception and generation that the beautiful effects" (*Symposium*, 206e). Recall that Socrates has learned that it is not so much the beautiful that is desired, but the good and the happiness it brings. Beauty is an instrumental intermediary to the Good. It is among the means to achieving the end of happiness. Rosen (1968/1987) believes that "the bridge between life and the Ideas [Forms] is represented in the *Symposium* by the theme of beauty" (p. 199). Beauty is the bridge erōs crosses as it moves between mutable life and the immutable Forms or Ideas. It functions for Plato as a receptacle, a place in this realm of time and chance (for instance, a womb or a creative image) where formless erōs, that all-beguiling power, can call the good it desires into existence. Beauty releases the human power to create. It is the paradoxical power of genesis that mediates between Being (the eternal forms) *and* not being. Beauty harmoniously structures spatiotemporal becoming, genesis, and growth.

For now let me note another surprising statement that follows immediately upon the connection between beauty and creativity. Diotima concludes, "And why all this longing for propagation? Because this is the one deathless and eternal element in our mortality. And since we have agreed that the lover longs for the good to be his own forever, it follows that we are bound to long for immortality as well as for the good—which is to say that Love is longing for immortality" (*Symposium*, 206e–207a). Human beings exist in the flux of becoming. The closest mortals come to the eternal (the Forms) is through continuous re-creation. Humankind reproduces itself in two ways: The first is biological; the second is cultural. If cultures did not reproduce their accumulation of learning, the efforts of millennia would vanish in one generation. Teaching is therefore a crucial social function of cultural reproduction. The propagation of children leads to one kind of immortality; the propagation of learning to another. The two go naturally together.

Procreative and creative immortality are, according to Diotima, what the acts of love offer to temporally finite and impassioned creatures like ourselves. It is here that Diotima begins to describe the ascent of erōs. In Plato's hierarchy of the procreative acts of erōs, the desire for immortality of the body by regeneration is at the bottom. According to Plato, humankind shares "the breeding instinct" with "the brutes." Higher than bodily erōs are the virtues of the *psyche* ("soul," or "mind"), beginning with the desire for fame and glory: "To win eternal mention in the deathless roll of fame" (*Symposium*, 208c). The desire is "to make a name for oneself" and have it repeated for generations. At the highest level are "those whose procreancy is of the spirit rather than of the flesh—and they are not unknown, Socrates—conceive and bear the things of the spirit. And what are they? you ask. Wisdom and all her sister virtues; it is the office of every poet to beget them, and of every artist whom we may call creative" (*Symposium*, 209a). Among the poets and creative artists who achieve immortality by calling into existence those things that propagate through the generations, Plato included educators such as his teacher, Socrates. At this point in the dialogue there is a pause before the higher or "final revelation." Diotima remarks to Socrates that so far "we are only at the bottom of the true scale of perfection" and wonders if he can follow her beyond "the more elementary mysteries of Love." (*Symposium*, 210a). Things are about to get a bit bizarre.

THE HIGHER REVELATION

If persons are ever to receive the higher revelation, they must be educated properly from the beginning:

For he who would proceed aright in this matter should begin in youth to seek the company of corporeal beauty; and first, if he be guided by his instructor aright, to love one beautiful body only—out of that he should create fair thoughts; and soon he will of himself perceive that the beauty of one body is akin to the beauty of another; and then if beauty of form in general is his pursuit, how foolish would he be not to recognize that the beauty in every body is akin to the beauty of another; and then if beauty of form in general is his pursuit, how foolish would he be not to recognize that the beauty in every body is one and the same! (*Symposium*, 210a–b)

This pattern, abstraction from all corporeal particularity and generalization of the resulting abstract universal to the whole, is repeated at the level of the psyche, or mind. One beautiful mind is as good as the next. Likewise one system of social laws (rules of fair practice) is as beautiful as the next as long as it serves the purpose of harmonizing society.

By the end of the lower half of the hierarchy constituting the final revelation, Diotima concludes:

Drawing towards and contemplating the vast sea of beauty, he will create many fair and noble thoughts and discourses in boundless love of wisdom, until on that shore he grows and waxes strong, and at last the vision is revealed to him of a single science, which is the science of beauty everywhere. (*Symposium*, 210d)

A single unifying science of beauty everywhere is the limit of the education of erōs within the everyday natural world of genesis, creation, and becoming. It is as far as speech and teaching can take us. The rest can only be pointed to in silence. It lies between the lines of written poetry and is beyond creation or calling into existence. It is the eternal, immutable realm of the Forms, which are the archetypes of creation governed by the Good itself. It is the point at which prophecy and poetry meet. For Plato it is a supernatural realm beyond time or chance. Because it is changeless, active participation in it is not possible. It is a realm that only philosopher kings may contemplate, and then only as passive, theoretical spectators.

Like the prophet she is, Diotima provides the young Socrates (a lover of wisdom) with a powerful intuition. It is found in the absences expressed by poetic silence. The final revelation is the negation of what can be said about genesis and becoming by finite mortals. The intuition points to an absolute, timeless, and changeless realm of reality. Some call it Platonic heaven. Diotima divulges the perfect revelation thus:

A nature which in the first place is everlasting, knowing not birth or death, growth or decay; secondly, not fair in one point of view and foul in another . . . or existing in any individual being . . . but beauty absolute, separate, simple, and everlasting, which is imparted to the ever growing and perishing beauties of all other beautiful things, without itself suffering diminution, or increase, or any change. (*Symposium*, 211a–b)

Platonic heaven is the home of the perfect Forms, the eternal archetypes of creation that cause change but do not themselves suffer it. They are beautifully ordered and eternally harmonized by "the Good." Only at the peak of Plato's hierarchy do the Good, the Beautiful, and the Harmonious become one.

The last words of Diotima recalled by Socrates are:

It is only when he discerns beauty itself through what makes it visible that a man will be quickened with the true, and not the seeming, virtue—for it is virtue's self that quickens him, not virtue's semblance. And when he has brought forth and reared this perfect virtue, he shall be called the friend of God, and if ever it is given to man to put on immortality, it shall be given to him. (*Symposium*, 212a)

For Plato, those who lived well could become, in a sense, immortal. I will return later to ask what it means to be called "the friend of God."

A DEWEYAN CRITIQUE OF PLATO

What is one to make of Plato's incredible revelations regarding erōs? Do they lead to heaven, or to hell? One thing is sure: They do not resemble everyday life and the familiar practices of teaching. I want to reflect on the indisputable fact that Plato's *Symposium* has had enormous influence on 2,300 years of Western thought. I rely on Deweyan pragmatism to first critique Plato and then reconstruct him. Our goal is a philosophy of erōs that appeals to the needs of classroom teachers. Dewey accepted the significance of Plato's themes. Their metaphysical and epistemological differences, however, led him to completely reconstruct Plato's theory in almost every detail.

The most important difference is between Plato's supernatural metaphysics and Dewey's mundane naturalism. Plato's supernaturalism seemed strange to Dewey, a naturalist who rejected any dualism between the natural and the supernatural. For Dewey all existence is a single whole, a seamless web of naturally occurring events. There is no supernatural realm for Dewey but only the natural realm that is un-known or not yet created. For Dewey, human nature is a part of nature and humankind a participant in a continuously creative, unfinished, and unfinishable universe.

Another substantial difference is that Dewey thought Plato's separa-tion of the theoretical and the practical a dangerous dualism. He denied any metaphysical domain containing unalterable objects of indubitable knowledge. He also explicitly denounced the Platonic distinction be-tween abstract theory and concrete, everyday practice. Practice always involves theory, and theory is a form of practice (see Nespor & Garri-son, 1992).

Recall that foolish erōs is full of practical skill, craft, and method and that his philosophical nature is manifestly practical rather than theoreti-cal. Presumably, if erōs were more theoretical, then he would be less foolish. If he were a philosopher king, he would be as wise as it is humanly possible to be. Dewey's rejection of the theory-versus-practice distinction becomes significant here. For Dewey all reasoning is practical means–ends reasoning conducted for some purpose or value. He re-jected all versions of essentialist metaphysics. For him everything that existed is a natural event like life in which everything is vague, indeter-minate, and subject to change. The practitioner's work is never-ending. Something always needs doing. While the children are at lunch, the teacher grabs a sandwich and reviews lesson plans. Analogous to erōs, teachers are forever needful and resourceful. Even those teachers pos-sessed of immense practical knowledge will remain needful, but not because they are foolish. Teachers must be forever needful and re-sourceful because the needs of those they care for are inexhaustible.

In Dewey's view the philosophy-versus-practice distinction serves the purposes of kings of various kinds (including some bureaucratic and technocratic experts and theoretical authorities) who assume some higher realm of reality and knowledge beyond reflection on ordinary practice. Dewey thought that Plato's metaphysics and epistemology emerged out of oppressive social practices.

Ironically, Plato made his teacher Socrates passively recite lessons learned from a woman, a deliberate and sinister irony because of the oppressed status of Greek women. Commenting on Platonic erōs, Ir-ving Singer (1984) concluded that Plato's conception of love "springs from the belief that all approaches to absolute beauty originate with a masculine object. . . . The sociological *setting* of Platonism makes it al-most inevitable. Greek civilization idealized masculinity. . . . Not only were women kept indoors as virtual household slaves, but also they remained uneducated" (p. 77). I address ancient Greek sexism to make

the following point: Unacknowledged cultural and sociological assumptions structure Plato's metaphysics, epistemology, and philosophy of
erōs. Love may be timeless, but how an epoch understands it is not.
Dewey also investigated the intimate relationship between the love of
wisdom and erōs. His answers, however, address the existential questions about living well in the natural world here and now.

As Dewey (1919/1982a) observed, "The [past] philosophies embodied not colorless intellectual readings of reality, but men's most passionate desires [erōs] and hopes, their basic beliefs about the sort of life to be
lived" (p. 44).[1] The moral quest for the good life and right action lies
beyond the quest for knowledge alone. It requires passionate action
guided by intelligent thought. Everyone reasons for the good life they
desire. Values guide practical inquiry. Different people have different
values. Those that seek practical wisdom desire values that contribute
to creating a better world, safer schools, and more creative classrooms.

Elsewhere in the same essay Dewey connected philosophy as the
genuine love of wisdom to gender and cultural domination. He recognized that different cultural roles lead to different types of experience
and different types of experience lead to different desires and values.
These in turn lead us to philosophize in different ways about our shared
world:

> One might rather say that the fact that the collective purpose and desire of
> a given generation and people dominates its philosophy is evidence of the
> sincerity and vitality of that philosophy. . . . Different hues of philosophic
> thought are bound to result. Women have as yet made little contribution to
> philosophy. But when women who are not mere students of other persons'
> philosophy set out to write it, we cannot conceive that it will be the same
> viewpoint or tenor as that composed from the standpoint of the different
> masculine experience of things. . . . As far as what is loosely called reality
> figures in philosophies, we may be sure that it signifies those selected
> aspects of the world which are chosen because they lend themselves to the
> support of men's judgment of the worth-while life, and hence are most
> highly prized. In philosophy, "reality" is a term of value or choice. (Dewey,
> 1919/1982a, p. 45)

Dewey insisted that all identities in nature are contingent, not just gender identity. He believed that our understanding of reality depends on
the various standpoints used to gather perspectives. He held a standpoint theory of knowledge. Everyone can only see from the various
standpoints they have occupied, including what they remember of
where they have been, where they think they are, and where they
imagine they are going. The power of imagination, however, lies in its

capacity to multiply perspectives rapidly. Dewey thought that reality is infinitely complex but that mortals can only gather a finite number of perspectives. Thus finite creatures can grow wiser only if they share perspectives, for seeing things from the standpoint of others also allows us to multiply perspectives. That is why Dewey thought dialogues across differences were essential for those who desire to grow. When a single standpoint excludes others, the result is a distorted view of reality. Monism is dogmatism.

Women who are not mere students of other persons' philosophies, theories, and research programs have only recently set out to write about teaching from their standpoints and perspectives in large numbers. Dewey emphasized the importance of human purposes and selective interests, driven by needs and desires, in arresting the rhythmic flux of events, fixing identities, and establishing values. He weaves human value and choice into the fabric of reality itself. "Reality" will be reconstructed, including the reality of schools and classrooms, when those with different purposes and values begin to speak and write about their experiences. Our understanding of what matters most will alter as women and so-called minorities increasingly participate in the public conversation. Later it will become evident how including women in the pantheon of pragmatists allows us to reconstruct Dewey in ways that lead to a better understanding of erōs.

Dewey (1934/1987) completely rejected Plato's hierarchy of fixed and eternal Forms:

> Plato's ladder is, moreover, a one-way ascent; there is no return from the highest beauty to perceptual experience. . . . The beauty of things that are in change—as are all things of experience—is to be regarded then but as a potential becoming of the soul toward apprehension of eternal patterns of beauty. . . . Sense [perception] seems . . . to Plato, to be a seduction that leads man away from the spiritual. It is tolerated only as a vehicle [intermediary] through which man may be brought to an intuition of immaterial and non-sensuous essence [the Forms]. . . . I know of no way to criticize the theory save to say that it is a ghostly metaphysics. (pp. 296–298)

Beautiful and harmonious aesthetic forms emerged for Dewey from everyday sensory experience and the ordinary affairs of life. Meanings and values are created out of the materials of mundane existence, while practical wisdom attends to the details of daily living. For beautiful forms are produced by practical reason, and constructive practical inquiry bestows value. Creating values in itself is a work of art. At first they are only glimpsed imaginatively while manipulating the sensuous material found in this changeable and imperfect world.

The troubles Plato attempts to alleviate do emerge out of the tragedies (and comedies) of daily living. His resolution, however, is lifeless
and irrelevant to mortals. It is an escape from living rather than an aid
in coping with the problems posed by daily practice. Dewey seems to
grasp the legacy of erōs' parentage better than Plato. He connects us to
the rhythms of life in ways that help us better understand the connections among desire, method, and practical wisdom.

Rosen (1968/1987) remarks, "Erōs' philosophical nature is manifestly practical rather than theoretical" (p. 235). Erōs is in the middle of
the major premise of practical deliberation and is a central part of all
practical reasoning. That is why a pragmatist such as Dewey insisted
that all reasoning begins in need and our desire to secure some value.
Intelligent inquiry achieves the end desired by transforming the needful situation into the value sought. Natural inquiry pulsates to life's
rhythms.

Dewey (1934/1987) wrote:

> The rhythm of loss of integration with environment and recovery of union
> not only persists in man but becomes conscious with him; its conditions are
> material out of which he forms purposes [values]. . . . Desire for restoration
> of the union converts mere emotion into interest in objects as conditions of
> realization of harmony. (pp. 20–21)

In troubled situations vague feelings of disharmony may become focused desires when the agent can imagine some idea (or hypothesis) of
a possible value that would restore harmony to the chaotic situation.
Once an actor foresees some value, he becomes practically interested in
those aspects of the practical context that might provide a means to
satisfying his desire. Dewey comprehended practical reasoning as an art
that involves creatively transforming distressing and needful situations
into more desirable ones. The rhythm of loss and recovery is the cycle
of expansive growth, genesis, and becoming.

For Dewey and Plato the beautiful, the harmonious, and the well-
formed are one. But instead of static supernaturalism, Dewey (1934/
1987) defended rhythmic growth:

> Life grows when a temporary falling out is a transition to a more extensive
> balance of the energies of the organism with those of the conditions under
> which it lives. . . . If life continues and if in continuing it expands, there is
> an overcoming of factors of opposition and conflict. . . . Here in germ are
> balance and harmony attained through rhythm. Equilibrium comes about
> not mechanically and inertly but out of, and because of, tension. . . . Form
> is arrived at whenever a stable, even though moving, equilibrium is

reached. . . . Order cannot but be admirable in a world constantly threatened with disorder. (p. 20)

All experience, Dewey believed, displays the rhythm of integration, disintegration, and aesthetic reintegration. For him, all forms are found or artistically created in the course of practical, lived experience, and all forms, including the formulas of science, bring a degree of aesthetic satisfaction. Ours is a world of rhythmic flux and change, but change can be threatening. Ours is a world where things are stable enough to be used to transform threatening situations into desirable, valued consequences. This occasionally happens as a consequence of good fortune. The ancient Greeks called good luck or fortune *tuchē*. The only alternative to luck is practical wisdom (phrōnesis) about what values are truly desirable and creative practical knowledge (technē) about how to actualize them.

There are other flaws in Plato's fantastic metaphysics that are obvious to any teacher. His oceanic vision ("the vast sea of beauty") drowns all uniqueness and particularity. One beautiful soul, body, or system of laws is as good as another. All values become homogeneous and intersubstitutable on the way to Platonic perfection. Nothing is irreplaceable. Everything differs only in quantity. Value judgment becomes simply a matter of calculation. If there are qualitative differences, they do not matter much since all values are positioned on a hierarchy that measures values along a common ruler. The values above are greater than those below. The ruler terminates in "the Good" that exists absolutely and lifelessly apart from all that suffers change. It may only be contemplated dispassionately with the detached soul of pure rationality. Philosopher kings have knowledge of this value ruler; that is why Plato believes they should rule. Few teachers view their students so dispassionately.

I have shown how Plato got to the Good, but why would anyone want to go? Life provides two compelling answers. If values were all homogeneous, commensurable, and measured along a single ruler, then value decisions would just be a matter of cost-benefit calculation of the quantities involved in any moral decision. That would be instant cookbook rationality. Our moral lives would be as simple as the recipes recommended by some bureaucratic school administrators or the technocratic test makers who label our children. The need is real, but the promise is false. Even the best administrators, and there are many, struggle at considerable personal and professional risk against state and federal rules, measures, and calculations to respond thoughtfully to the needs of individual students and teachers.

There is a second compelling existential reason to want to complete the quest for certainty and eternal perfection. Humanity desires invulnerability. If all bodies, souls, and minds were the same, we would be invulnerable to loss. No one would be so unique as to be irreplaceable; there would be no dependence on the intrinsic worth of special relationships. Everyone would be more self-sufficient, safe from pain, grief, fear, and despair. There would be little suffering. We would be in complete control. Above all, we would be beyond tragedy and loss, and we would not ever have to choose between incommensurable values, sacrificing one to obtain the other. It would be unnecessary to choose between parents and lovers, family and career, or giving precious class time to one child instead of another. We would be like God, or at least His friend. It is an attractive vision. It has seduced lovers of theoretical knowledge for millennia. It is not an alluring vision to the lovers of passionate, bountiful, and creative life who feel the wonder of existence in the continuing revelations of day-to-day living.

Tragic loss is a part of teaching that we all live with every moment of every day. As finite and limited human beings we must constantly choose between mutually exclusive goods. If we choose to give Mickie some of the personal attention that his emotionally deprived family denies him, then we must turn our back to Becky, who is struggling not to fall more than one grade level behind in reading. We must also ignore the remaining students in our class who would benefit by more personal attention. Do schools raise their academic standards to enhance academic performance, although self-esteem might suffer? Teachers constantly choose among incommensurable values in their classrooms. Incommensurable goods are those desirable but mutually exclusive values that cannot be simply computed by techniques of cost-benefit analysis. Teachers embrace the messiness of vital practice and seek practical wisdom to help deal with vagueness, uncertainty, and loss. Decision making here in the contingent realm of time and chance is inescapably difficult, tragic, and sometimes comic as well. Every teacher passionately desires help in making wise choices.

Teachers look into the faces of their students and know intuitively that Plato's otherworldly promise is not only false, it is ugly and undesirable. They know that Wes is not like Judy. Their bodies, minds, and personalities are different in many ways. They are unique in their fingerprints and personal history. Their needs, desires, and dreams are different, and teachers must strive to respond to that uniqueness in their own unique ways. Each of these children is irreplaceable. One cannot be substituted for the other even when their test scores are exactly the same. These children are unique selves; they are not ciphers. It would not be wise to respond to one exactly as to the other in similar situations.

Good teachers know all of this. They are not invulnerable. Loss and suffering are our lot, just as they are in any other role a passionate living being might play; for example, police officer, prophet, or psychiatric counselor. Indeed, classroom teachers perform all of these roles and many others. They may seek security behind test-score labels, but to do so is false, self-deceptive, and morally deficient. Each child is irreplaceable in ways that the Platonic pattern of abstract, universalized, and detached tests results cannot capture. It would be arrogant, inhuman, and destructive for teachers to be like philosopher kings in their classrooms. We live better if we learn to live with loss. It is better to be vulnerable.

Loss interrupts the wholeness and health of our organic functioning. It teaches us that many things and people may be external to our existence yet internal to our harmonious functioning. Loss allows us to become consciously aware of what we unconsciously have, are, and need. Each of us hungers for food and companionship. That is why the feast is such a powerful metaphor. Those who reflect intelligently on and inquire carefully into the losses life will impose inevitably grow wiser. Loss hurts, but it can emancipate us from vines that strangle growth. If love is for our growth, then surely it is for our pruning. In it each of us becomes aware of ourselves and others. Later we must send out new roots and shoots into the soil and sunlight.

I believe that vulnerable teachers are morally superior to safe, sure, and secure teachers. Vulnerable teachers are more perceptive. They are able to see the needs of the individual child and are more likely to respond for the best of all involved. Vulnerable teachers recognize unique persons and contexts and respond appropriately. They know that the class in February with four students out sick and three others who should have stayed home is entirely different from the "same" class in late spring when the weather is beautiful. They are also much more likely to know what to do about the situation on either occasion. Vulnerability leads to a virtue I will call "moral perception." It is the ability to see the unique needs, desires, and interests of our students in unique contexts and to respond to them with our own unique style so as to secure our and our students' best possibilities.

Moral perception requires sympathetic understanding. It is necessary to be in touch with our own needs and desires in order to perceive the needs of others. Such knowledge seems to involve suffering and careful reflection on what that suffering means. Moral perception also requires imagination. Rich moral imagination allows us to first see the child's present individual needs, desires, and interests, and then their future possibilities. Feelings and imagination are part of moral perception and, therefore, of practical logic. Feelings and imagination are simply part of tough-minded thinking. Abstract reasoning alone can only see static, universal, and abstract Forms. It cannot perceive concrete, contingent, and unique particulars, such as a student whose testing and administrative special education placement conflict with a teacher's perceptions.

For Platonists poetic imagination is too adventurous. It only distracts us from comprehending the Forms and the Good that structures them. For Deweyans, though, there is no wisdom without passion and imagination. All values are contingent social constructions. It is imperative to imagine alternative possibilities to the actual conditions in our classrooms if there is to be improvement. Without a lively imagination, there is no real freedom to make moral choices. Imagination alone, though, is not enough in a resistant world. It is necessary to have the desire to act, and effective action requires practical reasoning.

Tough-minded Platonic theoreticians, researchers, and administrative philosopher kings are afraid of reality. They often avoid the complicated and messy world of classrooms where change and uncertainty rule. Theoreticians often appear impractical spectators to practitioners because they operate in a perfect world apart. The ideal world of abstract certainty, precision, and immutability is a world unlike that in which teachers teach.

Platonic philosopher kings do not require sympathy or imagination. They have no need of moral perception. Only those at lower stages of development require such attributes. Kings calculate. Those at the highest level possess indubitable knowledge of eternal and immutable truth. Dewey, like Plato, preserved a place for poetry and prophecy, but he did not make them subordinate to some abstract philosophical theory of timeless theoretical "truth." Instead, Dewey insisted that poetry and prophecy actively contribute to continuing the creation of emerging meanings and values. For Dewey, unlike Plato, artistic creation and aesthetic appreciation is the source of all meaning and value.

A DEWEYAN RECONSTRUCTION OF PLATO

Plato's supernaturalistic metaphysics equated reality with eternal, unchanging objects of indubitable knowledge. The Forms subsist outside space and time and are beautifully harmonized by the principle of "the Good." The transitory events of nature are ultimately illusions. These objects of mere opinion are subject to moral corruption. Let us look at a naturalistic alternative.

In Latin, *natura* originally belonged to the language of agriculture and breeding. It derives from *nasci*, meaning "to be born" or "to spring up." It is useful to compare the second definition of *nascent* in the *Compact Edition of the Oxford English Dictionary* (1971) to Diotima's definition of poetry as "calling something into existence." The definition reads, "In the act or condition of coming into existence; just beginning to be; commencing to form, grow, or develop, etc." The Latin uses *natura* to translate the ancient Greek *physis*, which derives from the Greek *phyo* meaning "to bring-forth," "to put forth," or "to make grow." Nature did not indicate some object or thing, but a coming-to-pass, or an event (see Schadewaldt, 1979).

Dewey rejected Plato's supernaturalism, with its emphasis on the unchanging. Dewey preferred naturalism. For him all nature, including human nature, is an event. The purpose of practical reasoning is to cultivate nature to bring-forth the goods we desire. The purpose of practical reasoning in teaching is to cultivate human nature to bring-forth the best in young people and to help them grow. As already indicated, education is one of the most important cultural functions. Agricultural metaphors abound in education; the best known is probably "kindergarten," meaning "children" (*kinder*) "garden" (*garten*).

Erōs was a daimōn for Plato. It mediated between the upper transcendental realm and the region of time and chance here below. It moved upon the bridge of beauty. Rosen (1968/1987) argues that different daimōns handled "the split between the two worlds of Ideas [or Forms] and things" in different Platonic dialogues. Rosen (1968/1987) concluded: "In the Symposium the form of the bond is erōs. Erōs is one of the daimōns, and certainly one of the most important forms assumed by the divine principle of mediation between the lifeless Ideas and the mindless motion of matter or the spatio-temporal 'receptacle'" (p. 198).

Dewey's naturalism rejects all dualism, including the separation between the living organic realm of nature and Plato's lifeless supernatural abstractions. He was a holist. For Dewey there is no supernatural, only the natural that is not yet known or created. Still, erōs arising from need remained extremely important for him.

Plato's transcendental Ideas became *ideals* for Dewey. Ideals are possibilities that are desired. They are values, or what Dewey preferred to call practical "ends-in-view." Dewey (1925/1981) observed:

> In classic Greek thought, the perception of ends was simply an esthetic contemplation of the forms of objects in which natural processes were com-

pleted. In most modern thought, it is an arbitrary creation of private mental operations guided by personal desire. . . . In empirical fact, they are projections of possible consequences; they are ends-in-view. (p. 86)

Ideals are first perceived in imagination before being poetically called into existence. All practical reasoning departs from a desire to obtain some vision of the good, some valued object or state of affairs. As Dewey (1939/1988) put it, "Wherever there are desires, there are ends-in-view" (p. 237). The artistic process of creation connects to moral judgment. Ideals are possibilities that someone has judged *ought* to exist. Statements containing *should* or *ought* are moral statements. They are often counterfactual because the world is often not as it "ought" to be. For Dewey some actual state of affairs replaces Plato's "things" in the spatiotemporal receptacle. The ideally possible that someone desires to call into existence replaces Plato's Ideals or Forms. Similarly, the relationship is not between the natural and the supernatural: It is a naturalistic dialectic of the actual and the ideally possible. Creativity and genesis characterize cosmos for Dewey.

The moral dialectic between the actual and the possible is the dialectic of freedom. Expanding freedom is as much a creative aesthetic adventure as it is a moral duty. Practical reasoning connects the actual to the possible. Inquiry transforms a needful situation into desired possibility. To live better it is necessary to cultivate better values. Unless we are lucky (tuchē), values will not spring forth on their own. Practical reasoning is dialectical means–ends reasoning. The naturalist converts the role of daimōn into means that transform the present needful, doubtful situation into the desired end, value, or ideal. Finding means to desirable ends is a matter of inquiry, imagination, and creativity. It also requires technique.

Larry Hickman (1992), director of The Center for Dewey Studies, has suggested thinking about Dewey's entire philosophy as a philosophy of technology (technē). He encourages focusing on Dewey's instrumentalist logic and pragmatic theory of inquiry. Hickman (1992) begins with a bit of useful etymology: "Technē was for the Greeks a production, a leading toward, and a con-struction, a drawing together, of various parts and pieces in order to make something novel" (p. 18). He, like Diotima, recognizes that technē involves skill in calling something novel into existence. Hickman (1992) also indicates that technē serves to mediate: "The activities that Dewey called technology were for him a busy intermediary, a liaison between the resting places we call doubt on one side and resolution on the other" (p. 19). This liaison role may be understood as a dialectic between an actual situation and some ideal possibility (value) that someone seeks to call into existence. Hickman (1992) notes, "Productive inquiry is relative to an individual in a concrete situation" (p. 23). All inquiry is contextual. For example, I have worked with a teacher, Eva Moore (a pseudonym), in an elementary class in which a special-needs student was being fully included in all activities. This student was also physically powerful and sometimes difficult even for her to handle. She sought to make the classroom a safe place for other students while getting them to befriend the mainstreamed student. It required a great deal of complicated and productive inquiry. Eva values students' creative autonomy and self-expression; it is one of the most important goals she seeks to secure in her classroom. Given the ends she values, the means that some teachers might use to mainstream a child were not even something she would consider.

Inquiry is midway between ignorance and wisdom. It is a tool or instrument. Hickman (1992) finds that "the world of our experience is a real world, but a world that is in need of transformation in order to render it more coherent and more secure. Knowing an experienced world is instrumental to rearranging it and giving a [harmonious] form that is more useful to our purposes" (p. 37). Eva frequently had to send Randy (a pseudonym) to "time-out." One day Eva responded to the problem by using reading and writing workshop. She asked Randy's classmates to write to him requesting that he behave better so they could spend more time together. Several students even offered valuable suggestions describing what they do when they recognize they themselves are about to get into trouble. As the students learned to help Randy, they also learned to help themselves and others in the class, including the teacher. This teaching technique induced self-reflection in some students and resulted in practical advice about the various techniques students use to satisfy their desire to avoid time-out and remain in class with friends. It also contributed to a sympathetic, reciprocally caring attitude between Randy and the rest of the class. Eva's means fitted the ends of inclusion and her desire to foster students' creativity and autonomy. It also transformed and improved the classroom situation. That is the goal of teachers' practical reasoning.

Do not think of means–ends reasoning as linear, or as if means are separable from ends. Practical reasoning is inquiry into how best to transform an actual situation into a more desirable one. For Dewey the task requires *coordinating* means with ends. Means commonly constitute ends at the conclusion of inquiry. In the example above, Randy was fully included in class activities because of a county special education inclusion policy. Eva strongly believes that reading and writing workshop helps students become more thoughtful and reflective. Eva used a writing assignment as a means of inducing all her students to reflect not only on Randy's difficulties with self-discipline, but, more inclusively, on their own as well. Her selection of means was consistent with her values. Consistency is important because means do constitute ends. By including a student's discipline difficulties into the larger classroom context, Eva was better able to coordinate the larger situation and achieve her goal. The students and Eva learned something about a democratic ideal called inclusion. A less wise teacher might have blamed Randy and the county's policy and punished him regularly as a means for getting him out of the class. Because means constitute ends, everybody would have learned something from that lesson, too.

Inquiry for Dewey is a creative artistic activity, a part of poiēsis: Aesthetic forms emerge because of inquiry. This is a very different perspective from Plato's. Eva's inquiry was creative, calling into existence the classroom social structure she desired. Her practical inquiry was a response to a concrete situation. Another class in another year or county could have called forth a very different response. The form of her solution was an elegant, beautiful, and harmonious moment in the rhythm of classroom life and growth.

BEYOND ETERNAL BEING AND VALUE:
CREATIVE BESTOWAL

Irving Singer (1984) wonders, "How is one to understand such a way of talking" as Plato's? (p. 57). His answer is that "Plato's search for absolute beauty or goodness (*the* Beautiful or *the* Good) is related to what John Dewey called 'the quest for certainty'" (p. 57). The quest for certainty commonly turns on epistemological and metaphysical dualisms. Examples include Plato's dichotomies between illusion and reality, body and soul, matter and spirit. Plato confined matter and bodies (including our own) to the lower naturalistic realm. This is the realm of everyday experience, contingency, and uncertainty. He then consigned reality, necessity, and certainty to a supernatural realm of real, rational, and unalterable Being knowable beyond all doubt. Dewey (1932/1985b) entirely rejected any such eternal value hierarchy:

> The business of reflection [inquiry] in determining the true good cannot be done once for all, as, for instance, making out a table [ruler] of values arranged in a hierarchical order of higher and lower. It needs to be done, and done over and over and over again, in terms of the conditions of concrete situations as they arise. In short, the need for reflection and insight is perpetually recurring. (p. 212)

For Dewey there is no final revelation. There is no eternal cosmic table of values to discover. He understood values as contingent social constructions sensitive to context, circumstances, and occasion. That is why values are constantly open to reconstruction.

As Singer (1984) sees it, "The Platonic lover is not trying to create perfections that would not have come into being without his love. On the contrary, he is seeking union with an object of metaphysical analysis whose being precedes his own, as it also precedes the being of everything else" (p. 69). The Forms are eternal. Artists cannot create, but merely re-create, them. They can only re-create according to them. As Singer (1984) puts it, "To love beauty is to wish to bring forth in beauty; to possess it perpetually would be to recreate it endlessly" (p. 63). For Plato poets of all kinds only re-create images in this world of appearances that imitate metaphysical reality. Only philosopher kings know the real, although even they create imperfectly when they practice Plato's supreme art of statecraft.

Book X of the *Republic* presents a quarrel between poets and philosophers. Poets can re-create with passion but must be content with mere appearance. Philosophers have perfected their passion and calmly contemplate "the Good." In this confrontation, Plato relegates poets of all kinds to a status inferior to that occupied by the lovers of wisdom. He authorizes philosophers to censor the poets' work. For Dewey philosophers, genuine lovers of wisdom, are inquiring creators of needed goods. They are closer to poets in Diotima's sense. Dewey rejected dualisms such as that drawn by Plato between the poet and the philosopher, the researcher and the practitioner, or the fine and the practical arts.

Before turning to Dewey's own implicit philosophy of erōs let us look at one final criticism of Plato. Singer (1984) complains:

> Desire is always acquisitive and its object a mere commodity designed to satisfy. As Platonic erōs is the organism striving to overcome deficiencies, so too is desire an attempt to eliminate a state of need or want. Nor is Plato wrong to associate love with desire. The two are closely related. Without desire there would be no love. But loving something is not the same as desiring it, even though the element of bestowal itself entails various relevant desires. (p. 86)

Dewey, too, insisted on the importance of needs and wants to any theory of value. He did not conclude that desire seeks only commodities and cannot be creative. Singer (1984) concludes that "Plato's highest love is predominantly intellectual: possibly fervent but always a form of rational activity. Platonic erōs is basically a love of abstract science more than anything else" (p. 73). Deweyan pragmatism avoids this criticism by emphasizing artistic creation. For Deweyans, values are created during the course of practical reasoning. Singer agrees, although the rational-cognitive part of love, or what he calls "appraisal," is always important. That is how we distinguish what we merely desire from the truly desirable.

Singer (1984) sums up his own view this way: "Love is not primarily a way of knowing. . . . Appraisal is a way of knowing, and emotions may always interfere with its proper employment. But love is an imaginative means of bestowing value that would not exist otherwise" (p. 17). Elsewhere Singer (1984) speaks of bestowal as "a new creation of value" and concludes that love is "an artifact of the human imagination" (pp. 13, 22). Singer is suggesting that love is creative in the strong sense of Diotima's "calling something into existence that was not there before, so that every kind of artistic creation is poetry, and every artist is a poet" (*Symposium*, 205b). Creation in Singer's account is therefore genuinely creative and not just re-creative. It can create entirely new forms of "perfection" rather than merely copying eternal forms. Deweyan inquiry bestows value by creatively calling it into existence. Because it includes desire, creativity, and loving bestowal, wisdom for Dewey goes beyond knowledge.

Here is how Dewey (1919/1982a) understood wisdom:

> By wisdom we mean not systematic and proved knowledge of fact and truth, but a conviction about moral values, a sense for the better kind of life to be led. Wisdom is a moral term, and like every moral term refers not to the constitution of things already in existence, not even if that constitution be magnified into eternity and absoluteness. As a moral term it refers to a choice about something to be done. . . . It refers not to accomplished reality but to a desired future which our desires, when translated into articulate conviction, may help bring into existence. (p. 44)

The last three words of this long passage suggest that Dewey saw practical wisdom and knowledge as involving the *creation* of values in the same poetic sense as Singer and Diotima. Moral wisdom turns on our free choice about the kind of life we ought to live and what sort of world we should call into existence. The morally possible beyond the actual situation is the domain of wisdom. Such wisdom lies beyond knowledge of current actual circumstances. It leads to creative acts of bestowal. Practical wisdom in teaching determines what is most valuable for each person in the class, including the teacher. Practical reasoning deliberates about how to create and appraise valued goods.

The kind of wisdom Dewey has in mind is concrete practical wisdom, or what the ancient Greeks called phrōnesis. He did not mean abstract or theoritical wisdom, the Greek thēoria. The Deweyan scholar Raymond D. Boisvert (1985) explains nicely what Dewey intended:

> What Dewey wanted most of all was to eliminate this gap between learning [theory] and affairs [practice]. Pragmatism was meant to indicate the continuity between the two, to focus on intelligence in the Greek sense of phrōnesis, wisdom used to guide behavior . . . intelligence had as its task not the apprehension of standards already set forth and given prior to cognition, but the actual creation or construction of new goods or ends. (p. 348)

Later I examine in detail what Dewey meant by creative intelligence. Roughly, the idea is that intelligence involves creating and inspecting alternative value possibilities that go beyond the actual situation we are in, choosing the morally best possibility, and seeking means that may help bring it into existence.

In developing his view of philosophy, Dewey moved far beyond Plato. He proposed an alternative to Plato's static philosophy of eternal foundations. The alternative is:

> To deny that philosophy is in any sense whatever a form of knowledge. It is to say that we should return to the original and etymological sense of the word, and recognize that philosophy is a form of desire, of effort at action—a love, namely, of wisdom; but with the thorough proviso, not attached to the Platonic use of the word, that wisdom, whatever it is, is not a mode of science or knowledge. . . . It is an intellectualized wish, an aspiration subjected to rational discriminations and tests, a social hope reduced to a working program of action, a prophecy of the future, but one disciplined by serious thought and knowledge. (Dewey, 1919/1982a, p. 43)

Philosophy, the desire for wisdom, is beyond knowledge and the quest for certainty. It needs knowledge, but it needs poetry and prophecy as well. It is about the values we should morally most desire to live for. We engage in critical practical inquiry (appraisal) to distinguish objects of immediate desire from genuinely desirable objects. We engage in creative inquiry to bestow value. Practical wisdom, practical reasoning, and creativity are all part of the education of erōs.

The personal philosophy of Plato's teacher, Socrates, was a philosophy of daily living; he was not only comfortable in the uncertainty of the marketplace, he actively sought it out. In the next chapter we follow Dewey and Jane Addams as they, like Socrates, take their philosophy into the streets and stockyards of Chicago. Contemporary philosophers of education might do much better if they would follow them. Modernity, or even postmodernity, demands a return to a robust philosophy of everyday living and a philosophy that emphasizes emotions, imagination, and moral perception. Of course, that requires a critically reflective intellect and disciplined practical reasoning, but the result would be a more practical and naturalistic education of erōs. Such an education is largely creative, artistic, and aesthetic; but it is not the preserve of philosopher kings. It is precisely this poetic education of erōs that the following chapters strive to unfold.

Dewey (1932/1985b) acknowledged that "as Plato . . . said over two thousand years ago, the aim of moral education is to develop a character which finds pleasure in right objects and pain in wrong ends" (p. 209). Since Plato, the aim of the education of the human erōs has been to enable students to distinguish between something they might desire and the truly desirable. It is the single most important aspect of all education. Why? Because we become what we love. That is how we grow.

Care, Sympathy, and Community in Classroom Teaching: Feminist Reflections on the Expansive Self

Power to grow depends upon need for others and plasticity.
—Dewey 1916/1980a, p. 57

Because we become what we love, because that is how people grow, educating erōs to desire the greatest good with the greatest passion should be that aspect of education that receives the greatest attention. Ironically, the official curriculum, as well as most research on teaching, ignores the passions altogether. It is a strange and unnatural silence to the ears of teachers and teacher educators. For them, learning to recognize and cope with their students' moods, desires, and interests is a crucial part of good teaching. Teaching, along with nursing and counseling, is a caring profession. I follow the neopragmatist feminists in reconstructing Dewey's ethics of care in ways that emphasize expansive growth through reciprocal relations within nurturing communities.

Comprehending the reciprocity of expansive growth requires embracing a number of paradoxes that defy the logic of either/or. All those who seek wisdom desire expansive growth. I want to begin understanding expansive growth by returning to the ancient Greek and Latin senses of *physis* (to make grow) and *natura* (to be born). If human nature is a part of nature, then it is only natural that humans undergo the natural processes of cultivation, being born anew, and growing in every nascent spring they experience.

Growth, for Dewey, is the all-inclusive ideal, the greatest good. "Growth itself," wrote Dewey (1920/1982b), "is the only moral 'end'" (p. 181). Dewey (1920/1982b) underscored this conviction when he added, "Growing, or the continuous reconstruction of experience, is the only end" (p. 185). Embracing this supreme value was Dewey's way of answering the ultimate existential question: What is the meaning of life? The meaning of life is to make more meaning. Perhaps the supreme question with which educators struggle is: What is the aim of education? If the meaning of life is to make more meaning, then the aim of education must be more education. In *Democracy and Education* Dewey (1916/ 1980a) concluded, "Since growth is the characteristic of life, education is all one with growing; it has no end beyond itself" (p. 58).[1] Growth for Dewey is the all-inclusive and supreme value. How, though, is growth cultivated? The answer is, through reciprocal relations.

DEWEY AND FEMINISM

Teaching has relatively low social status compared to other professions. Some see the large number of women in teaching as a detriment to its status. Dominant social forces conspire to demean "women's work." These forces may eulogize it, but they do not materially reward it. Many assume that caregiving should be selfless and self-sacrificing, and too often it is. Determining exactly why caregiving has such low social status for both males and females is not my task, but I would like to make some conjectures.

Childrearing in homes or in schools is a confining activity. Even in public schools the activity is confined to small designated spaces, classrooms. However, in our society social status is usually acquired through social interactions in the public domain, especially through competition in the marketplace. Caring is not public competition. Marketplace rewards are explicit, tangible (e.g., money), and readily exchanged for status and power in comparison to the tacit, intangible, almost ineffable "psychic rewards" of teaching.[2] Teaching may have immense intrinsic value, but it lacks exchange value. Moreover, teaching is an unrelenting and immediately demanding activity. Children's needs, desires, and movements require constant supervision, reaction, and response. Researchers estimate that "on the average teachers make one interactive decision every two minutes. Thus, these data conclude that the decision-making demands of classroom teaching are relatively intense" (Clark & Peterson, 1986, p. 274). Ironically, however, ultimate decision-making power in schools lies outside the classroom. School boards, superintendents, and principals have the power to make institutional policy, while teaching dedicates itself to identifying and responding to the needs and demands of others. For reasons such as these, society frequently ignores the needs and demands of teachers. And too often teachers ignore themselves as they focus on the needs of others.

Teachers, male and female alike, share the sad consequences of a society foolish enough to care little for those who care so much. Good teachers desire the virtues and excellencies of their vocation. Since many of the virtues of teaching cluster around practical wisdom (phrōnesis) and competency in caring, it is not surprising that many teachers find the "ethics of care" far more attractive than the abstract, rule-governed "ethics of justice." It is also not surprising that so many of the pioneers of the ethics of care, scholars such as Carol Gilligan (1982), Jane Roland Martin (1985, 1992), and Nel Noddings (1984, 1992), are also educators. There are, however, difficulties with the ethics of care as commonly formulated. I will rely on the work of a number of neopragmatist feminists influenced by Dewey to address these difficulties. They find the resolution to these difficulties in the idea of the expansive personality and through an emphasis on personal creativity, genesis, and growth. Expansive personalities realize that they can grow only in reciprocal relation with others in their community.

Until recently, Dewey's philosophy has been accorded low status in the sphere of professional philosophy. It is significant that educators have embraced Dewey's thought while professional philosophers have tended to ignore it. Deweyan pragmatism challenges the patterns of social domination that denigrate caregiving and the caring professions. Charlene Haddock Seigfried (1991) suggests that pragmatism, and especially Deweyan pragmatism,

> was criticized and eventually relegated to the margins for holding the very positions that today feminists would find to be its greatest strengths. These include early and persistent criticisms of positivist interpretations of scientific methodology; disclosure of the value dimension of factual claims; reclaiming aesthetics as informing everyday experience; linking of dominant discourses with domination; subordinating logical analysis to social, cultural, and political issues; realigning theory with praxis; and resisting the turn to epistemology and instead emphasizing concrete experience. (p. 5)

I have already discussed many of these themes. Seigfried (1991) concludes, "On a scale of traits, assumptions, and positions that range from stereotypically masculine to feminine, pragmatism . . . appears far more feminine than masculine" (p. 10). Seigfried does not want to be caught up in these stereotypes; neither do I. It is enough to recognize that socially dominant institutions and discourses relegated Dewey to the margins of our culture for most of this century for many of the same reasons that are all too familiar to feminists.

The feminist aspects of Dewey's holism and organicism are seen as significant by Seigfried (1991):

> Dewey . . . responded to the Darwinian reconnection of humans with all of organic life. When separation, generalization, sharp boundaries, and the drive to reduce the multiplicity of experience into as few categories as possible are categorized as masculine, then inclusiveness, concreteness, vagueness, tolerance of ambiguities, and pluralism are seen as feminine. But these latter traits are also characteristic of pragmatist thinking. (p. 12)

Again, I do not want to harden contingent Western social constructions of gender into necessary and eternal Platonic essences. Instead, I will challenge many of them as this chapter unfolds. Dewey's philosophy allows us to develop an independent understanding of the ethics of care thus far associated almost exclusively with feminism and female experience. I want to develop an ideal of expansive personality that emphasizes personal creativity, growth, and becoming through reciprocal relationships regardless of sex or gender.

Seigfried (1991) augments the pantheon of pragmatic philosophers by including many women, such as Louise M. Rosenblatt, who developed the widely influential reader-response theory of literature; Charlotte Perkins Gilman, the author of *Herland*; and Nobel laureate Jane Addams, who achieved international fame as founder of Hull House. Dewey was closely associated with all three of these women. The close relation between Dewey and Addams will become particularly important when I develop Dewey's ideas about the caring community. Influenced by Dewey, these women seem, in turn, to have exercised influence on his philosophical thought, especially his social philosophy.

Dewey (1930/1984f) expressed disappointment that the modern moral perspective on love is an "almost exclusively masculine construction" and prophesied that "the growing freedom of women can hardly have any other outcome than the production of more realistic and more human morals" (p. 276). Gregory Fernando Pappas (1993) feels such passages show "how serious Dewey's commitment is to those aspects of experience that have been associated with women (or the 'feminine')" (p. 79). In a footnote Pappas (1993) points out that Dewey's interest in the "feminine" is part of a broader interest in "more human morals" (p. 91). A more human morality would be more inclusive of diverse voices. Pappas calls attention to three related aspects of Dewey's moral theory: (1) the role of the affective in moral inquiry, (2) the importance of "intelligent sympathy," and (3) the significance of relationships and community. These three aspects converge into an ideal of expansive growth through personal relationships wherein growth becomes the supreme, all-embracing moral value. I want to examine each of these aspects in turn. Combined they make it possible to develop a Deweyan understanding of loving bestowal.

THE ROLE OF FEELING AND INTUITION
IN MORAL INQUIRY

Intuition allows us to comprehend our current situation or context; let us see how. For Dewey, intuition is a part of "operative knowledge," that is, practical knowledge, the product of practical deliberation. Operative knowledge operates to transform some actual situation into one that is more desirable. Dewey (1932/1985b) begins a subsection of his *Ethics* titled "Sensitivity and Thoughtfulness" by saying:

> The permanent element of value in the intuitional theory lies in its implicit emphasis upon the importance of direct responsiveness. . . . Nothing can make up for the absence of immediate sensitiveness. . . . Unless there is a direct, mainly unreflective appreciation of persons and deeds, the data for subsequent thought will be lacking or distorted. A person must *feel* the qualities of acts as one feels with the hands the qualities of roughness and smoothness in objects, before he has an inducement to deliberate or material with which to deliberate. Effective reflection must also terminate in a situation which is directly appreciated if thought is to be effective in action. (pp. 268–269)[3]

It is evident from this passage that for Dewey all inquiry, not just moral inquiry, begins and ends with an affective intuition that involves a distinct feeling for the quality of a situation. In moral inquiry it is necessary to have an intuitive sense of the needs, desires, and interests of others. If one fails to *react* intuitively to the quality of another's needs and desires in the context in which they occur, then the data for subsequent moral inquiry will be deficient or distorted and the *response* will lack thoughtfulness.

The product of practical inquiry is knowledge or belief, that is, a disposition to act. Dewey (1932/1985b) wrote, "A moral judgment, however intellectual it may be, must at least be colored with feeling if it is to influence behavior. . . . Affection, from intense love to mild favor, is an ingredient in all operative knowledge, all full apprehension of the good" (p. 269). Affection is an element in the "operative knowledge" that realizes the good; it is simply a part of practical deliberation, including moral deliberation, and the knowledge it produces. Unlike most modern thinkers, Dewey entirely rejected any dualism of reason and emotion. For him affect is a necessary part of belief. He also rejected the dualisms drawn by logical positivists among theories, facts, and values. All these converge in his refusal to recognize a sharp theory-versus-practice dualism. Values are something that are desired, and people engage in practical reasoning to obtain them. They are present in all our thoughts, feelings, and actions.

Dewey felt that to desire some good, some ideal "end-in-view," is to simultaneously desire the means or operations needed to actualize the good. For him, the means are not detachable from the ends; that would be just another untenable dualism. Dewey's holism rejected the separations and sharp boundaries required by the logical positivists and other modern philosophers. Instead, he insisted that the means often constitute the end, just as the bricks and boards in a home are both means to the end of providing shelter and part of the shelter when completed.[4] It is best not to think of practical means–ends deliberation linearly. Instead, think of the relationship as transforming some situation to achieve a harmonious union of means and ends. Let us return to Dewey's idea that unreflective intuition helps us grasp "data" for subsequent thought.

For Dewey experience is holistic and undivided. It is not until after the discriminating activities of an inquirer's selective attention have operated on a qualitative whole that specific objects may be identified. People observing the same event often "see" very different things—just watch a cartoon with your children on Saturday morning or go to a football game with a fan from the visitor's school. The notion that experience is a bunch of atomistic "sense data" that are the same for everyone is just a bit of positivistic dogma that should be expunged from educational research. Dewey, following William James, found everyday experience a stream, an ever-changing flux. The needs, desires, and interests of finite and impassioned creatures govern selective attention, yet they must select from an infinitely continuous, ever-changing, vague, and indeterminate river of experience. Teachers selectively attend to things in their classroom environment according to their purposes and desires. So many things happen so quickly and in so many places at once in classrooms that it is impossible for any one person to attend to or recognize more than a small fragment of it all. If a teacher gives one student undivided attention, that teacher must, for a moment, ignore the rest of the class. We are finite beings, and classrooms, like life itself, are infinitely complicated.

Perceptive teachers see more; yet that, too, can present problems. Those who see too much may become distracted or overburdened with worry and concern. An endless number of things are happening moment to moment that even the best of teachers are too preoccupied to notice. Sometimes, though, especially if they are sensitive and "experienced," teachers can intuit a quality. Things are "flowing" well, or perhaps the teacher senses disruption. Wise teachers readily sense when things are suspiciously quiet. It is only after discriminating acts of selection occur, selections that follow the logic of their interests, that teachers may apply analytic categories learned in an inservice course or some such—if at all.

THE IMPORTANCE OF "INTELLIGENT SYMPATHY"

Dewey thought that emotional reactions are as necessary for knowledge of human beings as sensory reactions are for knowledge of physical beings. Dewey (1932/1985b) wrote:

> Our sensory reactions, of eye, ear, hand, nose, and tongue supply material of our knowledge of qualities of physical things. . . . *Emotional* reactions form the chief materials of our knowledge of ourselves and of others. Just as ideas of physical objects are constituted out of sensory material, so those of persons are framed out of emotional and affectional materials. (pp. 269–270) [emphasis in original]

Neither physical nor interpersonal data are "hard data." All data are subject to emotionally influenced, theory-laden, and value-biased selection according to the logic of our needs, interests, and purposes. Emotional selective attention determines what we recognize, react to, and respond to; these are the "data" that form our knowledge of other people. If our sympathetic intuitions are poor, it will not matter how perfect and exact our moral reasoning might be because what we will be thinking about will be irrelevant to the actual situation.

Sympathetic "data" used to understand others are at least as good as the sensory data used to infer physical objects. Of course people are often mistaken about the hopes, dreams, and wishes they identify (any database, or belief system, is fallible), but our sympathetic data, if carefully collected, are at least as reliable as any other kind of data. That our culture has not evolved highly refined methods of collecting emotional and sympathetic data, that researchers do not perform careful interpersonal experiments, that the theories of human thought, feeling, and action remain so remarkably underdeveloped and so lacking in critical self-reflection—all say something about the incredible complexity of the problems posed in coming to know people and what the dominant "scientific" culture of our day values.

Every successful practitioner has evolved idiosyncratic methods of collecting sympathetic data and relies on them more than on the impersonal, "objective" methods of positive science. This is especially the case in caring professions such as teaching. That so little theory has been constructed, or research conducted, using the sympathetic data most relevant to the topic of teaching, says something about what too many educational researchers, theorists, and technocrats value as opposed to what is, or ought to be, valued by classroom teachers. The concerns of classroom teachers are too frequently dismissed as soft-headed or sentimental by researchers. The ironies are incredible. Small wonder that practicing teachers tend to ignore educational theory and the results of research. Nevertheless, good teachers and teacher educators constantly engage in deliberation about their teaching. I want to explore how this is done.

As with the scientistic approach to research, a sense of sympathy seems entirely missing in Plato. There are only homogeneous bodies and souls whose worth is determined by calculating their position in an abstract value hierarchy. There is no need for sympathetic *reaction*, perception of unique persons in unique situations, or sympathetic *response*, because there is no significant uniqueness in Plato. In a passage that provides a direct rebuttal to Platonic thinking, Dewey (1932/1985b) wrote:

> The reasonable act and the generous act lie close together. A person entirely lacking in sympathetic response might have a keen calculating intellect, but he would have no spontaneous sense of the claims of others for satisfaction of their desires. A person of narrow sympathy is of necessity a person of confined outlook upon the scene of human good. The only truly *general* thought is the *generous* thought. (p. 270) [emphasis in original]

Dewey was not rejecting "calculating intellect" in responding to others so much as he was pointing to its limitations. Cost-benefit analysis without sympathetic reaction, understanding, or response is unlikely to satisfy the needs and desires of children, parents, or teachers. Only those doing the calculations will find satisfaction. Rational generalization in the social sciences should acknowledge individual differences. Need, desire, and interest constitute the threads out of which culture weaves the cloth of multicultural understanding and gender awareness. Platonic generalization relies heavily on abstraction that erases differences. Plato hypostatized abstractions, that is to say, he treated them as if they were concrete reality existing antecedent to all inquiry instead of the consequences of abstraction and inquiry. Platonic generalization is flawed because it is not generous.

Without sympathetic attention and response, researchers, including teachers conducting their own problem-solving inquires, intuit and select poorly in any qualitative context. When they select poorly in a moral context, they obtain flawed or irrelevant "data." If researchers gather the data of calculation improperly, it does not matter if the subsequent calculations are perfect (just as the calculations do not matter in physics if the experimentor identifies the wrong variables), operationalizes them poorly, or puts them in an improper relation. Without the "generous act" while collecting data, "the reasonable act" of practical deliberation will be blunted, forced, and perhaps foul. It is the lack of generosity that, in its extreme forms, creates Frankenstein monsters whose cold, nearly mechanical body parts are interchangeable for the responses of the supposedly dispassionate scientist, just as children's test scores are interchangeable for a technocrat's supposedly dispassionate categorizations, treatments, and responses.

A great deal of educational research, along with the educational policies we derive from it, is illogical because it lacks sympathy. For example, students' abilities and subsequently their access to educational possibilities are often dependent on their performance on pencil-and-paper, machine-graded, multiple-choice tests yielding a number that allows us to calculate and classify. Such research often fails to collect its data appropriately because it confuses the sensory material fit for investigating physical things with the sympathetic and emotional data appropriate for acquiring knowledge of persons. The mistake is then compounded when the results of the investigation are generalized into abstract classifications without being generous. Unsympathetic social science is simply bad science.

Dewey (1932/1985b) insisted:

> Sympathy is the animating mold of moral judgment not because its dictates take precedence in action over those of other impulses (which they do not do), but because it furnishes the most efficacious *intellectual* standpoint. It is the tool, *par excellence*, for resolving complex situations. (p. 270) [emphasis in original]

Sympathy is the best source of data in the social sciences and in moral deliberation. Intuiting data in qualitative contexts such as classrooms is a difficult task of intelligent selection and discrimination. Sympathetic insight is closely akin to aesthetic appreciation. Significantly, the sixth definition of "taste" in the *Oxford English Dictionary* (1971) reads: "Mental perception of quality; judgment, discriminative faculty." Sympathetic emotional intuition initiates practical social inquiry. The Latin word *intellectus*, from which we derive such words as *intellect* and *intelligent*, means "chosen among" or "understood." It derives from the compound *inter* ("among") and *legere* ("to choose"). For Dewey, "data" are intuitively chosen, or discriminated, from an infinitely complex qualitative context (e.g., classrooms) according to our cares, concerns, and interests.

Thus far we have talked about the role of needs, desires, and interests in guiding our selective attention and influencing our intuitions about the qualitative data of classroom contexts. Let us now focus on how we sympathetically intuit the needs, desires, and interests of others. We are about to enter an expansive circle of relationships between ourselves and others. It leads to the kind of bestowal (or value creation) appropriate to a caring profession.

Dewey (1932/1985b) wrote:

> It is sympathy which carries thought out beyond the self and which extends its scope till it approaches the universal as its limit. It is sympathy which saves consideration of consequences from degenerating into mere calculation, by rendering vivid the interests of others and urging us to give them the same weight as those which touch our own. . . . To put ourselves in the place of others, to see things from the standpoint of their purposes and values, to humble, contrariwise, our own pretensions and claims . . . is the surest way to attain objectivity of moral knowledge. (p. 270)

For Dewey, "objectivity" means intersubjective understanding, although not necessarily agreement. We all have different needs, desires, interests, purposes, wishes, hopes, perspectives, and values. These are the ingredients of self-knowledge as well as knowledge of others. There is always, though, the permanent possibility of interpersonal understanding regardless of how different our gender, race, ethnicity, culture, or social class may be. Without sympathy, however, there is always a danger of misunderstanding.

The sympathetic and generous recognition of the needs, desires, and hopes of others may propel us beyond the bounds of our fixed self, if we are generous, toward the ever-receding limit of universal humanity. When we recognize the perspectives and hopes of others we may begin to perceive new possibilities and hope for things we had never before even dreamed existed. It is an arduous and endless journey, though. If we allow ourselves to grow, we will lose our "selves," our personal identity, many times along the way. So, we wonder, why would anyone want to embark on such a journey of reciprocal becoming, genesis, and growth? One answer is that we desire to grow, and growth means undergoing change as we allow ourselves to be drawn out by others. This is especially so for those with the expansive need to care for the needs of others. To grow we must be vulnerable and risk ourselves in relationships of care and concern. We must open ourselves to and carry out transactions with the environment, especially our social environment. Eventually these answers combine to answer another question: Why be generous in our bestowal upon others.

THE IMPORTANCE OF RELATIONSHIPS AND COMMUNITY: SELF-TRANSCENDENCE, GROWTH, AND THE CREATIVE BESTOWAL OF VALUE

Dewey held that we come to have a mind and a self as we carry on transactions with the environment around us, especially as we participate in the social practices of a culture. Dewey (1925/1981) wrote, "Personality, selfhood . . . are eventual functions that emerge with complexly organized interactions, organic and social" (p. 162). The function of formal schooling in complex societies is to extend, broaden, and improve the cultural construction of emerging minds begun at home and in the community at large. Culture has us before we have it. The function of critical education is to make us aware of the contingency of this social construction of our minds and selves, and to aid us in taking possession of ourselves through a long process of self-reflective re-creation. Dewey was a "social constructivist" decades before the phrase became fashionable (see Garrison, 1995b).

Following Dewey, Pappas (1993) points out that if we recognize that "the self is relational, interactive, and processional," then "the self is always one with its activity, i.e., it is an agent, a participator. . . . For an agent in continuous formation 'being interested in' is not incidental or instrumental to its being but is what that being consists of. The self is not *behind* what one does, but *in* what one does" (p. 86). Pappas notes the role of interests in connecting the organism with its environment. Next he calls attention to the following passage: "Interest, concern means that self and world are engaged with each other in a developing situation" (Dewey, 1916/1980a, p. 132, emphasis in original).[5] People are participants in, and not spectators of, the world.

Pappas helps us locate an understanding of bestowal in Dewey's philosophy that provides an important insight into the nature of care in a caring profession. Pappas (1993) writes:

> Dewey can say that all interests are self-centered but only in the sense that they are organically related to a self. But not all objects of our interest are a means to possess some good (e.g., pleasure, survival, happiness, virtue) *for* a fixed self. A person can be *directly* interested or concerned for others or can have a genuine identification of her good and the good of others not as

a means to something else (for the self) but as an affirmation of what she is (constitutive of the self). (p. 86) [emphasis in original]

This is a direct rejection of Platonic possession and an affirmation of loving bestowal. Education requires self-transcendence and growth. That is the richer meaning of erōs. It is not enough that we desire to possess the good for ourselves, because we will not possess the good unless we can also give it away. Good teachers know we may give the gift without loss of self.

In creating the conditions necessary for a child to learn and grow, teachers are bestowing value (i.e., a good) on the child. In creating value teachers find self-expression, learning, and personal growth. By learning to recognize and respond appropriately to the needs, desires, and interests of each unique child in their class, teachers may have their own needs, desires, and interests fulfilled as well. Teachers and students must share interests and concerns; they cannot avoid each other in evolving classroom situations. In responding creatively to classroom problems, teachers may experience creative aesthetic expression.

In Diotima's terms, caring for the needs of others is poetic. It requires us to "call into existence" in our relationships those conditions necessary for appropriate response. These may range from giving a hug, to appropriate discipline, to better school lunches. Value is bestowed through acts of creation, and the process of creative bestowal involves aesthetic awareness and artistic creativity. Knowledge is also required to complete poetic acts of creation. Caring and creative teachers constantly engage in practical inquiry to improve their teaching. Practical reasoning is a part of bestowal. Teachers who say they care, but do not inquire, are fooling themselves by engaging in mere sentimentality. As Dewey (1932/1985b) put it, "The direct valuing which accompanies immediate sensitive responsiveness to acts has its complement and expansion in valuations which are deliberate, reflective" (p. 271). Caring is tough work and it calls for tough-minded thinking. Those who really care are eager to have valued colleagues thoughtfully appraise their work in the hope of enhancing it, just as they hope that intelligently criticizing their students' performance will promote learning. Learning to care well for others, creatively bestowing value, and mastering the necessary techniques (technē) of good care can be self-fulfilling.

Self-realization is reciprocal in the emergent model of the mind and self. Bestowing value, generating love, or creating goodness enhances others while affirming and expanding ourselves. That is why it is so important to receive as well as to give. Quality caring has a reciprocal and circular movement. Love may pass through us to others and through others to us. As with trees that benefit from the water cycle of rain, evaporation, clouds, and condensation into rain again, people grow and find nourishment through the coming, giving, going, and returning of the thoughts and feelings from ourselves to others and from others to ourselves. Should the rhythm break, lives would decay. Teachers find growth and self-affirmation in giving; but if they do not also receive, they dry up and burn out. The flames of passionate teaching die when not fueled by reciprocal care and creative opportunity.

Pappas (1993) observes, "A fuller, broader, and expansive self is one that has a direct personal interest in particular others and the relationships she shares with them" (p. 86). Dewey (1916/1980a) argued that "the kind and amount of interest actively taken in a thing reveals and measures the quality of selfhood which exists" (pp. 361–362). The expansiveness of a teacher's selfhood may be "measured" not by teacher evaluation instruments but by the interests he takes in his students. Being interested in students, caring for them intelligently, requires understanding their needs, desires, interests, dreams, and aspirations. Caring teaching must be sympathetic, imaginative, creative, inquiring, and critical. These are among the most important virtues of practical wisdom, or phrōnesis.

Pappas (1993) concludes:

> Those who find their own good in the good of others by virtue of having a direct interest in others are not, because of this, dependent, weaker, selfless, lacking identity, etc. They can still be said to sacrifice their "selves," but by that we must mean a narrow kind of self. On the contrary, Dewey thinks they are the most likely to become richer and growing selves, because the opportunities and demands for growth are found in relations. . . . The kind of character that is interested in growth . . . is one and the same with the one that is interested in the expansion and deepening of relationships. (p. 87)

Fixed selves, those that have reached their final identities, whether selfish or selfless, entirely misunderstand the expansive personalities commonly found in the caring professions. Fixed personalities are not expansive. Often they become obsessed with the will to power over others, although not over themselves. They may use selflessness as a secondary will to power that manipulates and controls the primary will through indirection and intrigue. Allowing narrow selves to dominate our personal and professional lives suppresses growth.

People learn and grow in relationship with others, but only if they are vulnerable. Others, especially others different from ourselves, educate us in the deepest sense of drawing us out. They allow us to explore our abilities and develop new ones. That is how lives expand and grow. Yet everyone is a unique and often unpredictable individual. The deeper and more intimate our relationships, the greater the potential risk and the greater the potential for growth. Those who desire to grow are vulnerable to suffering and loss in ways that cannot be calculated in advance. Perhaps there is no final accounting either.

Part of practical wisdom is recognizing that there are some whose needs cannot be met, while there are others who do not desire to grow but rather desire to control and inhibit the growth of others. It is also necessary to provide for and cope with the needs of others while having our needs met. What is it exactly about relationships that allows everyone to grow through them even when some do not end well? The answer lies in looking more closely at the reciprocal and potentially transformative interactions that occur in any relationship.

Persons, things, and events are constantly interacting with one another. These interactions are mutually modifying transactions for all participants. In all of nature, Dewey (1929/1984b) wrote, "Interaction is the primary fact, and it constitutes a *trans-action*" (p. 220). Human interactions are especially important. Just think of your own "love life" or the caring relationships that you sustain and that sustain you. Dewey (1922/1983) thought it a cruel abstraction that morals have been "discussed in isolation from the concrete facts of the interactions of human beings with one another" (p. 219). Reflecting on passages like these, Pappas (1993) concludes:

> The transactions in which we find ourselves are usually direct, unique, and reciprocal relationships with others. . . . There are occasions in which we need to distinguish our "selves" from our relationships, but it would be a vicious abstractionism to separate the self completely from these transactions and claim that it is somehow prior to them. . . . The self lives through and by social relations. . . . There are important implications of this new starting point for ethics. (p. 88)

Relationships are transactional and, therefore, potentially reciprocally transformational. Our minds and personalities emerge through interpersonal relationships. Children become the company they keep. Parents are right to worry about their children's playmates, and teachers ought to be conscious about the cliques in their classes—and in the teacher's lounge.

SOME PARADOXES OF TEACHING:
BEYOND THE EXCLUSIVE EITHER/ORS

Teachers need to be needed. How are we to understand such a paradoxical statement? I want to suggest that needing to be needed is how we all grow if we desire to flourish. It is through needing to be needed that good teachers grow in relationship with their students. At first the idea of needing to be needed sounds submissive; it seems to create an expectation of self-sacrifice and perhaps self-eradication. A self-centered public, and especially those segments composed of selfish fixed personalities, has often viewed the teaching profession in just that way. In a nation obsessed by false notions of purely negative freedom that assume a rational autonomous self entirely detached from connection with others, such attitudes come as no surprise. I appeal to the intuitions of those who know that they find out who they are only through reciprocal relations with others. To these people the paradox of needing to be needed is no paradox at all.

Teachers need to be needed. Appreciating this paradoxical statement about the expansive personality of good teachers leads to several other epistemological, metaphysical, and ethical paradoxes. The *Oxford English Dictionary* (1971) defines *paradox* as: "A statement or proposition which on the face of it seems absurd or at variance with common sense, though, on investigation or when explained, it may prove to be well-founded." The paradoxes of expansive growth are only paradoxical from the commonsense prejudice of the autonomous fixed self. Embracing the paradoxes of expansive personality proves well founded because it allows us to grow and create through relationship and community. What allows us to embrace them, however, defies the usual canons of philosophical common sense.

Dewey was very clear about where he stood regarding self-transcendence and growth, and he stated his position by pointing out the dangers of the popular, but often narrowly defined notion of self-realization. Dewey (1932/1985b) asserted:

> The *kind* of self which is formed through action which is faithful to relations with others will be a fuller and broader self than one which is cultivated in isolation from or in opposition to the purposes and needs of others. . . . The kind of self which results from generous breadth of interest may be said alone to constitute a development and fulfillment of self, while the other way of life stunts and starves selfhood by cutting it off from the connections necessary to its growth. But to make self-realization a conscious aim might and probably would prevent full attention to those very relationships which bring about the wider development of self. (p. 302)

Paradoxically, the vulnerability of needing to be needed, generous breadth of interest, and attentive relationships with others are among the most valuable virtues in cultivating expansive personal growth as well as practical wisdom. Those who grow expansively know how to bestow and receive. They also know that if so desired they may continue to grow, along with those others with whom they nurture reciprocal relations of mutual bestowal, for their entire life. They also know that they must learn to live with the paradoxes of growth.

Carol Gilligan (1982) identifies precisely what it is about the paradox of reciprocal relationships that defies the analytical logic of either/or when she contrasts the "ethics of justice" (with its emphasis on dispassionate and detached calculations conducted in a metrical hierarchy of moral rules, principles, and laws) with the "ethics of care" (concerned as it is with webs of personal connection, concern, and care for particular others and our self). Gilligan (1982) puts the paradox this way: "We know ourselves as separate only insofar as we live in connection with others, and that we experience relationship only insofar as we differentiate other from self" (p. 63). If we are generous, it is easy to generalize this into the following: We know ourselves only insofar as we know others, and others only insofar as we know ourselves. Such is the paradoxical epistemology of expansive personalities. It is by embracing the paradoxes of reciprocal relationships that teachers learn and grow by responding to the needs of others. This is the paradoxically circular logic of loving bestowal. More precisely, it is a spiral of expanding growth that can encompass entire communities. Teachers have seen it in their classrooms over the course of a good day, or a good year. Good schools may sustain it for their students, teachers, and staff; communities sustain it for their entire school system. To be good is to grow harmoniously within the classroom, but to grow teachers must exercise an intelligent and generous sympathy.

The paradoxical epistemology of personal growth is one that many teachers will recognize even if they find the process of professionally securing it frustrating. It is at least what many teachers hoped for when they entered teaching. Let us now provide an equally paradoxical metaphysic of expansive care that is as commonsensical as its epistemology. Such a metaphysic is required to understand not only how relationships can lead to discovery and knowledge of one's self and others as we and they actually are, but how relationships can poetically call new possibilities into existence, that is, how they can be truly self-transcending and transformative.

The metaphysic, like the epistemology, is Dewey's. Both are commonsensical. That is probably why neither has been popular with modern philosophers. I will develop Dewey's metaphysics more in the next chapter by describing the ways things may be created using Play-Doh modeling clay. The basic idea is that all of existence consists of events. Individual human existence is an event best recognized by its narrative structure. It has a beginning, a middle, and an end; a plot line; characters; a setting; and moments of active disclosure. All existence is a mixture of the actual and the potential. When two events interact, the actuality of the one may actualize the potential of the other, and conversely. Both events are transformed. Dewey was a "transactional realist." Let us concentrate on the relation between two events, the lives of a student and a teacher. In transactional relationships between teacher and student, the potential of the student is actualized when she learns. She may learn how to do something, or that something is true or false, or perhaps that some things are more desirable than others. Eventually the student may even learn that she becomes what she loves and set out to seek the wisdom of "artful living." It is the task of the teacher to possess the actual practical wisdom needed to initiate this transformation either by direct instruction or by creating a classroom and school environment in which students can develop self-knowledge, explore interests, develop abilities, and try new ideas and attitudes. The potential to possess these virtues can only be actualized through the transactions the teacher carries on with his students. The teacher and student transaction can be reciprocally transformative. Actualizing potentialities is creative. It bestows value on others by helping them to realize their unique potential. It resembles the sculptor shaping the stone to call forth the image hidden within. It is a perceptive and imaginative activity requiring us to "see" the possible in the actual.

Teachers are moral artists. They, too, have their potentials actualized by the students and by the creative activities in which they engage that allow them to respond in ways that promote the growth of their students. In an expansive caring relationship the roles of teacher and student can reverse in curious ways. In caring for others we not only come to know ourselves but we must explore our interests, develop our abilities, and try out new ideas and attitudes. Restricting ourselves to transactions between human events, we can put the paradox thus: We may actualize our potentials only if we actualize the potential of others and we may actualize the potentials of others only if we actualize our own. Expansive love lies beyond Platonic possession. This kind of love will not possess, nor will it be possessed. Expansive perception sees that whatever the actual state of its character, it can love itself only if it loves the lovable in all those who have influenced it. Expansive souls grasp the paradoxical truth that they grow only if they can bestow and receive gracefully. Expansive personalities realize that the ultimate aim of education can only be more education. There is an artistic logic to loving and living like this, if we can only perceive it, as good teachers, good teacher educators, and good practitioners of all kinds do. They do not need metaphysics to justify their faith or good acts, that is, those acts that are intelligent, sympathetic, and generous are sufficient. Philosophy may provide insight and understanding, but one senses that love is beyond the love of wisdom alone. There is poetry, then there is silence, then there is listening.

Conventional analytic rationality is unable to reconcile the creative tensions generated by contraries and paradoxes due to the constraints of either/or logic. For instance, the logical law of the excluded middle that says "A or not A" must necessarily be true. It asserts that either you are a sympathetic teacher (A) *or* you are not a sympathetic teacher (not A). Either Tony is learning-disabled (A) or he is not learning-disabled (not A). The laws of analytic, discursive rationality are assumed to be true *a priori*, that is, prior to all experience. Deweyans believe that truth and the laws of logic are always a *consequence* of empirical inquiry. I want to overcome exclusive either/or relationships. Such exclusive logical laws do not allow for becoming or growth. They lack the rhythmic temporality required to comprehend the idea of an emergent personality or the creative process of improving response. It is a logic suitable only for fixed selves incapable of growth through sympathetic reaction and creative response. The logic of practical reasoning, however, is daimōnic and therefore capable of coping with genesis, becoming, and growth.

The expansive self exhibits the "human erōs." What Alexander (1993) means by this phrase is the *"drive to live with a funded sense of meaning and value"* (p. 203). Human beings passionately desire to learn, create, and grow. Erōs is a daimōn. Formless and free-flowing, it lacks *logos*, that is, analytical structure and order. The beautiful imparts shape to erōs. The beautiful is the harmonious aesthetic order that gathers and structures the means for calling good "ends-in-view" into existence. Loving well requires a lovely logic. For Plato, erōs, as any other daimōn, mediated between heaven and earth. For the pragmatic naturalist, desire, sympathy, imagination, and caring inquiry mediate among actual conditions, including the current self, and future possibilities for others, self, and society. Erōs embraces the paradoxes and problems of creativity, genesis, and growth, including the teaching erōs.

Teachers need to be needed. That the teaching erōs, it is how teachers drive to live lives with a funded sense of meaning and value. Needing to be needed is a vulnerable condition, but in an ever-changing, vague, and uncertain world it is the wisest way to be. It allows us to be open to and perceptive of the needs of others, including our students and ourselves. It also allows us to respond more appropriately to unique, one-time-only situations rather than relying on cookie-cutter logic, abstract formal rules and laws, or unresponsive technocratic calculations. Desiring the good, striving for sympathetic understanding and response, and disciplining ourselves to the demands of hard practical reasoning allow us to transform and improve persons and situations. The fluidity and freedom of erōs can recognize and respond to the complicated, rapidly shifting, and uncertain classroom context in ways that theoretical abstractions can not.

THE RHYTHM OF GROWTH:
HARMONY, LOSS, AND RECONSTRUCTION

Expansive selves are much stronger, more agile, and far more fulfilled than those fixed and final selves that are already all they will ever be. Dewey (1925/1981) expressed it this way:

> Shared experience is the greatest of human goods. . . . God is love is a more worthy idealization than that the divine is power. Since love at its best brings illumination and wisdom, this meaning is as worthy as that the divine is truth. Various phases of participation by one in anothers's joy, sorrow, sentiments and purposes, are distinguished by the scope and depth of the objects that are held in common, from a momentary caress to continued insight and loyalty. (pp. 157–158)

Those who need to be needed find their own good in caring for others and providing for the good of their charges. If they are wise they will also allow others to care for them. If, however, they sacrifice by not caring for themselves or by allowing narrow fixed selves to control and manipulate them, then they will not grow. Eventually they will either burn out or, worse still, rust in place. The wise only sacrifice a relatively narrow kind of self to grow personally and morally, just as it is necessary to sacrifice part of a tree when it requires pruning. Those faithfully devoted to expansive personality share with Dewey a deep commitment to growth as the all-inclusive and supreme ideal for living. There is no denying it: Loss is a part of the natural rhythm of expansive growth. Sometimes pruning frees us from emotional vines that block sunlight and strangle growth. Let us not deceive ourselves, though: Growth involves real vulnerability and risk. Pruning sometimes permanently damages the person, as it does the plant.

Let us pause to fully appreciate the scope and importance of the paradox that arises from acknowledging loss as part of the natural rhythm of life and expansive growth. For many the notion of simultaneous loss and growth seems a paradox. They might well acknowledge that they cannot grow and remain the same, but they insist that growth is always cumulative. Sometimes it is, although that is not always for the best. Often, if we are to grow, we must stop being daddy's little girl or the wife who not only loves and honors but always obeys. Perhaps detachment and the suppression of emotion are not the masculine strengths some of us were taught. The Marine Corps taught me that "if you are a man, then you can take it," but sometimes if you are a man, you will not take it. No human being should. When we grow, even if we grow cumulatively, we must become someone else. When our personal identity changes, our relationships will change. Will those whose love sustains us—our parents, our friends, our children—continue to love us if we change? If we grow, not everyone in our web of relationships will respond to us as they did before. Why should they, since we are not the same?

Changes anywhere in the web will surely alter other relationships in unpredictable ways. Sometimes it is necessary to sacrifice friendship, love, and respect to grow. There is a kind of love that desires only to possess. Erōs alone, without a sense of self-transcending bestowal, is just such a love; it may smother growth. Sometimes growth is unrealizable without loss and even infidelity. It is always necessary to question loyalty. To what and to whom do we owe fidelity? Is it to our fathers, our calling, our community? Is it to our mothers, the Marine Corps, our country? Suffocating love and good intentions sometimes poison us. They demand unquestioned loyalty, honor, and obedience. The choice to grow is not an easy one. Sometimes to grow we must end or alter relationships. Knowing when and how to maintain and transform relationships, as well as when to accept the necessary losses, requires the greatest wisdom.

Loss is our human lot. There is only one world, the world of nature that includes human nature. That world is constantly evolving; nothing is permanent. If the possibilities for growth are endless, it is because we are able to find no fixed and final actualities in our fluid, ever-changing world. Existence is precarious, and death always follows life. Death may only stalk a living world. The paradoxes mount. Those that are only living may only die. We create children, we call into existence systems of education, and we make cultural meaning. The culture goes on, and so, too, do those who have creatively responded to the needs of others in this ever-moving world, each according to her own unique human capacities. Those who have committed themselves to the larger rhythm of life catch a glimpse of a larger kind of love. They find immortality in living well with and for others. Teachers devoted to the virtues of their practice are born again in each nascent generation, and it is only they who can guide others in their desire to grow. Teachers cannot serve as guides on a journey of creative growth unless they themselves have traversed part of the expanse themselves.

Let us develop a Deweyan understanding of the rhythm of expansive growth as a way of learning to cope with the paradoxical relation between expansive growth and loss. It involves an aesthetic movement from personal and social harmony, through disharmony and loss, and finally back to harmony again. The paradoxes arise from a vast groundswell whose deepest, constantly changing undercurrents bring forth ever-varied rhythms of life. We live in a world where senseless suffering, terrible and irreplaceable loss, and appalling affliction often prevail. In spite of our best efforts, some students who should succeed will not. Others suffer physical and emotional abuse. All these evils are terrifyingly real and undeniable; yet if these evils were not possible, the goodness of growth would not be possible either.

Practical wisdom chooses those possibilities that lead to growth and relies on practical reasoning to creatively call those possibilities into existence. Human nature is a part of nature, a participant in an unfinished universe. Human nature is that part of nature where the creation continues most intensely and passionately to create. Growth means the continued creation and creative unification of meanings and values. Evil is the decay of those values that sustain life and growth. Growth is the all-inclusive and supreme value because artistic creation (poiēsis, or calling into existence) is the most magnificent activity of the living creature.

The rhythms of nature are rhythms of growth, being born, and putting forth. It is the rhythm of loss and reintegration. Dewey (1934/ 1987) wrote:

> There are two sorts of possible worlds in which esthetic experience would not occur. In a world of mere flux, change would not be cumulative; it would not move toward a close. Stability and rest would have no being. Equally is it true, however, that a world that is finished, ended, would have no traits of suspense and crisis, and would offer no opportunity for resolution. . . . The live being recurrently loses and reestablishes equilibrium with his surroundings. The moment of passage from disturbance into harmony is that of intensest life. In a finished world, sleep and waking could not be distinguished. In one wholly perturbed, conditions could not even be struggled with. In a world made after the pattern of ours, moments of fulfillment punctuate experience with rhythmically enjoyed intervals. (pp. 22–23)

This is a remarkable statement of the paradoxical faith of a naturalist. It confronts with honesty and integrity the horror of a world in which there is no more meaning to make. We may experience extended periods of unity and harmony accompanied by an overall sense of well-being, but if we are to grow we must pass through periods of pruning, disunity, and disharmony. That is the rhythm of life and growth. The dawn of a new day of growth and an afternoon of harmonious delight may follow the night of loss, but those nights are long and chilling, and we are never sure if we will be there at daybreak. Even those devoted to expansive growth can sympathize with those fixed selves who choose to live in the calm twilight of dusk.

It is understandable that in a world of toil, trouble, and tragedy people would seek escape into a realm of perfection like Platonic heaven. It is a flight from freedom, living, and growth.[6] Only at the moment of loss and death would a perfect, eternal, and unchanging world look attractive when contrasted with the world of the living. Without the tacit contrast to a living world, a realm of unchanging perfection would appear what it is—infertile, fallow, and meaningless. Many want to preserve life forever but fail to consider that an eternally unchanging world is an already dead world. Only a living world includes loss and death, and only those who want to live and grow will acknowledge this fact and learn to live with it. Children can only grow in a living world.

Many who abandon the hope of transcendental salvation embrace pure contingency. They are called nihilists, yet that term might just as easily apply to those committed to unchanging eternity. Either way, life becomes inert, dumb, and meaningless. For nihilists, if there is no Platonic heaven, then life becomes senseless chaos. The paradox for these poor souls is that they are still in love with the Platonic quest for certainty and immortality. Life lies somewhere between eternal perfection and senseless chaos. Life is where the daimōns dance between the actual and the possible, and it is always possible to make more meaning in a living world.

Many so-called postmodernists stress the radical contingency of the self, our language, and our communities. They, like Dewey, refuse to let occasionally useful distinctions harden into dualisms. Derrida and Foucault, for example, emphasize that there are no eternal essences, fundamental meanings, or timeless truths. Richard Rorty (1979, 1989) remarks on the similarities between the postmodernists and the writings of Dewey. Derrida has developed a procedure called "deconstruction" that he uses to disclose the location in a text where it makes a transcendental or foundational claim. Deconstruction reminds us of the contingency of existence and the flux of events. It is also useful for destroying hegemonic structures. It would be unwise to forget that a world of mere flux is a meaningless world. Dewey (1925/1981) affirmed "the ineradicable union in nature of the relatively stable and the relatively contingent" (p. 56). Life, creation, and becoming occur between the Platonic, permanent, and immutable on the one side, and the chaotic, contingent, and adventitious on the other. Once this is recognized, the primary moral task for teachers becomes one of creating and rendering stable those values that contribute to bountiful flourishing for their students.

A world of genesis, growth, and becoming requires practical wisdom. Dewey (1925/1981) believed that "it is the intricate mixture of the stable and the precarious, the fixed and the unpredictably novel, the assured and the uncertain, in existence which sets mankind upon that love of wisdom which forms philosophy" (p. 55). When postmodernists fail to recognize the practical moral value of the "relatively stable," they fall into nihilism. Instead of enjoying the daimōnic dance, they deconstruct frantically. Ironically, if they were more morally responsible, they could be less serious. They lack phrōnesis. Such practical wisdom allows us to recognize the best possibility, the highest value, or end-in-view, in the precarious that may be actualized in the present. Practical reasoning, that is, intelligent inquiry, allows us to accomplish what wisdom recommends. "The striving to make stability of meaning prevail over the instability of events," wrote Dewey (1925/1981), "is the main task of intelligent human effort" (p. 49). Indeed, practical reasoning is part of practical wisdom, for it would be unwise to desire what is beyond our intelligent power at present.

While it is true that all essences, identities, and so on are contingent social constructions, it is a mistake not to recognize that some type of relatively stable structure is necessary to continue and exalt in our existence. Those who must struggle for existence without fang or claw should not deconstruct working tools (meanings) without need, and even then it is wise to reconstruct quickly. Only a privileged, secure academic could ever fall in love with constant deconstruction and the avant-garde as a way to avoid foundationalism and secure freedom. Such freedom is only negative. It is only freedom *from* something. It lacks the commitment, hard work, discipline, and above all faith necessary to sustain the struggle to actualize a valued end-in-view and obtain positive freedom through right action. Positive freedom, that is, freedom *for* some ideal end-in-view, requires immense discipline and responsibility. Constant and continuous deconstruction cannot be attractive to practitioners in a contingent, dangerous, and often destructive world.

Growing is the only ultimate end in life. If deconstruction can contribute to greater joy and meaning in life, then we should delight in it. If
it cannot, then it is destructive and we should shun it. To survive and
delight in our lives we need working tools, that is, made meanings. No
doubt these poetic creations are contingent, but so, too, are the creators
who created them to satisfy their needs and desires. There is always a
constant requirement for critique and possible deconstruction, but we
should immediately try to follow the act of deconstruction with reconstruction. The rhythm of construction, deconstruction, and reconstruction is part of the holistic rhythm of expansive growth.

Loss, decay, and death are real. They are part of expansive growth
in a living world. Each individual is a unique, one-time-only event. The
loss of one human being leaves a larger scar on the cosmos than if a
galaxy that contains no conscious beings should suddenly flame out.
For teachers, lesser losses may still leave emotional bruises. It can be as
simple as acknowledging that a student was not quite ready to serve as
a safety patrol or participate in a debate tournament, or it can be as profound as knowing and accepting that no matter what teachers do to
help a student they will not be able to save him from cruel circumstances
beyond their control. It is not always possible to plumb these depths,
but teachers can ride the rhythm of growth, suffer the losses, and delight in living and learning. For Deweyans, being made alive is among
the most wonderful things in all existence. The only thing better is to
grow and be made more alive, and that is the function of education and
the faith of the Deweyan educator. This is precisely why Dewey (1916/
1980a) could write, "If we are willing to conceive education as the process of forming fundamental dispositions, intellectual and emotional,
toward nature and fellow-men, philosophy may even be defined *as the
general theory of education*" (p. 338, emphasis in original). Philosophy
means the love of wisdom. Those who love wisdom love to grow.

Those who are in love with life desire to grow. Those who love to
grow love and care for others and let others care for them. That is the
paradoxical logic of expansive growth. Only the truly tough-minded
dare embrace this paradoxical truth. It is too much for the Platonic
transcendental logician or the modern epistemological escapist. It is too
much for the nihilist. It is just another paradox that those rigorous
analytic logicians who think they are so tough-minded with their exclusive either/ors lack the strength and courage to confront. It is the loving
champions of care, concern, and connected growth willing to remain
vulnerable and risk loss who are the truly strong. Each of us will grow
to the largest extent obtainable without despair. The supreme task of
education is to cultivate this growth. It is a difficult and dangerous task

to sustain this all-inclusive value. When the desire for expansive growth becomes instilled within the soul, then change becomes inevitable and action unavoidable. The passionate desire for growth accepts loving constraint, for it desires to grow straight and strong, but it refuses to accept hegemonic dominance and control. The desire for growth is threatening to many of the bureaucratic philosopher kings who control curriculum and mandate instruction in our schools.

Loss is the destiny of living creative creatures such as ourselves. Fixed personalities attempt to get beyond the power of love, loss, and pain. They deny the human predicament. It is an act of ultimate egotism for any individual to think she alone of all living creatures may transcend life. It is a terrible mistake, for being made alive, being made a human being, and continuing to grow is a miracle of existence. Loss of unique, irreplaceable, and one-time-only beings that we love, need, and desire is the most undeniable and painful truth that everyone knows. There is chaos and evil in the world. We will feel it even if we deny it. Love's losses frequently hurt deeply—they are like a living death—but if we can transcend egotism, we may catch a glimpse of the underlying rhythm of life and recognize that a deeper sense of love lies in expansive growth through commitment to life and especially through relationships with others. That is all we have, and for those in love with life that is enough. Good teachers feel the wonders of life, embrace them, and celebrate them with their students. For them that is enough.

A FEMINIST CRITIQUE OF JOHN DEWEY

Raymond D. Boisvert (1995) calls John Dewey "an old-fashioned reformer." Maybe he was too old-fashioned. What makes Dewey old-fashioned for Boisvert (1995) is that, "the whole challenge of Deweyan educational philosophy involved the attempt to preserve the best of home education in a world where schooling as a distinct institution had become a necessity" (p. 158). It is by participating in the functions of the family that a child's curiosity is first stimulated. The home is the setting in which the child first begins to learn cooperation and to refer his needs and actions to those of others. It is where habits of cooperation, industry, and responsibility are first formed. For Dewey (1916/1980a), "An occupation is a continuous activity having a purpose. Education *through* occupations consequently combines within itself more of the factors conducive to learning than any other method" (p. 319).[7] Dewey thought that "the occupations" found in and about the home—for example, cooking, gardening, or building—were particularly important and should be taught to boys and girls alike. As Boisvert (1995) puts it, ''The family serves as a springboard from which the child interacts with others, and through which the wider cultural and natural worlds are introduced'' (p. 158). Generalizing the virtues of participating in the occupational functions of a healthy family led Dewey (1899/1976b) to conclude:

> If we take an example from an ideal home, where the parent is intelligent enough to recognize what is best for the child, and is able to supply what is needed, we find the child learning through the social converse and constitution of the family. . . . There are certain points of interest and value to him in the conversation carried on. . . . There is no mystery about it, no wonderful discovery of pedagogy or educational theory. It is simply a question of doing systematically and in a large, intelligent, and competent way what for various reasons can be done in most households only in a comparatively meager and haphazard manner. (pp. 23–24)

Being intelligent enough to see what is best for our children involves compassionate sympathy, moral perception, and a desire to see them grow. The ideal family would be the caring, expansive family. The ideal family was, for Dewey, a valuable place to begin to catch an image of the ideal school. The ideal of the functions that a school should perform emerged for Dewey out of the social interactions, functions, and occupations of the ideal family.

Dewey (1899/1976b) was very clear in *The School and Society* that the upheavals of the Industrial Revolution at the turn of the last century required a reconstruction of society's system of education. Surely today's schools again require reconstruction as they move into another century and into the postindustrial and postmodern age. In *The Schoolhome: Rethinking Schools for Changing Families,* Jane Roland Martin (1992) calls attention to the modern home, where only 7% of families are of the traditional mother-stays-home-and-father-works variety while more than 65% of women work outside the home. She calls attention to the millions of latchkey kids and single-parent families as well as other nontraditional family structures. Dewey could not have anticipated such dramatic change, but he certainly would have insisted it was again time to reconstruct our schools. Ideally, for some, harmonious nontraditional families can continue to carry out the truly valuable occupations and functions found in the so-called traditional home, but in practice this is happening less and less.

Martin (1992) refers early and often to Dewey's *The School and Society* and is laudatory of the connection he makes between school and home. Nonetheless, Martin (1992) observes, ''The actual proposal Dewey made

. . . does not address our own situation. . . . The radical change in education he proposed was to put into the school the occupations of the earlier home. The critical factor in the second transformation of America's homes is the removal of parents, not work" (p. 7). She is correct, and she points to a place where Dewey's thinking surely requires reconstruction. However, Martin (1992) may be too critical when she concludes:

> Dewey apparently found it possible to remember home only by producing a heartless derivative thereof. In his eyes the household of an earlier generation was a place of work. . . . He paid no heed to the intimacy and affection of family relationships and to the shared day-to-day living that constitutes domesticity. . . . In recommending that the occupations of home be transplanted into school, he was tearing them from their domestic roots just as surely as the Industrial Revolution had done when it moved production out of the private home. (p. 126)

Dewey did tend to ignore "domesticity" and had relatively little to say explicitly about caring. Martin (1992) believes that, however right Dewey might have been for his day, what is needed now is "what Carol Gilligan, in her groundbreaking book *In a Different Voice*, has called an 'ethics of care.'" (p. 45). Dewey's philosophy, however much as it may need reconstruction, is compatible with an ethics of care. Dewey did not, however, explicitly refer to one particular form of caring associated with the family that has been especially important to some feminists, namely, feminine and maternal approaches to caring (see Gilligan, 1982; Noddings, 1984; Ruddick, 1984).

Sara Ruddick (1984) informs the ethics of care with a model of mothering:

> Maternal practice responds to the historical reality of a biological child in a particular social world. The agents of maternal practice, acting in response to the demands of their children, acquire a conceptual scheme—a vocabulary and logic of connections—through which they order and express the facts and values of their practice. In judgments and self-reflection, they refine and concretize this scheme. Intellectual activities are distinguishable but not separable from disciplines of feeling. There is a unity of reflection, judgment, and emotion. This unity I call "maternal thinking." (p. 214)

Ruddick is clear that maternal thinking is an activity engaged in by some men as well as many women. Maternal thinking displays the relationship among reflection, judgment, and emotion that characterizes the relationship among teaching, loving, and logic. It is a useful paradigm of practice, if not pushed too far, for a caring profession such as teaching.

Maternal practice concerns itself with meeting the needs of children for preservation and growth. Ruddick (1984) believes there are at least "three interests" that govern maternal practice. They are: (1) preserving the life of the child, which she insists requires humility and cheerfulness as practical virtues little appreciated by the male members of society; (2) fostering children's growth, which means that caregivers must welcome change; and (3) shaping a child acceptable to the social group in which the mother participates. The last can lead to internal conflict when the larger, dominant society demands that children have virtues of which the mother may not approve; for instance, preparing her daughters to be docile and her sons to be aggressive. The foregoing are all significant concerns for those in the caring professions, and all exhibit an element of expansive self-transcendence. Ruddick's three "interests" provoke a capacity that she calls "attentive love."

Attentive love is dependent on "selective attention" and contributes to "moral perception." It involves emotionally grounded selective attention directed toward the needs of those for whom we care. Ruddick borrows a line from Iris Murdoch to express what she has in mind: "The task of attention goes on all the time and at apparently empty and everyday moments we are 'looking,' making those little peering efforts of imagination which have such important cumulative results" (cited in Ruddick, 1984, p. 223).[8] The moral task in any caring activity is the desire to respond appropriately to the needs, desires, and dreams of others. Such sympathetic reaction and response require attentive love, moral perception, and self-transcending selective attention. That seems to be the message of all of those like Ruddick, Gilligan, and Noddings who rightfully champion an ethics of care. Understandably, many teachers find the ethics of care and models of maternal caring attractive.

A FEMINIST CRITIQUE OF THE ETHICS OF CARE

The pragmatist feminist M. Regina Leffers carries out a Deweyan pragmatic reconstruction of the ethics of care. She does so by reflecting on the feminist pragmatism of Jane Addams, extracting an ethics of care from Dewey's aesthetics, and then joining them. Leffers uses the results of her reconstruction to respond to two serious criticisms of the ethics of care.

Leffers (1993) notes, "The ethics of care has been largely characterized by a focus on responding to the real needs of others, and its 'primary virtue' is to be caring" (p. 65). Leffers refers with respect to the work of Carol Gilligan (1982), Nel Noddings (1984, 1992), and Sara Ruddick (1984), among others. Certainly perceiving and responding to the needs of others are central to teaching, loving, and logic. Leffers (1993) thinks an ethic of care has immense possibilities, but she believes it fails to realize them in at least two ways, observing:

> Thus far in the dialogue on the ethics of care, we have no theoretical foundation that will help us to understand why the caring response at the highest level of ethical behavior will include not only ourselves and those within our intimate circle of family and friends but also those human beings who would appear to be unconnected to us. We also have no understanding of what moves us from one level of moral reasoning to the next. (p. 64)

What especially concerns Leffers are the dangers of self-sacrifice, selflessness, and the lack of emphasis on caring for oneself in the ethics of care. Leffers notes that although the need to care for oneself is widely acknowledged by the champions of the ethics of care, exactly how to achieve it remains unclear. Her answer is a useful reconstruction of Deweyan ideas in support of feminist ethical projects that extends the notion of the expansive self we have been discussing.

Leffers (1993) believes that the ethics of care "is mired in the particular and cannot be generalized beyond close, personal relationships; the feminist approach should work toward a much broader understanding of what it means to care for" (p. 75). Dewey's notion about the most general thought being the most generous helps here. Leffers (1993) worries particularly about maternal models of caring and wonders "whether the morality of love as it derives from women's experience is worthy of being used as a paradigm for ethical behavior" (p. 65). Many see the paradigm of "maternal thinking" as just the opposite of a morality of love because the existing dominant social constructions of women, the family, and maternal care are representative of an oppressive system. Ruddick (1984) herself notes, "Obedience is largely a function of social powerlessness. Maternal work is done according to the Law of the Symbolic Father and under His Watchful Eye, as well as typically according to the desires, even whims, of the father's house. . . . Maternal thought will have to be transformed by feminist consciousness" (p. 222). Acting always in accord with the desires of others is emotional slavery. People who do not blaze with their own passions burn out.

Leffers does not care to be caught up in the debate over the practices of maternal caring. Instead, she would prefer to augment the pragmatist pantheon to include women such as Jane Addams and reconstruct it using Dewey's philosophy of art. The result tends to remove the ethics of care from rigid association with mothering. It might be better thought of as a model of parental caring. Given the large number of males who make so many important contributions to teaching in and out of class-rooms, parental caring seems a much more attractive perspective for a caring profession. The virtues of the ethics of care transcend gender boundaries. Augmenting the pragmatist pantheon allows Leffers to de-velop Dewey's insights into the importance of social connection. She also gains insight into why a more caring attitude allows us not only to understand caring for ourselves as part of caring for others, but why it is better for all to seek a more expansive sense of ethical response that extends the caring attitude beyond our intimate circle of family and friends. Leffers also believes that Dewey's emphasis on creative re-sponse to the needs of others allows us to understand better how people move from one rung of integration to another.

The notion of creative (poetic) response to the needs of others in-volves an ideal of love as the bestowal of value upon others, and thereby upon ourselves. Of heavy necessity and joyful lightness, we cultivate the arts of living well. Leffers, like Dewey and Addams, believes that bestowal is best understood as artfully creating better relationships, more democratic communities, and less oppressive scripts for perform-ing social roles such as caring. The idea of expanding ourselves through caring for and cooperating with others provides the reason to build relationships. Others have what we need. This reason becomes even more convincing when we recognize that we would have no sense of self (or even a mind) at all without social relationships. In the end, caring for others is a form of caring for ourselves and caring for our-selves is a form of caring for others.

In *Twenty Years at Hull-House,* Addams (1910/1981) described her frustration with social scripts that placed "cultured" young women of a certain social class such as herself in golden cages. Educated as social ornaments, they were expected to play the piano, go to the opera, read poetry, and visit art galleries. Indeed, in many ways they resembled the works of art in the galleries they visited: lovely to look at, but practically useless. She spoke of suffering the "shock of inaction." Addams (1910/1981) expressed the emptiness and world weariness of young women sensitive to social needs and problems, but forbidden to respond to them meaningfully: "You do not know what life means when all the difficulties are removed! I am simply smothered and sickened with ad-vantages. It is like eating a sweet dessert the first thing in the morning" (p. 65). These were the feelings of someone living the prescribed role of a woman of "privilege." Even the social scripts for culturally ad-vantaged women may deprive them of a sense of power and efficacy.

It was assumed that public problems were not among the concerns of "proper" young women.

Leffers (1993) expresses her understanding of what called Addams to create Hull House:

> Society was losing both the heartfelt and intelligent resources of young women, as well as the positive action the women could have taken in their desire to find solutions to human problems. Addams began the Hull-House Settlement in response to the need within herself and her contemporaries to use their skills and intelligence and the multiple needs of the community surrounding the Settlement. . . . Jane Addams had the distinctive ability to see individuals as wholes that are interconnected and interrelated parts of ever-larger wholes. (p. 69)

The desire to fulfill the need to be needed seems to be the emotional stance taken by Jane Addams. I think it is also the stance taken by teachers who creatively bestow value upon others as they seek to live valuable lives themselves. It is also the stance of those expansive personalities that grow by connecting with and caring for others, while reciprocally allowing others to connect with and care for them. It is the stance required for the self-transcending ethics of care. Love as bestowal goes far beyond simple enlightened self-interest. Enlightened self-interest would forsake vulnerability and loss as it calculates its selfish interest, like a banker appraising a loan applicant. The attitude of loving bestowal alone, however, will not assure quality care. The desire to give and receive care alone is not enough. We must be able to reason well to obtain the values we desire for others or ourselves; it is necessary to know how to make, create, and bestow love. That requires technē, the skill and knowledge of making.

The poetic arts of love require more than heartfelt care, concern, and connection. They also require intelligent sympathy, careful inquiry, and generous generalization. Mere sentimentality is often simply an escape from hard work and harder thinking. There is a logic to loving well. It is a practical logic that relies on erōs to initiate and internally motivate our inquiry into the practices that allow us to create those values that will satisfy the needs of others, and thereby our need to care. Remember, inquiry is a daimōn that mediates between ignorance and wisdom. Inquiry is a crucial teaching task.

Addams (1910/1981) stated that the philosophy of Hull House was founded

> in the solidarity of the human race, a philosophy which will not waver when the race happens to be represented by a drunken woman or an idiot

boy. Its residents must be emptied of all conceit of opinion and all self-assertion, and ready to arouse and interpret the public opinion of their neighborhood. They must be content to live quietly side by side with their neighbors, until they grow into a sense of relationship and mutual interests. . . . They are bound to regard the entire life of their city as organic, to make an effort to unify it. (pp. 98–100)[9]

Addams and Dewey were both committed to an organic holism that respected differences without allowing relationships to degenerate into alienating fragmentation or discord. Teachers care because they are connected, and they desire to be better and more creatively connected. Differences provide the creative tension and alternative possibilities; mutual relationship provides the hope for creative cooperation. Leffers (1993) believes that "Addams assumed a universalized caring standpoint, one that extends beyond the realm of personal relationships, in herself as well as in those who resided with her at Hull-House" (p. 70). A universalized caring standpoint requires the realization that "the only truly *general* thought is the *generous* thought." Dewey could well have learned this from his friend and colleague Jane Addams. Most likely it was an insight they both shared, or perhaps it was a product of their mutual inquiry.

Leffers (1993) concludes:

John Dewey expresses many values, imperatives, and purposes similar to those Jane Addams reveals in her work. This is not surprising, for they were like-minded colleagues who shared ideas with each other, talked about how those ideas could be actualized, and held a mutual respect for the other's work. . . . Just as Jane Addams did, John Dewey also saw life as it gets lived as an organic, contextually embedded whole. . . . Our projects are imbued with all of our hopes, fears, expectations, [and] values. (p. 70)

Addams and Dewey were fortunate to have had such a close and mutually reinforcing relationship. It is also our good fortune, for the collaboration of Addams and Dewey brought our society many needed goods. Communities exist in time as well as place, and they, too, may be expansive. That is why what happens within classroom and school communities can be so enduring.

Leffers (1993) believes that she could have used any of Dewey's major works to illustrate his belief that when holism, organic interconnection, and the contextual quality of all meaningful activities interpolate themselves into everyday human relationships, improving the quality of our lives must be a shared activity. She feels, though, that the most revealing choice is "Dewey's *Art as Experience* because it lends itself particularly well both to theory, why we can do something, and to practice, how we can do that same thing" (p. 70). Dewey's aesthetics allows us to connect theory with the practical arts, including practical reasoning. It does so because Dewey rejects any sharp theory-versus-practice dichotomy. Teaching is one instance of the mixing of moral practice and practical art.

Leffers moves perceptively to that part of Dewey's aesthetics that best explicates the way relationship and expansive creation fit together. Dewey concerned himself with how we have separated art from everyday life. Art has become something done by a few extraordinarily talented people called artists. So-called fine art separates itself from practical art primarily by means of a false criterion that says fine art (like the "fine" women of Jane Addams's social class) must be useless for daily living. Elite critics of fine art carry out appraisals, according to which they assign values to "objects of art." Others transform these objects into commodities to be bought and sold. These elites then display their artistic commodities apart from the ordinary workaday world, where those "cultured" elites educated to appreciate them view the works at their leisure. Dewey (1934/1987) observed that "the growth of capitalism has been a powerful influence in the development of the museum as the proper home for works of art, and in the promotion of the idea that they are apart from the common life. . . . Generally speaking, the typical collector is the typical capitalist" (p. 14). Dewey, Addams, and Leffers share Diotima's vision that creativity is constantly everywhere every day. For Dewey, the sharp distinction between fine art and practical art is yet another false dualism closely allied to the theory-versus-practice dualism. If an artist's work of art on a museum wall, or a student's work of art on a classroom bulletin board, effects upon us what Dewey called "the work of art," then it is possible to follow the unique logic of the individual creator's interests. As teachers, we can learn a new perception of the order of things and the infinite possibilities available for making meaning in this world. If the artifact works effectively upon us we may acquire insight not only into the life of the artist, but into our own lives as well. Teachers would comprehend their appraisals of their student's classroom artifacts, writing samples, worksheets, tests, and so forth, much differently if they looked at them this way. They would cease to comprehend judgment as exclusively cognitive. Aesthetic and moral aspects would become far more important.

Leffers (1993) observes:

> In *Art as Experience* Dewey describes the way in which we have separated art from life. We have dissected life in such a way that art has come to be an

object, something we have carefully placed inside a small cubbyhole of life—we no longer participate in it. We go to museums to look at it or we hang it on our walls. Art as a quality of the transactive experience of making and doing in our everyday lives is unknown to us. Art has become thing. Removed. Sterile. Commercial. Valuable. Separate. (p. 71)

Teachers should experience their practice as the art it is, although most intuitively recognize it as a transformational experience for both themselves and their students. Too many technocrats view classrooms as so many museums, that is, as places apart from the home and community where teachers and students go to do "school work." Teachers are practicing an art, whether they know it or not, and the transformations in their students are the artifacts of their artifice. Look on the tabletops and walls of a vibrant classroom community. Everywhere we see the artistic products of the class's collective aesthetic endeavor. If nothing is there but prefabricated bulletin boards and standardized worksheets stacked up on the desks, we can be sure that learning has become "a thing," something removed from what interests teachers and students in everyday life.

It is significant that Dewey titled his book on aesthetics *Art as Experience* and began it with a chapter titled "The Live Creature." As Dewey (1934/1987) saw it, the problem for aesthetics was "that of recovering the continuity of aesthetic experience with normal processes of living. . . . Even a crude experience, if authentically an experience, is more fit to give a clue to the intrinsic nature of aesthetic experience than is an object already set apart from any other mode of experience" (p. 16). Dewey concerned himself with the artistic experience of creation and the aesthetic experience of appreciation as lived out during everyday activities of work and play. Classrooms lacking in opportunity for creative expression and appreciation of everyone's work are sterile, uncreative, and reproductive of prescribed teacher-proof curricula. Such classrooms are separate and removed from the passions and activities of students' everyday lives. They are commercial when students and parents see classroom activity as valuable only for getting a job.

The idea of lived experience as a rhythmic tide of loss and reintegration informs Leffers' reliance on Dewey as she develops her theory of expansive growth through caring. I have shown that for Dewey life grows through natural transitions—through phases of stable equilibrium, disequilibrium (including loss), and back to equilibrium again. Further, it was shown that those periods of relatively stable equilibrium involve harmonious aesthetic forms. Finally, we also learned that for Dewey science and art, scientific law, and aesthetic form emerge out of the rhythms of nature and are in reality identical. As Dewey (1934/1987) put it, "All interactions that effect stability and order in the whirling flux of change are rhythms" (p. 22). Later we will return to review Leffers' own discussion of rhythmic transition and expansive growth.

Near the end of the section titled "Sensitivity and Thoughtfulness" in his *Ethics*, Dewey (1932/1985b) observed:

> One of the earliest discoveries of morals was the similarity of judgment of good and bad in conduct with the recognition of beauty and ugliness. . . . The sense of justice, moreover, has a strong ally in the sense of symmetry and proportion . . . a harmonious blending of affections into a beautiful whole, was essentially an artistic idea. . . . The Greek emphasis upon *Kalo-kagathos* [the good life], the Aristotelian identification of virtue with the proportionate [golden] mean, are indications of an acute estimate of grace, rhythm, and harmony as dominant traits of good conduct. (p. 271)[10]

Ethical and aesthetic appreciation have much in common. Recall the *Oxford English Dictionary* definition of taste as mental perception of quality, judgment, or discriminative faculty. This is also an extraordinary aesthetic expression of Dewey's holism. Dewey refused to disconnect the aesthetic, moral, and intellectual domains.

In *Art and Experience* Dewey (1934/1987) wrote:

> It is not possible to divide in a vital experience the practical, emotional, and intellectual from one another and to set the properties of one over against the characteristics of the others. The emotional phase binds parts together into a single whole; "intellectual" simply names the fact that the experience has meaning; "practical" indicates that the organism is interacting with events and objects which surround it. (p. 61)

This refusal has remarkable educational consequences. If teachers took it seriously, they would have to completely reconstruct their curriculum to emphasize the aesthetic and moral dimensions of our humanity. Furthermore, since a culture's philosophy may be defined as its general theory of education, curriculum reconstruction would require cultural reconstruction and the converse.

There is something else extraordinary about the way Dewey conjoins ethics to aesthetics and science. Many critics contrast the ethics of care, with its insistence on webs of relationship and the inclusion of the moral agent in ethical deliberation, with the ethics of justice and its emphasis on detached deliberation and hierarchy of rules, laws, and principles. Gilligan (1982) clearly rejects any such dualism; so, too, did

Dewey. Dewey's organic holism, by making room in its ethics for aesthetics as well as scientific inquiry, can comprehend justice as achieving harmonious caring relations with one's self and others.

Dewey's ethics emphasize erōs and the aesthetic. Consider the following passage:

> It is notorious that some moralists have deplored the influence of desire. . . . But reasonableness is in fact a quality of an effective relationship among desires rather than a thing opposed to desire. It signifies the order, perspective, proportion which is achieved, during deliberation. (Dewey, 1922/1983, p. 135)

Order and proportion are expressive of aesthetic form. Dewey's account of inquiry emphasizes art and aesthetics. Rationality is practical rationality, that is, the ability to transform the disharmonious into the harmonious. They bring the stable equilibrium and welcomed harmonious feeling described in the last chapter. In *Art as Experience* Dewey (1934/1987) explicated aesthetic form in terms of human relationships and feelings: "A social relation is an affair of affections and obligations, of intercourse, of generation, influence and mutual modification. It is in this sense that 'relation' is to be understood when used to define form in art" (p. 139). Dewey (1911/1978) understood form functionally: "Any process, sufficiently complex to involve an arrangement or coordination of . . . processes, which fulfills a specific end in such a way as to conserve itself" (p. 466). It is an achievement of a working harmony among diverse and mutually modifying processes. It is not some structure detachable from the person or the material situation she is in. Practical reasoning involves finding means functionally coordinated to construct a chosen end.

Social interaction is mutually modifying. Learning, for instance, is the explicit goal of the teacher–student relationship. A rational person is someone with an expanding number of ever more refined thoughts and passions that are diverse yet harmonized, and correspondingly for rational communities. That is why an ethics of justice that excludes the emotions involved in caring would not do for Dewey. Understood aesthetically, love, logic, and morality are complementary rather than conflicting. Rational deliberation seeks to secure the values we desire. Because of the rhythm of loss and recovery of integration, we never conclusively complete the task of practical deliberation. Expansive growth means continuously creating and re-creating new relationships and responses. New relationships mean loss of integration, and that initiates inquiry in the continuing quest for the creation of new and more expansive relationships. Those in love with life, and those who desire more of it by growing, would have it no other way. Expansive natural growth is poetic in Diotima's sense, or in that of *natura* and *physis*. In expansive growth we are born anew in every spring we experience. In the nascent state of a new self coming into existence we are sometimes awkward and clumsy. Those in love with life delight in "the creation," their own artistic creations, and aesthetically appreciate the creations of others. Those in love with teaching do the same. They recognize the nascent state of their children and forgive them their awkwardness, just as they forgive themselves when they, too, are growing.

Leffers makes much of the theme of loss and reintegration in Dewey's aesthetics, although she shifts to a metaphor that Dewey borrowed from William James. She cites the following passage from *Art as Experience*. I enlarge the citation to link it with some of the themes already discussed:

> In every integral experience there is form because there is dynamic organization. I call the organization dynamic. . . . Because it is a growth. . . . William James aptly compared the course of a conscious experience to the alternate flights and perchings of a bird. . . . Each resting place in experience is an undergoing in which is absorbed and taken home the consequences of prior doing. . . . If we move too rapidly, we get away from the base of supplies—of accrued meanings—and the experience is flustered, thin, and confused. If we dawdle too long after having extracted a net value, experience perishes of inanition. (Dewey, 1934/1987, p. 62)

The rhythm of experience must be steady. When we move too fast, things become chaotic. If we move too slowly, we do not grow, that is, extract the net value of our aesthetic experiences and artistic endeavors. Commenting on Deweyan passages like these, Leffers (1993) remarks: "We are alternately consumers and producers, receivers and makers. We undergo and we do, we perch and we fly. What is important is for us to grasp the union that exists between undergoing and doing—they are intimately tied together in experience" (p. 71). Analytic either/or logic cannot grasp the aesthetic union of opposites that occurs between perchings and flights, undergoing and doing, because it does not accommodate the tensions of becoming, genesis, and growth. The context of classroom practice, however, is always changing; children are always growing. The practical logic of everyday classroom teaching is far more complex than discursive theoretical logic can grasp. It must be sympathetic, imaginative, and prophetic. Leffers distinguishes two distinct but dialectically paired qualities associated with each aesthetic moment of undergoing and doing. They are perception and response.

In the undergoing phase of aesthetic experience, it is the capacity to receive, our ability to take in that is crucial. Dewey (1934/1987) calls this "perception" and contrasts it with mere recognition:

> In recognition [re-cognition] we fall back, as upon a stereotype, upon some previously formed scheme. . . . Perception replaces bare recognition. . . . The perceived object or scene is emotionally pervaded throughout. . . . The esthetic or undergoing phase of experience is receptive. It involves surrender. But adequate yielding of the self is possible only through a controlled activity that may well be intense. . . . Perception is an act of the going-out of energy in order to receive. . . . We must summon energy . . . to *take* in. . . . For to perceive, a beholder must *create* his own experience. (pp. 59–60)

Self-transcendence or self-eclipse (as opposed to self-sacrifice or dominating self-assertion) means that the present, relatively stable self is open to new possibilities for growth. Self-eclipse is not a passive activity; it creates its own expansive experience in conjunction with others.

Perception is crucial for an ethics of caring. It allows us to perceive the needs, desires, interests, wishes, and hopes of others under our care. It involves sympathy. Perception provides the "data" for creative moral response. Perception for Dewey is active and passive. It involves self-eclipse but not self-eradication and allows for growth and becoming. It is like a daimōn that moves beyond the usual either/ors of the conventional logic of self-assertion or self-sacrifice. That is important if caring is to cease contributing to an oppressive social system. One of the principal reasons for Leffers' championing a Deweyan aesthetic for the ethics of care is that it allows ethical agents to consider their own needs as well as those of others in the context of formulating a caring response. Self-sacrificing teachers tend to burn out quickly, while self-assertive ones slowly rust in place and seem never to retire.

Leffers (1993), who calls attention to many of the sentences from Dewey's aesthetics cited above, comments on them this way:

> When we perceive, we do not merely recognize, but see with fecundity. Our physicalness and all funded ideas are involved in the process of perception. . . . Thus, we get the very clear picture of aesthetic undergoing as a fertile, active, creative, responsive, and directed process, one in which we are completely absorbed and in which we open ourselves to being *vulnerable* to meanings, intensity, and change. (p. 72) [emphasis added]

There is no need for an ethics of care for the Platonist or any others who seek certainty and invulnerability. For them there can only be an ethic of dispassionate justice, meted out according to a detached, ordered hierarchy of rules and laws. To perceive the needs of others, we must be vulnerable enough to know that we, too, are needful. Leffers is also right to call attention to the fact that not only the response but the perception is fluid, fecund, and creative; it can give birth to relationships, and it bestows value upon the perceived. The ethics of care involves sympathy, imagination, poetry, prophecy, and inquiry.

"In the doing phase of aesthetic experience," writes Leffers (1993), "the quality of how we do what we do is at issue" (p. 72). Practitioners want to know how to get things done, how to arrange seating in this class, how to hold down lunchroom noise, or how to assign grades. Answering questions such as these in the context of practice requires creative activity. Practice involves action: We desire something, or the situation we are in needs transforming. Leffers (1993) describes these creative activities this way:

> We begin the doing phase of aesthetic experience with an impulsion—a desire to create. Next we get an idea [ideal value] of what it is that we want to create; Dewey calls this our "end in view." When we are creating something imbued with the quality of art, we gain emotional satisfaction in and from our work. It represents . . . a genuine desire in us to be moved, to grow. . . . What results is sincerity and rhythm in the work and emotional satisfaction in us. (p. 72)

Teachers wonder, How can I get Natasha to stay on-task? How can I make language arts more interesting for Steve? These questions define problems requiring solutions. We desire to move from ignorance to answers. When approached aesthetically, creative activities such as these can bring a satisfaction difficult to describe. Perhaps creative and caring connection is what teachers mean when they describe the psychic rewards of teaching. Perhaps that is why creative autonomy is so important to them. Creative problem solving requires calling novel things into existence, perhaps even things that have never existed before in our school or classroom.

Leffers (1993) draws two conclusions from her reflections. Both turn on Dewey's idea that the only general thought is the generous thought. Leffers (1993) states:

> The work of Addams and Dewey can explain why the caring response in moral reasoning is capable of becoming universal, including the self, those who are close to us, and those who lie outside of our circle of personal

relationships. . . . For if we see ourselves connected to everyone and everything, then problematic social conditions are problems for us in our environment . . . problematic world conditions are problems for us in our world;
and so on. (p. 74)

Yes! Problematic social conditions are problems for us in our school and
classroom environment. Because we are connected, we care best for
ourselves only if we care for others, and care for others only if we care
for ourselves. In a holistic, organic, and growing world, good care is
expansive. Expansive caring is loving bestowal. It bestows value not
only on others but also on ourselves. If we are vulnerable we are open
to loss, but we are also open to becoming, growth, the need to care for
ourselves, and the need to be needed.

Leffers' (1993) second conclusion is a practical suggestion:

> The work of Addams and Dewey can also give us some direction in how we
> might begin to put into practice ourselves a level of moral reasoning that
> includes a universal caring response. This matter of following our own
> creative impulses is important for both Addams and Dewey because it
> honors our differences. As philosopher-writer-teacher-artist, my impulse
> will lead me to work on the theoretic underpinnings of connection and care
> and to try to translate theory into method. I want to figure out how we can
> teach connection and care; then I want to figure out how we can teach
> teachers to teach connection and care. (pp. 74–75)

Teachers and teacher educators should teach connection and care. Leffers provides a powerful and convincing Deweyan reconstruction of the
ethics of care that allows her to overcome two serious criticisms. She
shows how the caring response includes both self and other and how it
is capable of moving beyond particularity to wider human circles. Caring must be perceptive and creative if it is to be fully responsive. The
idea of teacher as artist is crucial to loving bestowal as a creative teaching act.

Let me sum up how the work of Pappas and Leffers allows us to
construct a Deweyan ideal of self-transcendent loving bestowal. The
logic of needing to be needed and loving bestowal is paradoxical. Episte-
mologically, we know ourselves only if we know others and we know
others only if we know ourselves. Metaphysically, we actualize our
potential for growth only if we actualize the potential for growth of
others, and we actualize the potential for growth of others only if we
actualize our own. Finally, in the ethics of care, we care best for ourselves only if we care for others, and care best for others only if we
care for ourselves. Loving bestowal requires constructive *criticism*, and

discriminating judgment of the artistic efforts of others and ourselves. It does not only discover and appraise values; it creates them. Loving bestowal relies on moral *perception*, that is, the sympathetic capacity to perceive the needs, desires, interests, hopes, and dreams of others. Finally, loving bestowal calls for aesthetically appreciative recognition and artistic creative *response* to the needs, interests, and values of all of those, including ourselves, caught together in some shared social context. Needs, desires, values, dreams, and aspirations comprise problems. For those of us who need to be needed, the problems of others are our problems. Their world connects to ours. Loving bestowal concerns itself with moral perception, constructive criticism, and creative response. Creative response, constructive criticism, and moral perception are part of practical reasoning and are, in that order, the topic of the next four chapters. Creative response often requires us to call into existence things that have never before existed. Dewey called these original creations "ethereal things."

CHAPTER 3

Play-Doh, Poetry, and "Ethereal Things"

Only imaginative vision elicits the possibilities that are interwoven within the texture of the actual.

—Dewey, 1934/1987, p. 348

I begin this chapter with a description and a discussion of an activity that I use to start the first day of my philosophy of education seminar. The example illustrates Dewey's transactional metaphysics while playfully dramatizing that his realism is naturalistic and immanent within everyday living rather than supernaturalistic, Platonistic, and otherworldly. The example involves each student playing with the possibilities inside a small canister of Play-Doh, a modeling compound appropriate, as the label indicates, for "ages 2 & up."

THE METAPHYSICS OF PLAY-DOH

Many teachers know a recipe for creating a noncommercial near-equivalent of Play-Doh. I use the commercial product because it comes in a wide variety of colors and includes a kind with little silver sprinkles that get all over the students' clothes and in their hair where it is hard to get out. Telling the students that the sprinkles help the lesson really stick with them brings a groan from the class. As you read my description of this activity, try to imagine yourself as a student in the class.

What color did you pick? Over the years I have noticed my tendency to choose earth tones; it is green today. We open the canisters. Ahh. As they squeeze the material; it warms in their hands. Regularly someone will spontaneously note that it smells like elementary school. Several usually admit they like the smell; others concur. Commonly there is a brief exchange of memories, mostly pleasant. Getting "a feel" for the material (the "data") seems to occur simultaneously on the sensory, tactile, and the emotional levels. Light-hearted silliness seems to flood the room as we play. This is fun.

Once the material has warmed to their touch, the students and teacher make something out of the clay. I explain that no artistic talent is necessary and urge the students to relax. Some students show remarkable command of technique as they mold the clay. Others are very clever in their conception. A few are both. Some, such as the teacher, are neither. It does not matter. Almost everyone becomes surprisingly intent on their pro-duction.

The activity takes five to eight minutes. When everyone has created something, they display it on their desks. We then take turns telling each other what we have created. Frequently students volunteer an explanation of what they made. It is remarkable how often the artifact expresses a meaning or a mood from deep within. The teacher admits that he made his usual elephant, dog, or pig without much emotional investment—perhaps because he knows what is coming.

Without warning, the teacher *shouts*: "Crush it! Smash it! Destroy it now!" Instantly the mood alters. Frequently someone will refuse; many hesitate. They are the ones who immediately feel the cruelty of the command. It *is* cruel. Why? Because even when it may appear trivial to others, it is cruel to devastate anyone's artistic creation. Who cares about a hunk of Play-Doh? The creator cares. It is an emotional assault to demolish self-expression. Teachers know that this happens all too frequently. I have never met a teacher who enjoys evaluation, especially when it concludes in some summative final grade. Critical appraisal of the value of the goods our students create is necessary, but teachers sense that it may easily slip into the destruction of our students' sense of artistic efficacy and self-worth. There are exceedingly difficult issues involved in artistic appraisal. I will explore them later. For this lesson, though, it is only a notable aside. At this point the teacher announces that the students have been "doing" Dewey's transactional metaphysics. There is usually an unusual silence.

THE POETICS OF PLAY-DOH

Whatever the artifact produced with the Play-Doh, I claim it is only one actualization of an infinite number of possibilities within the material. In calling these possibilities into existence (poiēsis), there are limits other than our imagination and practical skill (technē). The material the artist has to work with constrains actualizable possibility. Artists cannot construct just anything they desire from a small canister of Play-Doh.

For instance, they cannot construct a working computer or a comfortable chair. Still, the possibilities are unlimited. Similarly, although imaginative and creative teaching can produce remarkable results, material conditions do provide real constraints. Teachers should only be expected to accomplish so much in seriously underfunded and understaffed schools. The larger society must share responsibility. Good teachers can only do the best with what they have. That does not mean that as meliorists teachers should not seek to actualize the best possibilities they can. Material conditions provide real limits, but finite creatures such as ourselves cannot say with certainty what may become possible in the future. We do not want to fall into romantic escapism by refusing to acknowledge that present material conditions constrain real possibility. At the same time, we do not want to be mere realists chained like slaves to the limits of what actually exists at this moment. It requires wisdom to determine what is really possible given current conditions. Such wisdom is clearly beyond mere knowledge of current actual states of affairs. At the very least, it involves an imaginative grasp of possibilities beyond present actualities.

Dewey was a naturalist and transactional realist. Both the Play-Doh and the living artist are distinct natural events that begin to interact when the artist removes the Play-Doh from the canister. The Play-Doh and the artist are a mixture of the actual and the potential. The artist's existing thoughts, ideas, ideals, feelings, imaginings, and embodied technical skill actualize the Play-Doh possibilities, just as the Play-Doh actualizes the artist's potential and limits what she can do.

The same transactional relation holds between teacher and student. To master the medium, the artist must actualize her own potential to think more clearly, imagine more creatively, feel with more taste and refinement, and practice more intelligently. It is useful to think about teaching as an artistic practice—the teacher as artist and the student as medium. Teaching, though, is transactional, so it is not unusual for the aesthetic roles to change. For example, a high school drama coach brings to a proposed theatrical production a certain technical and philosophical impression of a particular play. But the student actors, the "medium" if you will, also bring a certain degree of expectation and imagination to the work. Together, students and teacher push the limits of one another's experience and manage to actualize through performance something none of them envisioned at the start.

Part of refining one's technique is mastering the tools of production, including the instrumental logic of practical means–ends reasoning. Another part is knowing the medium. In teaching that means knowing the students. Refining and mastering the tools of production require practitioners to refine and master themselves through expansive growth. Dewey (1925/1981) remarked on the instrumental importance of the practitioner when he urged us to "understand operations of the self as the tool of tools, *the* means in all use of means" (p. 189). The most important tool available to any artist in any context of practice is the practitioner himself.

Teachers desire to call into existence the good of their practice. That means the good of their students. To call into existence the good of their students they must, reciprocally, desire to call into existence their own good. The most important thing practitioners can do to improve the quality of their practice is to improve themselves. That involves developing the habits, abilities, thoughts, ideals, technical mastery, and virtues of the practice. Becoming an expansively more competent practitioner requires disciplined practice and eventually self-creation, that is, calling into existence a new and better self. Subject-matter knowledge is only a small part of the discipline of teaching. Mastering the latest classroom disciplinary technique, or knowing how to use the latest instructional technology, may be worse than useless if teachers do not grasp what it is good for, that is, what value or end-in-view it is a means to actualizing.

Understanding what a technique is good for—indeed, whether it is genuinely good at all—requires practical wisdom (phrōnesis). Such wisdom lies beyond just knowing how to apply the tool. Practical wisdom about the use and purpose of tools is the most prized possession of the self, the tool of tools. Persons who declare their dedication to teaching, but are not constantly working to improve, are deceiving themselves. Tragically, and ironically, many teacher education programs devote themselves entirely to the technical knowledge of how to teach without any particular concern with the practical wisdom and the content of the character of the practitioner. They fail to treat teaching as a vocation requiring constant personal and professional growth.

After pausing to reflect on the artistry that shapes Play-Doh and students, I then change the subject slightly. It is relevant here to note that teaching is a vocation. *Vocation* derives etymologically from the Latin *vocare*, "to call." It denotes a summons or a bidding to do something or become somebody. Teaching is a call to respond to the needs, desires, and interests of children (see Hansen, 1995). Faithfully answering the call to teach requires mastering the practical art of teaching, including its tools, to produce the goods of the practice. Mastering one's self, the tool of tools, requires improving the content of our character and acquiring the virtues of the practice.

A vocation like teaching chooses to call us as much as we choose to answer. At some time in their lives, most teachers have sensed that teaching calls out to their natural and acquired capacities. Many teachers experience their desire to teach as a calling. Listen to student teachers try to articulate this call; most cannot. Nor can many experienced teachers fully explain teaching's call to them. There is an eloquence to this ineffability. The call is vague and indeterminate, yet persistent and powerful. Try explaining the wonderful feeling of connecting with students to someone who has never had the experience.

Teachers become this call only if they answer with persistence and care. By answering in a disciplined way, we create ourselves. There is no certainty in advance that what we hear is calling for us. We must be careful. For a unique individual to answer a call authentically and responsibly, she must partially annul it by making it her own. An authentic answer to a general summons must be an expression of one's own unique style. A responsible answer questions the call. Where is it coming from? Is it authentic? Is it truly good? Self-reflective value critique is among the virtues of any practice.

To answer any calling responsibly is the work of a lifetime. Student teachers who are beginning their inquiry into the vocation of teaching will have to discipline and re-create themselves considerably just to achieve an entry-level poetic competency in responding appropriately to the needs, desires, and dreams of their students. This may mean a reconstruction of their own needs, desires, and dreams. Many good people take a few teacher education courses and understand that teaching is not for them. That is not what they desire to become. It does not satisfy a deep need or lofty dream. Others will teach for a few years and conclude the same thing, or realize that they have actualized a great deal of their potential in answering the call but that the newly created self must answer other voices. These choices are all good. It is only those who lose their sense of calling and still remain in classrooms that do harm.

To care for ourselves we must care for others, and to care for others we must care for ourselves. Caring for ourselves requires participating in reciprocal relationships that allow us to bestow as well as secure value. It is easy to criticize the ethics of care in teaching because it seems to demand too much not only from teachers, but students as well. It is unreasonable to count on our students to give comfort, sustenance, and good advice, although sometimes they do. The relationship between teacher and student cannot always be entirely reciprocal. That would be an unfair expectation. Reciprocity in relationships need not be shown merely by simple mirror reflection. The vocation can act as daimōn or intermediary in the reciprocal bestowal of value between teacher and student. Practicing the virtues of the vocation, including the development of practical wisdom and the refinement of practical reasoning that allows teachers to call into existence the values of their practice, can sustain them and help them grow even when relationships with their students, or colleagues, cannot.[1]

In summary, the metaphysic of Play-Doh exposes the transactional and transformational nature of all artistic construction. It allows us to appreciate that in producing its artifact, any social practice such as teaching is attempting to actualize the ideal possibilities within some material. The most desirable possibilities are the goods of the practice, that is, the values it strives to create. All vocations should be constantly debating the goods of the practice.

PLAY-DOH PARADOXES

Teachers seek to respond creatively to the needs, desires, and dreams of their students in ways that actualize their students' potential for growth as well as their own. The good of teaching involves creatively bestowing value on others. The caring vocations bestow value on those who practice them when the practitioners bestow value on others. The virtues of a vocation like teaching require practitioners themselves to become refined instruments of the practice. Becoming a master practitioner requires teachers to actualize and refine their potential for intelligent, creative, and responsible response to their students, helping them in actualizing their potentials. Good practicioners are always working at becoming teachers.

There are no Platonically perfect practitioners in the vague and mutable world of everyday practice. In striving to master, refine, and reconstruct the techniques and tools, including themselves, required of their form of poetry, that is, bestowing the good of the practice on their charges, teachers also bestow value on themselves. Transactional realism allows us to appreciate this paradox: To bestow value on students teachers must expansively bestow it on themselves, and to bestow value on themselves teachers must expansively bestow it on students. This does not mean that teachers should expect students to always bestow value on teachers; that is unfair. Society should bestow value on teachers, but often it does not; that is unfair, too. Still, teachers should expect the vocation to bestow value if they respond to its call and discipline themselves to its demands.

Social transactions transform us and those with whom we interact forever. Creative practitioners may permanently transform the virtues,

goods, and techniques of the practice itself, just as the practice transforms them. To see this, just think about the lasting impact of those
with whom you have interacted intimately: lovers, parents, offspring,
close friends. They have all left a lasting impression. Now think about a
valued mentor, inspirational book, or talk. Think about your students. I
am thinking about my students throughout the Play-Doh demonstra-
tion. Remember, this is the first session. There is still more to do with
the Play-Doh, and yet we have already been at it for over half an hour.
What in the world are they thinking? What can metaphysics have to do
with the real world of teaching? All teachers know the feeling of emptiness when we see that blank look of uninterest in our students' eyes.
Two or three will drop the class after the first session. What *does* Play-
Doh have to do with reality? Maybe they are too smart for this nonsense. Where am I to go from here? I am about to say realists are weak,
and perhaps worse.

It is important to note another paradox before moving on to explore
the limits of commonsense realism implied by Play-Doh metaphysics. I
will call it the poetic paradox: Answering the call of the vocation to teach
with discipline, dedication, and deliberation allows the practitioner to
call into existence within herself the poetic capacity to call into existence
the goods of the practice in others. Each vocation is its own style of
poetry in Diotima's sense of poiēsis. There is also an aesthetic dimension. Each unique individual must respond to the call with his own
unique artistic style. It is individual style that allows the most able practitioners to call into existence what Dewey called "ethereal things,"
those remarkably original creations the vocation needs to renew itself.

PLAY-DOH, REALITY, AND IMAGINATION:
THE CALL TO TEACH

The metaphysical recognition that whatever the artist actualizes in the
Play-Doh is only one of an infinite number of possibilities has at least
two significant consequences for realists. First, when realists say humankind must act according to the structure of reality, they are usually
just saying that they must conform to some current, historically contingent state of affairs. Reality for the transactional realist includes both the
actual and the infinite transformational possibilities that lie within the
actual. This is not romantic escapism that thinks it can ignore the actual
state of affairs. Most realists present themselves as tough-minded, task-
driven doers. Ironically, they are often just docile conformists with weak

imaginations. For without imagination, people are slaves of the actual. Shaping any actual state of affairs, from Play-Doh to public schools, is done by those who have the power, for good or evil, to put things into the form they desire. Realists are often either the powerful who want to keep things as they are, or too oppressed in imagination, thought, or action to transform the situation. It is here that the metaphysics and aesthetics of Play-Doh open up substantive ethical issues.

If we can imagine alternative aesthetic possibilities to an actual state of affairs, then we can conceive alternatives to the contingencies of any given situation. Who, we might wonder, shaped this situation and why? This is the metaphysical and moral understanding needed for free choice. Lacking imagination, commonsense realists think they are free when they feel no restraint. Maybe they are accustomed to their manacles. Simply following social rules and laws constructed by the masters of the art of statecraft does not of itself make one moral; it may just make one a docile and compliant slave.

If our imaginations are rich, we may decide that the way things are now is not how they ought to be. We may decide that things should be better. Metaphysical statements are about what exists or could exist. Moral statements are about what should or ought to exist. Prophecies about conditions that ought to exist but do not are counterfactual claims. Recall Dewey's description of wisdom cited earlier: "Wisdom is a moral term, and that like every moral term refers not to the constitution of things already in existence." (1919/1982a, p. 44). Wisdom is beyond knowledge of the actual constitution of things, although such knowledge is part of wisdom. Commonsense realists mistake part of reality, the actual, for the whole of reality, that is, the actual and all of its transformational possibilities. The commonsense realist can be powerful and wealthy, but to be wise one must be able to see the possible in the actual, able to pick the possibilities that ought to exist, and able to pursue them with a passion by applying the tools of good practice. Nurturing wisdom means seeking insight into morally desirable possibilities concealed by the actual. It also means the ability to unconceal them. Such ability dwells within already actualized vocations that involve preexisting techniques and continuous inquiry that, when combined, allow us to call into existence "ethereal things." Significantly, *teaching* derives etymologically from the Middle English *techen*, "to show how to do," or simply, "to show." Vocations like teaching provide a place for the exercise of practical wisdom as Dewey defined it: "A social hope reduced to a working program of action, a prophecy of the future, but one disciplined by serious thought and knowledge"

(Dewey, 1919/1982a, p. 43). It is hard work to envision what is concealed beneath politically approved ignorance and prejudice and show it to students.

Teaching is a moral art that requires the greatest degree of practical wisdom. Wisdom is beyond systematic and proven knowledge of actual existing facts and truths; it is even beyond knowledge of what could possibly exist. Practical wisdom requires insight into those possible values that *ought* to exist if we are all to live the good life. Wisdom demands that we understand not only what we should call into existence, but how to do it. Finally, wisdom requires insight into what needs calling out of existence.

So here I am. The first hour of the class is over. We are staring at the Play-Doh or off into space. Some express excitement, others boredom, and many seem confused. Teachers, including teacher educators, all know what these awkward silences feel like. We have held infinity in the palm of our hand and eternity in an hour. Some will not return after break. Others are thinking that this can only go on for two more hours. Some understand that it could go on forever. Let's take a break.

THE LIVE CREATURE AND ETHEREAL THINGS

Dewey (1934/1987) titled Chapter 2 of *Art as Experience*, ''The Live Creature and 'Ethereal Things.''' Exploring the implications of this title helps clarify the core of Dewey's thinking about the relations among erōs, action, and rationality. It also helps explain his thinking about the relationship between poetry and philosophy in ways that will greatly surprise those who misread Dewey as scientistic. In explaining the second part of his title, "Ethereal Things," Dewey (1934/1987) acknowledged that he "took the liberty of borrowing from Keats the word 'ethereal' to designate the meanings and values that many philosophers and some critics suppose are inaccessible to sense, because of their spiritual, eternal and universal characters—thus exemplifying the common dualism of nature and spirit" (p. 38). To Dewey, Plato's division between the elementary and the perfect revelation in the education of erōs is yet another instance of this dualism. Plato's philosophical construction is a social construction distinguished only by its historical influence. Dewey's naturalism puts the wonder of existence, the miracle of creation, not merely re-creation, into the daily activities and details of our contingent, evolving, and unfinished world. Nature for Dewey is a place where new things are constantly being born or springing forth out of the course of events. Whether creating with Play-Doh, or writing and dramatically performing our own stories in the language arts classroom, these acts derive their remarkable power from the miracle of creation wherever it occurs, however mundane the act. Imagination and creative action release possibilities and transform the commonplace instantly.

The passage of Keats's poetry from which Dewey's chapter title is derived recommends that the artist should gaze "upon the Sun, the Moon, the Stars, and the Earth and its contents as material to form greater things, that is ethereal things—greater things than the Creator himself made" (Dewey, 1934/1987, p. 38). This way of thinking seems to reverse the causal order of creation as described by Plato and places the role of poets above that of philosophers. Dewey himself, however, did not see any special need to engage in combat for supremacy between poetry and philosophy. For him philosophy could be creative and poetry critical. Both functions are needed to continue the evolutionary process of intelligent creation. The fertile earth may bear fruit never seen before on vine or tree. Humans, who are themselves the fruit of the earth, are able to care for the nascent blossoms and graft fruit never before found. If Diotima is correct, then both cultivating the land and teaching kindergarten are poetic acts. If Dewey is correct, poetry can create ethereal things and thereby the created can continue the creation.

For Dewey, humanity is a participant in an unfinished universe rather than a spectator of a finished one. To survive and exalt our existence, humans must evolve practices that creatively solve their practical problems and produce life-affirming values, perhaps ones that have never before existed. Original solutions to problems and the genesis of values are creative. Creation perpetuates and refines those prior acts of cultural meaning and value creation that fund the human erōs. There are an infinite number of possibilities in a handful of Play-Doh, only a limited number of which will ever be actualized. Finite and impassioned creatures, we desire only a few of the infinite possibilities and evolve only some of the practices needed to realize our passions. Still, in our creative action we find what is most godlike within ourselves, the expression of passion and power in acts of continued creation and bestowal. We are created creators. When it is said that we are created in the image of God, perhaps it is meant that the divine passion and power to create have been bestowed on us. When teachers bestow value on their students, the passion and power come *through* them as much as *from* them. We share the power and the passion with other living creatures.

Dewey (1934/1987) makes much of the fact that Keats "identified the attitude of the artist with that of the live creature" (p. 38). Dewey (1934/1987), who held a better opinion than Plato of "the breeding instinct" we share with "the brutes," refers us to a passage from Keats that begins with remarks on the commonalties between the love-making and home-making habits of hawks and humans. He concluded with Keats' observation, "I go out among the Fields and catch a glimpse of a stoat or a fieldmouse hurrying along—to what? The creature has a purpose and his eyes are bright with it. I go amongst the buildings of the city and see a man hurrying along—to what? The creature has a purpose and his eyes are bright with it" (cited p. 39). Recall that the Latin *natura* originally belonged to the language of the farmer and breeder. All living creatures exude passionate desire and, so animated, their actions may be graceful and attuned to their purposes.

Dewey was quick to follow Keats in drawing a remarkable conclusion from the above analogy. When human action, like that of other living creatures, is guided by goals, purposes, or ends-in-view, we may gracefully achieve what we desire. Purposeful action desires to creatively harmonize means with ends: "There may be reasonings, but when they take an instinctive form, like that of animal forms and movements, they are poetry, they are fine; they have grace" (Dewey, 1934/1987, p. 39). Recall how Diotima taught Socrates the universality of the "renowned and beguiling power" of love that includes every kind of longing for happiness and the good. The desire of the hawk, the strivings of the fieldmouse, and the habits of the human erōs all passionately and with a beguiling power long for the happiness that the good promises.

PASSION, POETRY, AND PRACTICAL WISDOM

Passion is a part of practical reasoning; nothing is called into existence without it. It is the possibilities that we desire to actualize that drive us to rearrange the world. The human erōs is at the center of the major premise of practical reasoning, all of which arises out of our human need and desire. Guided by our interest in the desired value, we seek means for transforming our environment and actualizing new possibilities. The human erōs must actively arrange and organize its habits, actions, and environment as means for accomplishing the "ends-in-view" or values that it desires. Such passionate activities are part of practical reasoning.

Since we are the tool of tools, the means to any end we may choose, the actions of the able practitioner are instinctive; they are poetry; they are fine; they have grace. Watch the eyes of a good teacher in action. Note how easily he sees a discipline problem before it occurs, how he looks away from minor transgressions so as not to interrupt a group's enjoyment in rehearsing a dramatic story. The left arm embraces the child needing the hug, while the right hand confiscates the baseball cards being traded during class time. More deliberately, the teacher rearranges class seating or reorganizes small group participants to reduce cruel teasing. All these acts establish good, harmonious social relations conducive to learning, and that is beautiful. The supreme power of human passion, unconscious habit, and conscious thought lies in a capacity to move quickly beyond the mundane and call "ethereal things" into existence.

What the passions contribute to this process may be gleaned from the chapter of Dewey's (1932/1985b) *Ethics* entitled "Ends, the Good and Wisdom." Dewey asserted, "Thinking has to operate creatively to form new ends" (p. 185). These are ends-in-view, goods, and values. The subsection, "Ends and the Good: The Union of Desire and Thought," elucidates what Dewey meant by "end-in-view." Here we find such bold statements as, "there can be no separation morally of desire and thought because the union of thought and desire is just what makes an act voluntary" and "the Good is that which satisfies want, craving, which fulfills or makes complete the need that stirs to action. In its relation to *thought*, or as an *idea* of an object to be attained, it imposes upon those about to act the necessity for rational insight, or moral *wisdom*" (Dewey, 1932/1985b, pp. 189, 191, emphasis in original). Wisdom about ethereal things is far beyond knowledge. It is about those desirable imaginative possibilities that morally ought to be actualized even though they are not here now and may never have been before. Practical wisdom is desire expressed as moral conviction disciplined by the artistic techniques of sound practice. It possesses the poetic power to actualize the good in everyday affairs. Thought originates in need and desire and, following the logic of our interests, seeks the coordination of means to ends that, even at the level of unrefined, unreflective, impulsive, and habitual action, may embody intelligence and grace.

Dewey (1934/1987) developed two points about the origins and limitations of cognition from the following passage by Keats: "The simple imaginative Mind may have its rewards in the repetitions of its own silent workings coming continually on the Spirit with a fine Suddenness" (cited p. 40). The first point we have already considered. It is the conviction that reasonings "have an origin like that of the movements of a wild creature toward its goal"; that they, in becoming instinctive, become poetic. The second point has implications for our understanding of the kind of curriculum needed for the education of wisdom. Dewey (1934/1987) said:

> No "reasoning," that is, as excluding imagination and sense, can reach truth. Even "the greatest philosopher" exercises an animal-like preference to guide his thinking to its conclusions. He selects and puts aside as his

imaginative sentiments move. "Reason" at its height cannot attain complete grasp and a self-contained assurance. It must fall back upon imagination—upon the embodiment of ideas in emotionally charged sense. (p. 40)

Imagination and selective interests can confer a vision of values, ideals, and ideas of things that do not actually exist anywhere, but that could be here now. Imagination images possibilities beyond the bounds of the actual. A beneficial, erotic education would stimulate the imagination to create new and genuinely desirable values.[2] Erotic teaching would require imagination to creatively bestow value on students. Those with rich imaginations are also better able to bestow value on themselves.

Dewey (1934/1987) remarked:

Art is thus prefigured in the very processes of living. . . . But all deliberation, all conscious intent, grows out of things once performed organically through the interplay of natural energies. . . . The conception of man as the being that uses art became at once the ground of the distinction of man from the rest of nature and of the bond that ties him to nature. (pp. 30–31)

Like a small stoat or a fieldmouse, we embody thinking, living, and natural desire, but our ability to engage in intelligent, conscious, and reflective deliberation allows human nature to give birth to creations that go far beyond those of the other creatures of nature. We select creatively with a passion and a purpose. Imagination gives us a creative vision of novel goods, new values, and ends-in-view to guide our inquiries. Imagination gives us freedom "in the sense of unity of impulse, desire, and thought which anticipates and plans" (Dewey, 1932/ 1985b, p. 176). Imagination and dramatic action may transform the world by actualizing its hidden potential, thereby calling into existence "ethereal things." As participants in an unfinished and unfinishable universe, human nature, as a part of nature, can continue "the creation."

Dewey did not believe that either emotions or imagination interfered with intelligent thought. Rather, they are integral to intelligent functioning. If love is "an imaginative means of bestowing value that would not exist otherwise" (p. 17) as Singer (1984) indicated, then Dewey's and Keats' notion of calling "ethereal things" into existence *is* bestowal of meaning and value and a fulfilling of the human erōs. Part of bestowing value on students involves reflecting on our emotional reactions to students' actions, collecting sympathetic data, and inquiring carefully that we may know student desires and dreams before responding. Teaching is an infinite, often frustrating, but also a fine and graceful art.

Poets not only perceive actualities, but imagine possibilities with a passion. They desire to actualize their imagined ideals. Even Play-Doh poets may strive to call "ethereal things" into existence. Wise poets rely on fine reasoning to realize their values, but it is hardly a detached and dispassionate logic. Value-neutrality and detached rationality are passions whose very purposes ironically deny their own realization. For Dewey and Keats, acts of reasoning are just paving stones on the roadway to making more meaning. If we must reconstruct "rationality" itself to reach our destination, then we should do so.

Imagination for Dewey and Keats is a daimōn mediating aesthetically between constructed truth and harmonious beauty until the two become whole in wisdom. Dewey introduced this mediation by reflecting on what may be Keats' most famous lines:

Beauty is truth, truth beauty—that is all
Ye know on earth, and all ye need to know.[3]

Dewey (1934/1987) connected this passage to a letter written two years earlier in which Keats attested, "What Imagination seizes as Beauty must be Truth" (cited p. 40). Dewey (1934/1987) clarified the basis for this connection by observing that in Keats' "tradition, 'truth' never signifies correctness of intellectual statements about things, or truth as its meaning is now influenced by science. It denotes the wisdom by which men live, especially 'the lore of good and evil'" (p. 40). At first this observation might not seem to help. If, however, we remember that nowhere is the ancient Greek influence that acted on Keats more evident than in his "Ode on a Grecian Urn," which concludes with the two famous lines above, then we have a clue. By truth, Keats and Dewey were, I suggest, thinking within the Greek tradition of *alētheia*, which we can translate only roughly as "truth." By alētheia the ancient Greeks meant the disclosure of something, or the unconcealment of some being. The closest thing we moderns have to the idea of unconcealment is the word "revelation." The Deweyan pragmatist would prefer to talk about imagination as unconcealing, or calling into existence, the potentialities within an infinite qualitative whole.

The artist's work reveals beauty. Intelligent selection, understood as the exercise of discriminating taste that permits choice among the various possibilities, can reveal the truth. Beauty for the ancient Greeks, including Plato, meant some harmonious form that organized and structured things and situations into an ordered, balanced equilibrium. Plato attributed real existence to the idea of aesthetic form by abstracting the mutable and temporal from everyday existence and placing them in a supernatural world apart. Dewey and Keats refused to do any such thing. Both thought beauty was the functional form or structure that transformed some needful, doubtful state of disequilibrium into harmonious equilibrium by revealing (alētheia) the possible in the actual. The truth of art, of poetry in Diotima's sense, is that it can disclose the beauty of extraordinary possibilities concealed beneath the cloak of the actual, the ordinary, and the everyday. Similarly, teaching is a lovely art whose beauty is often concealed beneath bureaucratic forms, teacher-proof curricula, and tests. This potentiality is as real in making love, making children, homemaking, or the making of good classroom community (statecraft) as it is in sculpting, painting, or literary composition. Dewey saw no simple or sharp difference between so-called fine art and practical arts such as teaching.

So how does art release concealed possibilities? The immediate agent is imagination; the mediate is wisdom. It is imagination that first images the bare possibility, that catches a glimpse of things, meanings, and values that are not now, but that could be. At first such imaginative insight into new values can only be vague, inexact, and imprecise. The beginning of wisdom lies in envisioning ethereal things, however elusive. As Dewey (1934/1987) put it, "Ultimately there are but two philosophies. One of them accepts life and experience in all its uncertainty, mystery, doubt, and half-knowledge and turns that experience upon itself to deepen and intensify its own qualities—to imagination and art" (p. 41). The other philosophy tries to complete the Platonic transcendental quest for certainty that removes all mystery and resolves all doubts forever.

GOOD TEACHING, COMFORT, AND DOUBT

Vagueness, mutability, and indeterminacy are an unavoidable part of teaching. The word *teaching* describes an intentional act. So, too, does the word *loving*. Tragedy and comedy both turn on the vicissitudes of human intention. One turns quickly into the other. Just think about dating, or that "foolproof" lesson plan you made up your first year. Knowing the truth of teaching or loving is a process of long and difficult inquiry in which the most relevant data are sympathetic data and the most important thing to know is ourselves. Good teaching practice demands many of the same traits required of good loving: care; concern; connectedness; moral perception of the needs, desires, and dreams of others (and ourselves); courage; moral commitment; faith and faithfulness; intelligent inquiry to solve problems as they arise in relationship;

aesthetic appreciation; responsiveness; and, above all, wisdom. Teaching, like loving, is difficult because of its vicissitudes, its vagueness, its mutability, and its indeterminacy. Making love, its pro-duction and con-struction, in the etymological sense of those words already discussed, often requires the creation of ethereal things. Moreover, each love is unique unto itself yet inextricably connected to all that came before and all that are to follow. It is much the same with teaching. Good teachers accept life in all its uncertainty, mystery, doubt, and half-knowledge, then strive for practical wisdom and mastery of practical reasoning to transform conditions for the better. Tough-minded Platonists plod on toward the ever-receding goal of certain knowledge of eternal and immutable truth. In the end there truly are only two philosophies.

Teachers often cannot tell what their influence has been. Monitoring change and growth in students is difficult since it emerges so unevenly, unpredictably, and haltingly. It takes time to become familiar enough with students to interpret their individual actions as indicating different needs, desires, or involvement in the subject matter. It takes just as long to learn how to respond appropriately. Often the growth that teachers impel does not manifest itself until much later, perhaps not until the student has moved on to another grade level, or even beyond formal education. Good teachers never become comfortable with the doubts and uncertainties their practice engenders, but they do come to realize that the tensions are not only part of the vocation, but may sometimes be the best part. It takes courage and faith in the future to persist in such an essentially uncertain occupation. But faith and courage alone are not enough. We must constantly be reflecting on our responses and their consequences. Inquiry is never complete. Since every student is unique, teachers must constantly inquire into what will work with this student in this class today. Those who continue to answer the calling to teach realize that it is precisely because we never know for certain that we have gotten it right, and because every class every year poses its unique challenges, that teaching is a worthy lifelong calling in which we can appease our expansive need to be needed, thereby fulfilling our own potential. Still, it is sometimes good when the day ends or summer comes.

Plato did not even venture to speculate about the possibility of actualizing the potential of authentically unique persons or relationships. He did not seek to call into existence truly ethereal things, that is, "greater things than the Creator himself made" (Dewey, 1934/1987, p. 38). Where in the world may we find the continuous creation of ethereal things? Everywhere, although the elementary school language arts classroom is one of the more remarkable places. Let us look for it there.

CHAPTER 4

The Aesthetic Context of Inquiry and the Teachable Moment

It is no more possible to eliminate love and generation from the definition of the thinker than it is thought and limits from the conception of the artist.
—Dewey, 1903/1976a, p. 186

Most educational theorists and researchers recognize that all knowledge and inquiry are context-dependent. In spite of this recognition, the exact definition of *context* remains unclear. The first part of this chapter discusses some of Dewey's notions about qualitative thought and context.[1] The last part tries to disclose the context of reading a text in an elementary school classroom. Good teachers must have an intuitive understanding of the context of practical reasoning. This chapter defends the validity of practitioners' reliance on their feelings and intuitions. Providing a fuller understanding of the context of practice allows us to clarify the elusive situation that teachers call "the teachable moment." I rely heavily on three of Dewey's most important, although largely ignored, essays: "Affective Thought" (Dewey, 1926/1984a), "Qualitative Thought" (Dewey, 1930/1984d), and "Context and Thought" (Dewey, 1931/1985a).

Dewey asserted that some largely noncognitive, qualitative situation provides the necessary "background" for all inquiry, whether quantitative or qualitative in focus. He believed that the "foreground" of cognitive thought (i.e., ideas, rules, and identities) *emerges*, or springs forth, naturally from a noncognitive qualitative background. Indeed, there can be no foreground without such a background. I want to call attention to the many noncognitive components such as need, desire, selective interest, sympathy, and imagination in the background of thought that precede the emergence of the cognitive problem-solving foreground. During the emerging inquiry, once inquirers translate some contextual situation into a problem stated as a linguistic proposition—say, a question—they have already left the precognitive background and entered the cognitive foreground phase of inquiry. Nonetheless, the cognitive phase of the inquiry remains perpetually *qualified* by the noncognitive background, or what Dewey also called "the context of thought."

As Hickman (1990) indicates, inquiry for Dewey is "a busy intermediary," a liaison between wisdom and ignorance, doubt and resolution. Dewey himself identified science and art as technē, a matter of artistic pro-duction and con-struction.

Dewey understood form as an aesthetic creation emerging from natural events. In *Art as Experience* Dewey (1934/1987) wrote, "The first characteristic of the environing world that makes possible the existence of artistic form is rhythm. There is rhythm in nature before poetry, painting, architecture and music exist" (p. 152). This statement may appear to have nothing to do with practical inquiry. As the following passage illustrates, though, Hickman is accurate about Dewey and "pro-ductive inquiry." Dewey (1934/1987) wrote:

> Thus, sooner or later the participation of man in nature's rhythms, a partnership much more intimate than is any observation of them for purposes of knowledge, induced him to impose rhythm on changes where they did not appear. . . . The reproduction of the order of natural changes and the perception of that order were at first close together, so close that no distinction existed between art and science. They were both called *technē*. . . . The idea of law emerged with the idea of harmony. . . . What is not so generally perceived is that every uniformity and regularity of change in nature is a rhythm. The terms "natural law" and "natural rhythm" are synonymous. (pp. 153–154) [emphasis in original]

Natural laws are forms. Many of them are so formal they are expressed as mathematical formulas. Some rules, such as the statement "students learn more if teachers begin class on time," are also forms. They are formulas for good teaching as well as part of the technē of teaching. Forms are created to help harmonize practice. These formulas express natural rhythms and are the product of natural inquiry. Participation that creatively couples the rhythms of human nature with the rest of nature calls new forms into existence. In this way creative inquiry allows humankind to continue the creation. Children learn and grow in biological and social rhythms. Teaching, loving, and logic must resonate and modulate these rhythms.

There is no ultimate separation between art and science, just as there is no deep distinction between theory and practice. It becomes increasingly evident that all inquiries are practical inquiries and all inquiry is an art. Science is a cultural creation. It is a product of human need and desire. In turn, the product of science is truth, or what Dewey preferred to call "warranted assertion."

In Dewey's opinion, art and science are best comprehended as poiēsis and technē. All inquires, including mathematical science, are practical inquiries. They are, therefore, practical arts. Teachers are practical artists, poets in Diotima's sense. Cognitive meanings, including the warranted assertions produced by the labor and instruments of scientific workers, are conducive to making (poiēsis) situations better. This aesthetic, artistic, and poetic sense of making will become increasingly important as we strive to understand loving bestowal.

Erōs, the son of Poros and Penia, is full of technē. He lives in the major premise of practical reasoning midway between people and their values. Recognizing this provides a powerful way to grasp Dewey's instrumentalist understanding of inquiry. Inquiry is an instrument, a technology, that is used for rearranging the world to satisfy our desires. It is especially potent because inquiry is an instrument that produces other powerful tools. Inquiry understood as technē is also a daimōn. It artistically mediates between the actual and the possible, just as it cognitively mediates between ignorance and knowledge. It provides the means to poetically call ideal values into existence. Educational science cannot determine eternal and immutable educational laws good for all students in all classes, cultures, and occasions. That is just another version of the philosopher king's quest for certainty.

Inquiry, including inquiry into education, serves practical interests arising out of life's rhythms. It moves from confidence, satisfaction, and equilibrium, to doubt, need, and disequilibrium, and back again to dynamic harmony. Practical inquiry contributes to this rhythm in the phase that restores the desired equilibrium. Recall that erōs is a daimōn and that daimōns, for Plato, are intermediaries between heaven and earth. Naturalizing Plato's supernatural understanding of the daimōns allows us to comprehend them as mediating between some actual although undesirable state of disequilibrium and some possible desired state of equilibrium and harmony. Even for Plato inquiry is a daimōn mediating between ignorance and wisdom, although for him ignorance means being bound by our opinions of natural, everyday experience rather than knowing the supernatural Forms and the harmony of the Good. Inquiry involves erōs for both Plato and Dewey. Erōs, though, is only one of the daimōns involved in the artistic, mediating activity of inquiry. I think other noncognitive notions such as interest, selective attention, sympathy, and imagination are daimōnic. Surprisingly, the most cognitive component of inquiry (i.e., ideas) also mediates between the actual and the possible.

Practical reasoning is means–ends reasoning in which the means mediate between where we are and where we want to be. Dewey (1939/1988) declared, "*Means* are by definition relational, mediated, and mediating, since they are intermediate between an existing situation and a situation that is to be brought [called] into existence by their use" (p. 214). Means mediate between the actual and the possible by poetically calling the latter into existence.

Most modern thinkers—and especially Dewey's contemporaries, the logical positivists—considered the factors of artistic creation and aesthetic appreciation in inquiry (such as affect, intuition, and imagination) to be irrational; consequently, they consigned these elements to the domain of psychology and confined them to what they called "the context of discovery." Rational thought, logical analysis, and the enterprise of epistemology occurred for them in an entirely different domain called "the context of justification" (see Reichenbach, 1938, p. 6 ff.). Cognitive epistemological and psychological models, or what Jean Lave (1988) calls the "functionalist/positivist position" for comprehending thinking and knowing, currently dominate theories of inquiry.[2] These theories usually treat the so-called context of justification as a logical category and comprehend creativity and rationality as distinct modes of thought requiring entirely different types of investigation. If, as Dewey maintained, the cognitive foreground of inquiry emerges or grows without break in continuity from a precognitive aesthetic background, then any attempt to destroy the functional dependency between creative thought and rational thought is a false dualism. Artistic creativity and discriminating aesthetic appreciation form an integral part of the qualitative background in Dewey's paradigm of inquiry as an emergent organic process.

Dewey's philosophy is organic and holistic. That fact makes it difficult to divide his thought into analytical units, although for the sake of discussion that is what I will do. What Dewey means by context cannot be grasped apart from what he means by the context of inquiry. I begin, therefore, with a brief discussion of his conception of inquiry. Next I consider the importance of the unified qualitative whole of primordial experience, or what Dewey sometimes called a "situation," in establishing the context of inquiry. I will then identify a number of context-setting constituents in this theory of inquiry. These include desire, intuition, selective interest, and imagination. Dewey's theory of art is the key to his entire philosophy (see Alexander, 1987; Garrison, 1995c;

Hickman, 1992; Shusterman, 1992). This is especially the case with Dewey's theory of inquiry.

DEWEY'S THEORY OF INQUIRY

For Dewey, human nature is an integral part of nature (see Garrison, 1994a). That means that inquiry is a natural endeavor engaged in by that specific manifestation of nature called human nature. Dewey posited no supernaturalistic, transcendental, or *a priori* ideas, identities, or principles of rationality (see Dewey, 1938/1986, p. 3). According to Dewey, all that we will ever have or know arises out of everyday practical experience, and even the most abstract of theoretical inquires must return there for final adjudication. Truth, or what Dewey preferred to call "warranted assertability" to indicate that truth claims are always revisable, is a *consequence* of inquiry; so, too, are the very laws of logic (see Dewey 1938/1986, pp. 11, 15). Dewey did not mean, however, that the consequences of inquiry once warranted cannot serve as a context for further inquiry.

The cognitive consequences of prior inquiries can influence the background of subsequent inquiry, just as the precognitive background influenced earlier inquiry. There are two different phases of emergent thought, background and foreground, but to think we can separate them functionally is to commit ourselves to an unwarranted dualism. The belief in something like Platonic heaven—that is, some supernatural realm of exact, eternal, and immutable logical laws (what Plato called "the Forms")—and the belief that we can get outside space and time, or beyond luck and fortune, are equivalent to saying that we can completely decontextualize understanding.

For Dewey, human nature is not only a part of nature, but it participates in the ongoing creation of an unfinished and unfinishable universe; consequently "the creation" continues to create. Influenced by Darwin, Dewey (1920/1982b) argued that "change rather than fixity is now a measure of reality," or again, "natural science is forced by its own development to abandon the assumption of fixity and to recognize that what for it is actually 'universal' is *process*" (pp. 114, 260). As living organisms, *Homo sapiens* constitutes a species—perhaps a fleeting one since "it has been estimated that 99% of all species that have ever lived are now extinct" (Parker, 1992, p. 570, emphasis in original). Thus the purpose of inquiry is not, for Dewey, to discover timeless truths. Rather inquiry seeks to arrive at temporarily "warranted assertions" that aid in transforming the environment so that humanity may maintain and enjoy its precarious existence. Patterns of inquiry must themselves evolve in an evolving world; they must respond to human nature's evolving needs, desires, and interests.

Belief for Dewey is a product of inquiry, and for him beliefs are dispositions to act. Because of his naturalism, beliefs did not exist for Dewey in some mental realm apart from other naturally occurring events. There was no mind versus body distinction for him. If they are so different, we might well wonder, then how do they interact? Dewey insisted that habits of action embody belief. Further, because they are dispositions to act, habits (embodied beliefs) have an affective constituent. What distinguishes vague feelings or innate impulses from emotions is that the latter are intelligent and intentional, that is, directed by habit. Dewey fused the constructs labeled as belief, the body, and emotion into a single construct—habit.

Dewey (1922/1983) contended, "Man is a creature of habit, not of reason nor yet of instinct" (p. 88). By instinct Dewey meant innate neurophysiological impulses such as tropisms. Such impulses are too uncoordinated to be called responses, but they do give us the motive power to act. Our learned habits of response channel and refine our innate affective impulses. They are modifications of our neurophysiological system acquired from prior experiences as participants in the customs of some sociocultural tradition and in our natural–biological environment. They allow us to respond systematically to subsequent situations resembling the one(s) that shaped the original habit. Habits are attitudes, beliefs, and dispositions toward certain modes of action. They are not detachable from their social and physical environment. To grow, individuals must integrate minor elements of action into ever-expanding webs of habitual coordination. Inquiry aids integration.

For Dewey (1922/1983), habits compose the "mind":

> Concrete habits do all the perceiving, recognizing, imagining, recalling, judging, conceiving and reasoning that is done. "Consciousness," whether as a stream or as special sensations and images, expresses functions of habits, phenomena of their formation, operation, their interruption and reorganization. . . . Yet habit does not, of itself, know, for it does not of itself stop to think, observe or remember. (p. 124)

Habits are intelligent, but they are not inquisitive, reflective, or knowledgeable. For teachers or ballet dancers, good performance requires large repertoires of solid and well-practiced habits. In practice, in situations in which the right response must come quickly, too much reflective thought may even be dangerous. According to Dewey, conscious thought and inquiry only occur when established habits fail us. At such times the disruption of habitual action is experienced physically as feeling.

Chapter 2 of Dewey's (1938/1986) *Logic* concerns itself with "the biological natural foundations of inquiry" (p. 30). Dewey was having recourse here to the ancient Greek and Latin definitions of the words *natura* and *physis*, discussed earlier. Biological ideas such as "being born," "springing up," "bringing forth," and "making grow," or what Dewey preferred to call emergence, was a major concern of his naturalistic metaphysics. Human nature is a part of nature, so we must participate in all the functions characteristic of other natural events. The living creature is constantly acting and reacting. Dewey (1938/1986) observed that "living may be regarded as a continual rhythm of disequilibrations and recoveries of equilibrium. . . . The state of disturbed equilibration constitutes *need*. The movement towards its restoration is search and exploration. The recovery is fulfillment or satisfaction" (p. 34, emphasis in original). This biological rhythm is part of the natural rhythm earlier identified that "makes possible the existence of artistic form" and "natural law." It is the same rhythm whose discovery or creation allows us to refer to both science and art as technē.

Reflection and inquiry are intermediate between need and satisfaction, ignorance and wisdom. Recall the major premise of practical reasoning. The cycle of need, desire, inquiry, and satisfaction leads us to Dewey's (1938/1986) aesthetic definition of inquiry: "Inquiry is the controlled or directed transformation of an indeterminate situation into one that is so determinate in its constituent distinctions and relations as to convert the elements of the original situation into a unified whole" (p. 108). This definition manifests the Deweyan themes of aesthetic unity, harmony, and holism. Life grows through the rhythm of harmony, disharmony, and restoration of harmony. Equilibrium is restored when a stable form is reached. Inquiry mediates between being in some undesired present actual situation and looking toward a desirable future possibility of some better situation, some stable form, some end-in-view, that each of us strives to create through intelligent transformative practice.

The rhythm of inquiry is from doubt (ignorance of how to act) to the restoration of habitual functioning (knowledge of how to continue). Rhythm is the rhyme and reason that led Dewey to understand all inquiry as practical reasoning and all reasoning as instrumental. Tools are intermediaries between the self and the world. The plow that divides the fertile earth and the chalk that divides the chalkboard connect the hand to the world for a purpose. Dewey comprehended inquiry as a daimōnic tool for restoring harmony to our lives. The rhythmic cycle of inquiry has the passionate potential for genesis and expansive growth. Humankind must seek to cultivate "conceptions" of all kinds, culturally or agriculturally.

Ordinarily, habitual activity accomplishes the movement from disequilibrium to equilibrium. Conscious inquiry occurs only when habitual ways of acting fail us. Dewey (1938/1986) went on to observe, "A state of tension is set up which is an actual state (not mere feeling) of organic uneasiness and restlessness. This state of tension (which defines need) passes into search [inquiry] for material that will restore the condition of balance" (p. 34). Need that cannot be readily satisfied results in a disruption of habitual action. It is not simply a subjective feeling. Environmental stress is real and the habits (embodied beliefs) that must respond to that stress are natural neurophysiological, organic functions of the body only partially constituted by emotion.

The disruption of the habits that ordinarily structure vague feelings into intentional emotions occasions the onset of vague and indeterminate feelings; we are uncomfortable and ignorant about what course of action we ought to take. Everyday nervous tension is like this. Something is disturbing us, even if we cannot name what it is. Similarly, when fulfilled and satisfied we may feel a vague sense of well-being. Such feelings of disequilibrium and equilibrium are part of the beginning and ending of inquiry. According to Dewey, when we are in a state of relatively stable equilibrium, the body, the passions, and the mind constitute an organically unified whole.

For Dewey the purpose of inquiry is not to disclose timeless truths. Instead, the purpose of inquiry is to help us cope with the stress of living and to aid us in delighting in our lives wherever possible. It serves the needs and desires of living beings. Inquiry serves to educate us to discriminate objects of desire from the genuinely desirable. It may also mediate between ignorance and wisdom about the values man and woman ought to live by.

The feeling of organic unity is primordial aesthetic experience. As Dewey (1934/1987) put it:

> In a world like ours, every living creature that attains sensibility welcomes order with a response of harmonious feeling whenever it finds a congruous order about it. For only when an organism shares in the ordered relations of its environment does it secure the stability essential to living. And when the participation comes after a phase of disruption and conflict, it bears within itself the germs of a consummation akin to the esthetic. (p. 20)

Think about how it feels when we finally understand how to handle complex disciplinary difficulties, or when we reconcile relationship problems among students or cliques of students. It feels good to go through an entire lunchtime or recess without serious bickering, and it feels especially good to connect with our students and feel them learn and grow.

We reason to resolve the tension of need. In his essay "Affective Thought," Dewey (1926/1984a) concluded that "reasoning is a phase of the generic function of bringing about a new relationship between organisms and the conditions of life, and like other phases of the function is controlled by need, desire, and progressive satisfactions" (pp. 105–106). For Dewey (1922/1983), "'Reason' is not an antecedent force which serves as a panacea. It is a laborious achievement of habit needing to be continually worked over" (p. 137). The kind of labor this achievement demands is suggested by the following contrapuntal prescription:

> The conclusion is not that the emotional, passionate phase of action can be or should be eliminated in behalf of a bloodless reason. More "passions," not fewer, is the answer. To check the influence of hate there must be sympathy, while to rationalize sympathy there are needed emotions of curiosity, caution, respect. . . . Rationality . . . is not a force to evoke against impulse and habit. It is the attainment of a working harmony among diverse desires. "Reason" as a noun signifies the happy cooperation of a multitude of dispositions. (Dewey, 1922/1983, p. 136)

These are aesthetic definitions of rationality. A rational person is someone with an expanding number of ever more refined passions that are diverse yet harmonized. The same may be said for rational communities. To fully appreciate what Dewey was prescribing here, it is essential to comprehend the embodied, passionate nature of belief (that is, habit) in his theory of inquiry.

Dewey believed that all inquiry begins in doubt. Because of what belief meant for Dewey, doubt is a living, embodied, and impassioned condition, a state of need and active seeking. It is not some passive, exclusively intellectual state. Dewey (1938/1986) pointed out that "it is of the very nature of the indeterminate situation which evokes inquiry to be *questionable* . . . or . . . uncertain, unsettled, disturbed. The peculiar quality of what pervades the given materials, constituting them a situation, is not just uncertainty at large; it is a unique doubtfulness which makes that situation to be just and only the situation it is" (p. 109). The qualitative whole is the only thing "given" in inquiry. Unusual situations frustrate habitual ways of acting. Frustration, even anger, can impel inquiry. Inquiry and deliberation occur only when the situation becomes uncontrollable by the actions of prior habit; hence coordination with the environment requires reconstruction.

Conscious reasoning for Dewey is the center of the redirection and reconstruction of action, although it accounts for only a small part of our intelligent lives compared to the activity of unconscious habits. "Reason pure of all influence from prior habit," wrote Dewey (1922/1983), "is a fiction" (p. 25). Conscious reasoning, for Dewey, emerges naturally out of a background of intelligent, although unconscious, habits. Conscious deliberation seeks to restore the harmony of habitual functioning. When effective, instinctive, and habitual behavior is interrupted, an affective tension arises because of the unsettled, needful, and doubtful situation. Inquiry is initiated to resolve the situation.

Vague feelings of tension evolve and become more focused, more specific, and more namable as the cognitive idea of how and toward what one should act become more definitely fixed by inquiry. For Dewey, emotional clarity and intellectual clarity emerge together in the larger unity of the act in our effort to coordinate some situation. Dewey established the primacy and unity of activity at least as early as his 1895 reconstruction of William James' theory of emotion. Dewey (1895/1971) wrote:

> In Mr. James's statement the experience is . . . split up into three separate parts: First comes the object or idea that operates only as stimulus; second, the mode of behavior [activity] taken as discharged of this stimulus; third, the *Affect*, or emotional excitation, as the repercussion of this discharge. No such seriality or separation attaches to the emotion as an experience. . . . We are easily brought to the conclusion that *the mode of behavior [activity] is the primary thing, and that the idea [hypothesis, object, or objective] and the emotional excitation are constituted at one and the same time; that, indeed, they represent the tension of stimulus and response within the co-ordination which makes up the mode of behavior.* (p. 174) [emphasis in original]

Reflecting later on the initially unified experience of activity, it becomes possible to distinguish between activity, the feeling, and the idea. Yet this is only a functional distinction, useful for practical purposes. Dewey warned against allowing such useful practical distinctions to harden into untenable dualisms between mind (ideas, etc.) and bodily activity (behavior, etc.). Contrary to unfocused feelings, emotions have intentional objects (ideas, images, etc.). As Dewey (1895/1971) put it, "Emotion in its entirety is a mode of behavior which is purposive, or has an intellectual content, and which also reflects itself into feeling or affects, as the subjective valuation of that which is objectively expressed in the idea or purpose" (pp. 170-171). Because human nature is part of nature, the terms *subjective* and *objective* here are just two ends of the same naturalistic stick. They are only—like stimulus and response, feeling and thought—action and feeling, or action and thought, useful functional distinctions. Both are parts of a larger unified experiential whole that the organism is attempting to coordinate. Within the unity of the act, no feeling or thought is ever complete without its companion.

Dewey (1922/1983) described the search for the right idea or hypothesis to relieve the felt tension of some situation in this way:

> The habit denied overt expression asserts itself in idea. It sets up the thought. . . . This thought is not what is sometimes called thought, a pale bloodless abstraction, but is charged with the motor urgent force of habit. . . . It has its source in objective conditions and it moves forward to new objective conditions. For it works to secure a change of environment. . . . A habit impeded in overt operation continues nonetheless to operate. It manifests itself in desireful thought, that is in an ideal or imagined object which embodies within itself the force of a frustrated habit. (p. 39)[3]

It is desire that propels the inquiry. "Desireful thought," or erotic inquiry, seeks to restore a stable working harmony between and within the human organism and its environment. It is important to be clear about the connection between "desireful thought" and some "ideal or imagined object."

THE AESTHETICS OF INQUIRY: IMAGINATION
AND THE ART OF SCIENTIFIC INQUIRY

Imagination, for Dewey, explores alternative possibilities for action within a selected context of ongoing activity. Imagination enables the search for ideas that can possibly reconstruct the situation. It takes the context and its "data," including emotional sympathetic data, as intuited and determined by selective interests and transforms them into a plan of action, an idea that if acted upon might allow the agent to achieve the desired ideal in reality. Dewey (1934/1987) wrote:

> No "reasoning" as reasoning, that is, as excluding imagination and sense, can reach truth. . . . [The inquirer] selects and puts aside as his imaginative sentiments move. "Reason" at its height cannot attain complete grasp and a self-contained assurance. It must fall back upon imagination—upon the embodiment of ideas in emotionally charged sense. (p. 40)

Ideas emerge, or are brought forth, from an affective, intuitive background and imagination involves many things, including the body and social relations. The above passage clearly indicates that Dewey understood imagination as having an intrinsic role in the emergence of more structured phases of the developing experience. For Dewey, imagination mediates in the conscious reconstructive phase of a continuously developing experiential situation. Indeed, imagination is the point of transition between the background of inquiry (e.g., disrupted habits, needs, cares, desires, selective interests, and sociocultural traditions that go into intuiting a context) and the more developed, more structured, cognitive foreground of experience (e.g., categories, concepts, essences, identities, and logical rules).

Dewey's naturalistic and emergent theory of inquiry allows us to see that thinking is not a set of context-independent forms, principles of formal logic, or calculations. It also allows us to see that inquiry is inherently a creative, productive, and constructive process of transforming some actual, although undesirable, situation into some desired possibility. The aesthetic artifacts of creative imagination, and all that precede it, are original ideas and novel hypotheses, the consequences of which are testable by further inquiry. Inquiry on such an account is an artistically creative endeavor. As Dewey (1925/1981) put it, "The idea [the artifact of inquiry] is, in short, art and a work of art" (p. 278). Ideas are themselves daimōns mediating between the actual and the possible, ignorance and wisdom. "Every idea," wrote Dewey (1934/1987), "is by its nature indicative of a possibility not of present actuality" (p. 246). Dewey was thus able to provide a crucial role for artistic con-struction and creative use of imagination without falling victim to the romantic view that imagination and all the penumbra of the noncognitive context-setting daimōns are so wild, chaotic, or irrational as to be uncontrollable. Noncognitive, intuitive, and context-setting daimōns are a phase of the *intelligent* development of experience controlled, as they were for Plato, by the beautiful; that is, the harmonious form of some erotically sought equilibrium.

The following passage is a condensed but concise expression of Dewey's entire theory of emergent natural inquiry:

> The rhythm of loss of integration with environment and recovery of union not only persists in man but becomes conscious with him; its conditions are material out of which he forms purposes. Emotion [feeling] is the conscious sign of a break, actual or impending. The discord is the occasion that induces reflection. Desire for restoration of the union converts mere emotion into interest in objects as conditions of realization of harmony. . . . The artist cares in a peculiar way for the phase of experience in which union is achieved. (Dewey, 1934/1987, pp. 20–21)

With the loss of integration we have a vague, unconscious feeling of actual or impending disequilibrium. We are in doubt and ignorant about how to continue. When reflective imagination alights upon an idea (or ideal) for restoring equilibrium, that idea then becomes an object of desire. Once we have an object of desire we become interested in identifying means in our environment for obtaining the end-in-view. Selective interest then drives selective attention to extract the necessary discriminations from the otherwise infinitely complicated world that we find ourselves in. As Dewey (1934/1987) put it, "The directive source of selection is interest. . . . An artist is ruthless, when he selects, in following the logic of his interest" (pp. 100–101). Pedagogically, following the logic of a student's interest, rather than our own or that of a preplanned curriculum, allows us to understand the background patterns of our student's thinking. Often when students make even grievous errors it turns out that their reasoning was intelligent and logical. There is a logic of intelligent error. The teacher perceptive enough to detect this logic may greatly facilitate learning by detecting systematic errors that are often easily correctable. Sometimes the failure to obtain a predetermined answer occurs because the student uses creative rather than conforming intelligence. Unfortunately, many educators seem obsessed with the stupidity of error.

Oddly enough, educational theorists and researchers usually interpret Dewey's theory of inquiry and instrumentalist logic in a manner that makes him resemble the logical positivists or other idolaters of scientistic methodology. This tendency is ironic, since Dewey opposed positivism from the start. There is no quicker way to dismiss this false impression than by going straight to his aesthetics. In *Art as Experience,* Dewey (1934/1987) maintained that "science itself is but a central art auxiliary to the generation and utilization of other arts" (p. 33). In a footnote to this statement, Dewey referred the reader to the following passage from an earlier work: "Art—the mode of activity that is charged with meanings capable of immediately enjoyed possession—is the complete culmination of nature, and . . . science . . . conducts natural events to this happy issue" (Dewey, 1925/1981, p. 269). Indeed, Dewey (1925/1981) insisted that "science [itself] is an art, that art is practice, and that the only distinction worth drawing is not between practice and theory, but between those modes of practice that are not intelligent . . . and those which are" (pp. 268–269). Science is a cultural artifact. It is a technē, whose artifact, in turn, is warranted assertions.

Hickman (1992) argues that Dewey understood "knowing as a technological artifact" (p. 17). Knowledge, for Dewey, is demystified as an artifact produced by the labor of "the scientific *worker*" using the tools of logic (see Dewey, 1925/1981, p. 268, emphasis in original). In *Logic: The Theory of Inquiry*, Dewey (1938/1986) wrote, "All controlled inquiry and all institution of grounded assertion necessarily contains a *practical* factor; an activity of doing and making which reshapes antecedent existential [i.e., qualitative] material which sets the problem of inquiry" (p. 162, emphasis in original). How practical doers and makers imaginatively reshape the antecedent qualitative material is dependent for the most part on what kind of persons they are—their needs, habits, and desires.

Dewey's theory of inquiry challenges the usual purely intellectual accounts of thinking and knowing. That is why it seems so strange to some. For Dewey, affect and habit do much of the work most assume done by higher intellectual functions. In "Affective Thought," Dewey (1926/1984a) suggested:

> We may begin with the field of reasoning, long supposed to be preempted by pure intellect, and to be completely severed, save by accident, from affectivity and desire and from the motor organs and habits by which we make our necessary practical adjustments to the world about us. (p. 105)

Dewey, as previously discussed, attributed many of the supposedly rational functions normally "preempted by pure intellect" to the agency of natural biological functions that embody habit and affect.

The following passage emphasizes the erotic, biological basis of Dewey's (1926/1984a) theory of inquiry as including feeling, reasoning, and environmental transaction throughout an organic whole:

> What is summed up here under the idea of "affectivity" is that an organism has certain basic needs which cannot be supplied without activity that modifies the surroundings; that when the organism is in any way disturbed in its "equilibration" with its environment, its needs show themselves as restless, craving, desiring activity which persists until the acts thus induced have brought about a new integration of the organism and its relation to the environment. (p. 105)

Any activity that modifies our surroundings constitutes creative, artistic activity. The routine and rhythmic cycle of need–desire–satisfaction repeats itself constantly, moment to moment, every day of our lives. Erōs and habitual response mediate our every movement. If the failure of habitual responses to restore "equilibration" initiates inquiry, then the creative need–desire–*inquiry*–satisfaction rhythmic cycle often results in learning and growth. Inquiry introduces conscious, reflective mediation into the rhythm of life. Thus one possible consequence of inquiry is the acquisition of new habits of action. In both routine and creative cycles the organically modified dispositions, attitudes, and habits resulting from prior inquiry constitute a plateau that grounds action and informs subsequent inquiry.

The creative need–desire–inquiry–satisfaction rhythmic cycle closes what Dewey (1926/1984a) called "the great gap which is traditionally made between the lower physiological functions and the higher cultural ones. . . . Desire, interest, accomplishes what in the traditional theory a pure intellect was evoked to accomplish" (p. 106). Said differently, erōs and other fluid daimōns perform the functions ordinarily reserved for the pure and precise Platonic Forms, or the abstract schemas and scripts of the functionalist/positivist position. Dewey (1926/1984a) followed this observation with an equally controversial contention, writing:

> Reasoning and science are thus obviously brought nearer to art. The satisfaction of need requires that surroundings should be changed. . . . Art also explicitly recognizes what it has taken so long to discover in science; the control exercised by emotion in re-shaping natural conditions, and the place of the imagination, under the influence of desire, in re-creating the world into a more orderly place. When so-called nonrational factors are found to play a large part in the production of relations of consistency and order in logical systems, it is not surprising that they should operate in artistic structures. (pp. 106–107)

Any deliberate transformation within nature, including human nature, is artistic. Enjoying the results of re-creating the world is the germ of aesthetic appreciation. Among the "nonrational factors" are such daimōns as desire, intuition, effectively charged selective interest, and imagination. These precognitive factors frame the context of inquiry by artistically identifying and discriminating the conditions of inquiry.

Alexander (1987) contends, "The search for an adequate aesthetics of experience is what drives the development of Dewey's philosophy" (p. xvi). Certainly the passages cited above seem to document such a reading. So, too, does Dewey's essay "Qualitative Thought." Alexander (1987) describes the significance of that essay:

> But the sense of the world depends ultimately, in whatever context we are in, upon the felt, qualitative, and non-cognitive dimension. This theme is the central topic of Dewey's highly significant essay, "Qualitative Thought." Without the role of quality to create the sense of the situation, inquiry would be impossible. By "quality" Dewey is referring not primarily to particular discriminated qualities *within* a situation, but to the distinctive, unnamable uniquely characteristic feel of *that* situation. The qualitative

sense of the whole situation provides the fusion of part and whole in experience which, in terms of meaning, is the integration of "text" and context.
(p. 179)

All inquiry for Dewey, whether quantitatively or qualitatively focused,
depends on how the inquirer originally feels, intuits, and selectively
frames noncognitive qualities.

Activities that reshape antecedently given qualitative materials are
creative, artistic activities. The architecture of Dewey's theory of creative
inquiry has three major moments. Inquiry emerges from a largely precognitive "background"; evolves into a statable cognitive problem in
the foreground of inquiry; and concludes with the solution of that problem, the answering of the question, and the satisfaction of that need.
This process of inquiry is a continuous and unbroken emergence from
background to foreground wherein the cognitive foreground remains
permanently dependent on earlier precognitive intuitions. The rhythmic
cycle then repeats itself, with the cognitive products of earlier inquiries
influencing emerging background intuitions. The cycle continues as
long as the individual or the larger culture survives.

THE QUALITATIVE WHOLE OF PRIMORDIAL EXPERIENCE

Dewey (1930/1984d) began "Qualitative Thought" boldly by implicitly
defying prevalent assumptions about the nature of thought:

> The world in which we immediately live, that in which we strive, succeed,
> and are defeated is preeminently a qualitative world. . . . This world forms
> the field of characteristic modes of thinking, characteristic in that thought is
> definitely regulated by qualitative considerations. (p. 243)

Let us examine what Dewey means by living immediately in a qualitative world whose immediate quality regulates all thinking.

For Dewey, our primary relation to antecedent reality is *immediate*
and aesthetic. It is not primordially a knowledge relation. Knowledge,
for Dewey, is a consequence of inquiry, hence secondary, and *mediate*,
in that it connects one discriminated object to another. Dewey was a
transactional realist. For him, existence is an event, an indeterminate
temporal process, defined as a transaction between organism and environment. Transactions occur when we transform the environment (such
as students or Play-Doh) and it transforms us (e.g., our habits). Dewey
saw objects, things, and even logical essences as artistic products of the

transactions between human beings, themselves existential events, with other existential events (see Garrison, 1994a).

Dewey (1930/1984d) insisted, however, that the immediate aesthetic experience of reality always precedes such artistic production:

> The only thing that is unqualifiedly given is the total pervasive quality. . . . "Given" in this connection signifies only that the quality immediately exists, or is brutally there. In this capacity, it forms that to which all objects of thought refer, although . . . it is never part of the manifest subject-matter of thought. In itself, it is the big, buzzing, blooming confusion of which James wrote. (p. 254)

The immediately experienced qualitative whole is vague, inexact, and indeterminate, yet it influences the later discriminations of thought. Qualities envelop us. We are enwrapped—rapt—within them, as within a powerful piece of music, and they are within us. For each of us, the qualitative whole has a unifying theme that is captivating, compelling, and pervasive, yet inarticulable. The qualitative whole seizes us. It is well to say that we fall in love, likewise, that hatred consumes us, or that we feel anger grip us. In their intensity such passions possess us. Qualitative experience is thus first *had*, and only later, if ever, known. Enthralled by the power of an aesthetic quality, we are initially inarticulate. The qualitative whole leaves us speechless at the limits of language.

Dewey (1925/1981) indicated, "Immediacy of existence is ineffable. There is nothing mystical about such ineffability; it expresses the fact that of direct existence it is futile to say anything to one's self and impossible to say anything to another" (p. 74). When we exclaim Oh!, Huh!, or Ugh!, such exclamatory utterances are not necessarily nonsense. They indicate that the exclamatory whole needs investigation to disclose its aesthetic, moral, and cognitive meaning and potential. As Dewey (1930/1984d) put it:

> The full content of meaning is best apprehended in case of the judgment of the esthetic expert in the presence of a work of art. But they [ejaculatory judgments] come at the beginning and the close of every scientific investigation. These open with the "oh" of wonder and terminate with the "Good" of a rounded-out and organized situation. Neither the "Oh" nor the "Good" expresses a mere state of personal feeling. Each characterizes a subject-matter. (p. 250)

What is the meaning of a qualitative experience? Initially we do not know because qualitative experience is precognitive. Clarifying feelings of all kinds is part of the task of scientific, aesthetic, and moral inquiry upon the path to the "Good."

The qualitative is "given." We immediately enjoy it or suffer. The qualitative whole is immediately had, had but not yet known. Dewey (1925/1981) wrote:

> *Being* and *having* things in ways other than knowing them . . . exist, and are preconditions of reflection and knowledge. *Being* angry, stupid, wise, inquiring; *having* sugar . . . occur in dimensions incommensurable to knowing these things which we are and have and use, and which have and use us. Their existence is unique, and, strictly speaking, indescribable; they can *only be* and be *had*, and then be pointed to in reflection. . . . Their existence is . . . qualitative. All cognitive experience must start from and must terminate in being and having things in just such unique, irreparable and compelling ways. (pp. 377–378) [emphasis in original]

The immediately given qualitative whole is, however, knowable, but only by the mediating process of inquiry. The wise seek knowledge. Is some event that they have experienced "truly" good, or bad? They reflect on the causes of their suffering to avoid future pain and on the sources of their joys so that they may soon experience them again. Reflection, though, must begin with the felt quality of the immediate qualitative whole.

Dewey (1930/1984d) declared:

> If we designate this permeating qualitative unity in psychological language, we say it is felt rather than thought. Then, if we hypostatize it, we call it *a* feeling. But to term it a feeling is to reverse the actual state of affairs. The existence of unifying qualitativeness in the subject-matter defines the meaning of "feeling." (p. 248) [emphasis in original]

In other words, the feeling we have is the feeling of a quality. Dewey's (1930/1984d) example is anger: "When . . . anger exists, it is the pervading tone, color, and quality of persons, things, and circumstances, or of a situation" (p. 248). When angry, we are not immediately aware of the anger per se, but only of the pervasive quality of our current situation. The qualitative unity is felt before it can be cognitively identified. We must experience anger before we can know it. Only later, upon reflection, may we analytically discriminate determinate objects and relations from the qualitative whole of the original situation by specifically naming a feeling as a distinct psychological "fact," or the object of anger as a distinct physical or environmental "thing." Controlling anger requires prior reflective awareness of the conditions that have anger as their consequence. It resembles Randy learning to avoid time-out.

The antecedent qualitative experience is passively had; it possesses us. More pointedly, Dewey (1934/1987) suggested that we must "begin with what may be called a total seizure, an inclusive qualitative whole not yet articulated, not distinguished into members" (p. 195). Quality is experienced; initially it is felt, a matter of mood and affect, rather than known. The reflective consequence, the artistic product of inquiry, is knowledge. Feeling, as a distinct and determinate object of psychological analysis, occurs in a situation other than the original qualitative experience. To hypostatize something—say, a feeling or an object of knowledge—is to attribute real identity to an abstract concept. It is the most common error of Platonic metaphysics. Dewey (1925/1981) described the error this way: "It consists of objects of immediate enjoyment hypostatized into transcendent reality. . . . The technical structure of the resulting metaphysics is familiar. The cosmically real is one with the finished, the perfect or wholly done" (p. 78). Objects of knowledge, while quite real, are secondary artistic artifacts of productive, reflective inquiry, a consequence of discrimination and analysis within the original qualitative whole given to the inquirer. Hypostatization involves mistaking the consequences of inquiry for it antecedent conditions. Quality is the immediate "given." It is what we have and are. Knowledge, on the other hand, is created or constructed (including knowledge about our own moods and feelings) as the mediate product of inquiry. Self-knowledge, like all knowledge, is an artifact of inquiry. It, too, is constructed.

Dewey (1930/1984d) declared:

> To say I have a feeling or impression that so and so is the case is to note that the quality in question is not yet resolved into determinate terms and relations. . . . All thought in every subject begins with just such an unanalyzed whole. . . . It is a commonplace that a problem *stated* is well on its way to solution, for statement of the nature of a problem signifies that the underlying quality is being transformed into determinate distinctions or has become an object of articulate thought. (pp. 248–249) [emphasis in original]

The qualitative whole is what is *given*; however, "the 'given,' that is to say the existent, is precisely an undetermined and dominant complex quality" (Dewey, 1930/1984d, p. 253). It is a mistake to think that inquiry begins in something so precise as a stated cognitive problem. It begins in an ineffably vague qualitative situation. As Dewey (1938/1986) put it, "The unsettled or indeterminate [qualitative] situation might have been called a *problematic* situation. This name would have been, however, proleptic and anticipatory" (p. 111, emphasis in original). *Proleptic* means treating a future development as if it were already existing or accomplished. Ignoring or forgetting the context of a problem, its background, destroys the qualitative unity from which it naturally emerges. Dewey (1934/1987) asserted,

> The undefined pervasive quality of an experience is that which binds together all the defined elements. . . . It cannot be a product of reflection. . . . For unless the sense were immediate, we should have no guide to our reflection. The sense of an extensive and underlying whole is the context of every experience. (p. 198)

A linguistic description that translates the exclamatory qualitative situation into a precise statement of the specific objects and relations constituting a problem allows reflective cognitive inquiry to begin reconstructing the situation, but we should not forget the primordial quality on which we are reflecting. Dewey used the terms "qualitative whole" and "situation" interchangeably. In his *Logic*, Dewey (1938/1986) wrote, "A contextual whole . . . is what is called a 'situation'. . . . There is always a *field* in which observation of *this* or *that* object or event occurs" (pp. 72–73, emphasis in original). Intuition and selective attention conjointly discriminate objects from the felt unity of the qualitative whole. We can only intuit the initial quality, however.

INTUITION, AFFECTIVITY, AND SELECTIVE ATTENTION

Dewey maintained that our primary relation to reality is not cognitive. Rather the experience of the qualitative unity of a situation, the contextual whole, is immediate. According to Dewey, one of the gravest errors of epistemology is the assumption that our primary relation to reality is one of knowledge. Recall that, for Dewey, knowledge is a mediated consequence of inquiry, whereas the primordial qualitative whole is initially grasped immediately and intuitively through action and feeling. Dewey (1930/1984d) declared:

> The word "intuition" has many meanings. But in its popular . . . usage it is closely connected with the single qualitativeness underlying all the details of explicit reasoning. It may be relatively dumb and inarticulate and yet penetrating; unexpressed in definite ideas which form reasons and justifications and yet profoundly right. . . . Intuition precedes conception and goes deeper. . . . Intuition, in short, signifies the realization of a pervasive quality such that it regulates the determination of relevant distinctions or of whatever, whether in the way of terms or relations, becomes the accepted object of thought. (p. 249)

Hypostatizing occurs when the inquirer fails to realize that intuition precedes conception and goes deeper. The question remains: How does the indeterminate existential quality become conceptually discriminated and fixed? How does one determine the relevant distinctions? How is it possible to analyze the unanalyzed inarticulable whole? Dewey's answer is by selective interests that, in turn, are dependent on our affective, caring, and concerned involvement in the antecedent qualitative situation.

It is the affective sense of a unified quality that ultimately frames a contextual whole, or situation. Dewey (1930/1984d) defined "situation" this way:

> A complex existence that is held together, in spite of its internal complexity, by the fact that it is dominated and characterized throughout by a single quality. . . . The situation as such is not and cannot be stated or made explicit. It is taken for granted, "understood," or implicit. . . . The situation controls the terms of thought; for they are *its* distinctions, and applicability to it is the ultimate test of their validity. (pp. 246–247) [emphasis in original]

For Dewey, the quality of a situation is neither "in" us nor "in" the environment. "The qualities," wrote Dewey (1925/1981), "never were 'in' the organism; they always were qualities of interactions in which both extra-organic things and organisms [such as human beings] partake" (pp. 198–199). The quality of any situation is determined, in part, by the organism's needs, desires, and interests interacting with its environment. Living creatures are always already involved in the world of events. Feelings, such as anger, are the "tensions" that arise when the organism is in a state of disequilibrium. The feeling is not isolated in "the brain." It is distributed throughout the organism in conducting transactions with its environment.

For example, anger is an emotion that sometimes accompanies need. One "idea" may identify the object of anger. Another may serve as a hypothesis for designing a plan for transforming disequilibrium into equilibrium, resolving the doubt and relieving the need. Resolving a difficult disciplinary problem with a student perceived as irritating is a need all teachers have felt. The solution may evolve as a product of the "progressive satisfactions" of inquiry. Such progressive inquiry is emergent. Dewey (1934/1987) indicated:

> Not only does the "mood" come first, but it persists as the substratum after distinctions emerge; in fact they emerge as *its* distinctions. Even at the outset, the total and massive quality has its [affective] uniqueness; even when vague and undefined, it is just that which it is and not anything

else. If the perception continues, discrimination inevitably sets in. (p. 196) [emphasis in original]

The creative transactions of inquiry begin with an intuition of quality, involving need and desire requiring satisfaction; move through discrimination and analytic selection; and eventually produce everyday objects, logical objects, essences, and truths (warranted assertions) that, taken together, guide our action.

For Dewey, the context for all inquiries is *taken* from the antecedent qualitative whole, the given. All subsequent meanings depend on the inquirer's original selections. Dewey (1931/1985a) wrote, "There is selectivity (and rejection) found in every operation of thought. There is care, concern, implicated in every act of thought. There is some one who has affection for some things over others. . . . As a thinker, he is still differentially sensitive to some qualities" (p. 14). Rather than immaculate conceptions of theory-neutral, value-neutral, and context-independent interpretation and understanding, Dewey believed that all reasoning is for a purpose and that biases in the guise of intuitive care, concern, and involvement are an integral part of emergent knowledge. Dewey and Bentley (1949/1989) felt that the notion of care in inquiry "ranges from solicitude, through caring *for* in the sense of fondness, and through being deeply stirred, over to caring *for* in the sense of *taking* care, looking after, paying attention systematically, or *minding*" (p. 247, emphasis in original).[4] Those who do not care do not inquire. Good inquiry must be careful. When concerned about somebody or something in some situation, we may recognize our ignorance and desire wisdom, or at least knowledge. Yet to obtain wisdom, we must inquire carefully. Such "bootstrapping" is incomprehensible using the fixed categories of discursive analytic logic, although we may easily grasp it using the paradoxical logic of artistic creation, genesis, and becoming.

Analytic selection and discrimination require intuition and selective attention derived from affective involvement in a situation. Good selection requires a sense of taste. (Recall again the *Oxford English Dictionary* (1971) definition of taste: "Mental perception of quality; judgment, discriminative faculty.") The conditions of life that lead to our needs, desires, and necessary biases control care and concern. To live at all, and surely to live well, the organism must carry out successful transactions with its environment. That means that we must select carefully for our purposes from the unity of the contextual whole. Dewey (1930/1984d) wrote:

The logic of artistic construction and esthetic appreciation is peculiarly significant because they exemplify in accentuated and purified form the control of selection of detail and of mode of relation, or integration, by a qualitative whole. The underlying quality demands certain distinctions. . . . Scientific thought is, in its turn, a specialized form of art, with its own qualitative control. (pp. 251–252)

For Dewey, all reasoning is practical reasoning carried out for our human purposes. He considered scientific inquiry to be a particularly successful way of satisfying life's needs and desires, including the passionate desire to live a life of expanding meaning and value in relationship with others.

Care, concern, and affection arising out of the organism's involvement in a qualitative situation begin setting the emergent context of natural inquiry. Dewey (1934/1987) wrote that "the penetrating quality that runs through all the parts of a work of art [including the aesthetic quality that initiates inquiry] and binds them into an individualized whole can only be emotionally 'intuited.' 'Parts' are discriminated, not intuited" (p. 196). Purposive involvement transforms the vague, inexact, and unsettled qualities in question into discriminated and determinate parts, relations, and eventually objects that help resolve the affective tension arising from the struggle to coordinate stimulus and response. Initially contexts are selections from an aesthetically intuited qualitative whole. The finite living creature seeks to maintain and enjoy its existence; therefore, it selects from the infinite number of aspects of existence according to its cares, needs, and desires—the necessary biases of living creatures. All living organisms, including teachers, educational researchers, and theorists, select according to their purposes and ignore the rest.

THE FALLACIES OF IGNORING CONTEXT

For Dewey, facts, objects, and our knowledge of them are all artifacts of inquiry. Dewey considered the assumption that there is a fixed world of facts, things, or essences existing antecedent to inquiry fallacious. To mistake the constructed *consequences* of inquiry for the qualitative whole, given *antecedent* to inquiry, is to commit what Dewey (1925/1981) called "*the* philosophic fallacy" (p. 34, emphasis in original). Whatever may exist before inquiry, all that we can ever "know" are the mediated consequences of inquiry, and these consequences continually change as the context changes. Dewey (1931/1985a) maintained that "the most perverse fallacy of philosophic thinking goes back to neglect of context" (p. 5). Mistaking the cognitive consequences of inquiry for the infinitely complex, precognitive qualitative background from which we have selected aspects to attend to for particular human purposes, committing "*the* philosophic fallacy," and "the neglect of context"—all amount to the same perversion.

Thinking becomes perverse when it ignores or forgets that all inquiry originates in either an affective intuition of the unity of a situation or in the subsequent selections that discriminate objects from within the qualitative whole. Dewey (1925/1981) wrote:

> Selective emphasis, choice, is inevitable whenever reflection occurs. This is not an evil. Deception comes only when the presence and operation of choice is concealed, disguised, denied. Empirical method finds and points to the operation of choice as it does to any other event. Thus it protects us from conversion of eventual functions into the antecedent existence: a conversion that may be said to be *the* philosophic fallacy. (p. 34)

An instance of the philosophical fallacy occurs when we forget the inarticulate but penetrating feelings of care and concern that pervade the original qualitative whole (see Garrison, 1994b). Qualitative intuition and selective attention precede conception. Purposeful selective interests, arising out of need, care, and concern, develop the intuition and continue to determine the context of later thought. Selective interest makes its choices and more fully determines the context. Only then can inquiry continue. Remember, *intellectus* derives from the verb meaning "to choose among." Dewey's theory of intelligent inquiry rejected any form of "rationality" that relied on *a priori* categories, concepts, and essences—oblivious of their origins as products of inquiry—as just another instance of the philosophical fallacy.

Categories, concepts, and essences are themselves historically contingent products of inquiry and differ from culture to culture and from research tradition to research tradition. Noncognitive choices do not determine the final consequences of inquiry, but they do continue to influence its course. The philosophical fallacy consists of adopting the consequences (artifacts) of inquiry, forgetting their derivation from careful artistic selection, and acting as if categories, objects, or knowledge of them existed antecedent to inquiry. Objects (and statements of truth about them) are no less the created artistic products of intelligent inquiry. Although Dewey respected the daimōns, he was no romantic celebrant of irrationality. If our primary relation to reality is physical, emotional, and intuitive, then the artistic products of scientific inquiry, such as truth or "warranted assertability," are intelligent and busy intermediaries employed in educating our aesthetic sensibility to make wiser context-setting selections. To remain bound to the immediate affective intuition is to remain cognitively and emotionally immature. Nonetheless, inquiry does begin with the intuition of a quality. Let us return again to examine Dewey's notion of quality in more detail.

Dewey believed that the qualitative given was infinitely diverse and confused. Dewey (1895/1971) asserted:

> [We] start from the assumption of a sensory-continuum, the "big, buzzing, blooming confusion," out of which particular sensory quales are differentiated. Discrimination, not integration, is the real problem. In a general way we will admit that it is through attention that the distinctions arise, through selective emphasis. (p. 179)

Reversing the actual state of affairs—ignoring the antecedent qualitative whole and assuming that integration, not discrimination, is the real problem—leads to another contextual fallacy, which Dewey called "the analytic fallacy."

The analytic fallacy occurs when we begin our inquiries as if the original "data" are distinct bits of a sensory given or "atomic facts" readymade for sorting out according to *a priori* logical categories. For Dewey, "facts" are "artifacts" of inquiry. For Dewey (1930/1984d), since "the original datum is always . . . a qualitative whole," it is illegitimate to "continue talking about 'data' in any other sense than as reflective distinctions" of the original datum (p. 250). Dewey became embroiled with Bertrand Russell, the most famous of the logical positivists, over precisely this issue (see Dewey 1915/1979; Russell, 1919/1977). Russell insisted on the objective reality of hard (positive) facts or "sense data," as he called them. He maintained that these discrete atomic facts could be integrated using the supposedly eternally valid *a priori* laws of logic. For Dewey, supposedly hard, positive, highly discriminated, atomic "sense data" are really the soft contingent consequences of background selections. This analytic fallacy is just another instance of the fallacy of ignoring the context. In this case it involves ignoring the selective discriminations that have led to the construction of the so-called "hard facts." They are eventual functions resulting from a long process of discrimination, involving needs, desires, and purposeful interests, that Russell mistook as an antecedent starting point.

Experientially, the only "given" is the indiscriminate unity of a qualitative whole; however, as Dewey (1915/1979) put it:

> The original datum is large but confused, and specific sensible qualities represent the result of discriminations. In this case, the elementary data [of

Russell], instead of being primitive empirical data, are the last terms, the limits, of the discriminations we have been able to make. . . . Knowledge grows from a confusedly experienced external world to a world experienced as ordered and specified. (pp. 94–95)

The original qualitative datum is emotionally intuited. It is not some known "thing." For Dewey, the original "datum" is large and confused, not discriminated, atomic, and exact.

A decade and a half after his initial response to the tenets of positivism, Dewey (1929/1984e) made himself clearer:

Scientific inquiry always starts from things of the environment experienced in our everyday life. . . . This is the ordinary qualitative world. . . . Experimental inquiry treats them as offering a challenge to thought. They are the material [datum] of problems not of solutions. They are to be known, rather than objects of knowledge. (p. 83)

There is an intermediate stage between the qualitative existential "datum" and something so cognitively determinate as a stated "problem"; that something is "data" in Dewey's sense. Dewey (1929/1984e) declared:

By data is signified subject-matter for *further* interpretation; something to be thought about. *Objects* are finalities; they are complete, finished; they call for thought only in the way of definition, classification, logical arrangement, subsumption in syllogisms, etc. But data signify "material to serve"; they are indications, evidence, signs, clues to and of something still to be reached; they are intermediate, not ultimate; means, not finalities. (p. 80) [emphasis in original]

There are no hard data, including the sympathetic data of moral perception. It is all quite soft—soft but substantial. What we identify as data change with our selections. Data are not the antecedently *given* qualitative whole. They are an intermediate consequence of our *taking*; we select them. We may select poorly. Perhaps we "felt weird," or worried too much, and selected improperly from the qualitative space. Our intuitions are sometimes poor and we make inappropriate (given our purposes) rather than wise distinctions. Sometimes qualitative selections are mistaken. We craft our mistakes with the same care and concern as we make anything else. One reason we tend to become wiser as we become older is because we become more emotionally mature about that to which we should selectively attend. The preeminence of logical positivism for most of the twentieth century prompted most research methodologists to ignore such considerations, entirely glossing over the role of selective interest and attention in determining the data, the "facts," of inquiry.

Dewey pioneered the recognition that between the existential quali- tative whole and the determination of ideas and objects there come the contextual "data," discriminated by a particular observer having a cer- tain emotional involvement and selective interest. The following anal- ogy drawn from the practical art of manufacturing helps us better un- derstand what Dewey (1916/1980b) meant by "data":

> Let us take the sequence of mineral rock in place, pig iron and the manufac- tured article, comparing the raw material in its undisturbed place in nature to the original . . . experience, compare the manufactured article to the objective and object of knowledge, and the brute datum to the metal under- going extraction from raw ore for the sake of being wrought into a useful thing. (p. 341)

The indeterminate qualitative situation is grounded within nature, much as the iron ore that is "given" to us. The pig iron is the refined subject- matter for further interpretation, something to be thought about (or used) further, such as facts. Because it is people rather than pig iron that we are talking about, we will need intelligent sympathy to identify the data, not just sensory stimulation. These "facts" are created artifacts of some theoretical and methodological refining process. Finally, we create manufactured articles, whether watch springs or knowledge. Both are products, artifacts of the process of inquiry. Inquiry itself is something that is "brought forth" or "springs up" naturally from the needs and desires of living creatures.

The following statement connects what Dewey (1938/1986) meant by refined facts or data within the emergent inquiry with the formulation of problem-solving ideas or hypotheses:

> A *possible* relevant solution [imaginative hypothesis] is then suggested by the determination of factual conditions [data] which are secured by observa- tion. The possible solution presents itself, therefore, as an *idea*, just as the terms of the problem (which are facts) are instituted by observation. . . . An idea is first of all an anticipation of something that may happen; it marks a *possibility*. (p. 113) [emphasis in original]

Ideas emerge out of a background of biological need and affective dis- equilibrium. Ideas that determine possible solutions to the contextual problem are pro-ductions of imagination. The idea is fulfilled when acted upon in the lived drama of everyday living. We must constantly reflect on the consequences of acting on ideas. Are they instrumental for our purposes? Do they truly solve the problem? Do they only make matters worse? Educational theories, facts, and policies may be experimentally confirmed, but never validated irrevocably. They are the results of prior selections, and we may always select differently. A good experiment requires us to select and control *all* the relevant variables. Fully comprehended, that requirement is impossible. So who is privileged to decide which variables are most relevant, and why and how they are related? It is a matter of selection.

Though dismissed as "irrational" by many theories of rationality, the background aesthetic elements of developing experience, including the refinement of the larger, confused datum into data, nonetheless do determine and extensively influence the foreground of cognitive inquiry. That is why Dewey preferred to speak of freeing the intellect within the world of experience to refine and reconstruct it rather than applying *a priori* rational principles from outside the world that supposedly predetermine and control it.

Dewey (1931/1985a) identified a kindred fallacy: "The counterpart fallacy to that of analysis (as wrongly interpreted because of denial of context) is that of unlimited extension or universalization. When context is taken into account, it is seen that every generalization occurs under limiting conditions set by the contextual situation" (p. 8). The conditions of the original circumstances within which the inquiry originated limit the scope of the resulting universal. Different selections establish different conditions of inquiry. The resultant universal principle is valid only under specified conditions. Dewey (1931/1985a) called the consequences of ignoring the conditional character of universal generalization "the fallacy of unlimited universalization" (p. 8). For Dewey (1931/1985a), "All statements about the universe as a whole, reality as an unconditioned unity, involve the same fallacy" (p. 8). Dewey urged us to recognize our limited perspective as finite and impassioned creatures and advised us to abandon the swaggering desire to make sweeping statements embracing all space, time, and circumstance. The fallacy of unlimited universalization is perhaps the most serious barrier to dialogues across differences. We assume that statements universally warranted in the domain of our daily action must be true for all people in all places and times. The only general thought, though, is the sympathetically generous thought that considers the context of others and what we would do if we were they in their situation.

Dewey had earlier identified a fallacy he termed the "psychologist's fallacy" during a discussion of the nature of self-expression. His point here is that the observer's interpretation should not be confused with the actor's interpretation, if any, of the action. Dewey (1895/1971) wrote:

> We call it expression when looking at it from the standpoint of an observer—whether a spectator or the person himself as scientifically reflecting upon his movements, or aesthetically enjoying them. The very word "expression" names the facts not as they are, but in their second intention. To an onlooker my angry movements are expressions—signs, indications; but surely not to me. To rate such movements as primarily expressive is to fall into the psychologist's fallacy: it is to confuse the standpoint of the observer and explainer with that of the fact observed. (p. 154)[5]

It is, of course, necessary for researchers to make their own discriminations and theoretical assumptions for their research purposes. Fallacies occur when researchers confuse their own research perspective with that of the subjects or assume some God's-eye, transcendental view of the subjects' action.[6] Indeed, researchers must be wary of their subjects' "first-person" accounts because these are usually the subjects' own "second intention"—reflective and retrospective explanations of, say, their earlier anger or misbehavior. The psychologist's fallacy is perhaps the single most common flaw of bad educational research. It is also one of the most serious fallacies of flawed teaching.

Many now reject positivism, with its presumption of "hard facts" existing antecedent to inquiry, yet many educational researchers, including many "qualitative" researchers, continue to commit the psychologist's fallacy. Facts, or data, are never "hard" precisely because they change when the needs, intuitions, and selective interests that determine the initial selections of data change. Said differently, the "facts" will change whenever the context changes. Multicultural and gender inquiry have brought this lesson into the laboratory of the contemporary classroom. Many qualitative researchers, strangely enough, are still not careful about observing how their subjects grasp the quality of the whole, or how their subjects' desires and interests select the context according to their own individual idiosyncratic needs and biases. Mistaking the researcher's or teacher's selections for those of the research subjects is an instance of the neglect of context. It involves a self-deception that occurs when we conceal, disguise, and deny the presence and operation of the "subjects" choices. Dewey called it "the psychologist's fallacy." It could just as easily be called the sociologist's, anthropologist's, or teacher's fallacy or, more generally, the inquirer's fallacy.

There is another element of context that deserves comment. According to Dewey (1931/1985a), "There is no thinking which does not present itself on a background of tradition. . . . Traditions are ways of interpretation and of observation, of valuation, of everything explicitly thought of" (p. 12). In different scholarly traditions—for example, the psychologist's and anthropologist's—researchers intuit and select their subject matter in different ways even within the same country, town, or classroom targeted for research.[7] As Dewey (1931/1985a) put it, "There is the background of the experimenter. This includes the antecedent state of theory which has given rise to the problem" (p. 7). Prior education of the researcher in a particular theory influences the background of inquiry. Since theory and a cultural tradition contain cognitive components, there will always be some cognitive component in the background just as there is precognitive material in the foreground. That is why it is necessary to repeatedly use qualified descriptions, such as "largely noncognitive qualitative situation." Ignoring cultural traditions or the personal history of the practical inquirer, including the folk and scientific theories they contain, is in itself some kind of fallacy. Let us call it the "ahistorical fallacy."

IMAGINATION, EMOTION, AND INQUIRY: THE TEACHABLE MOMENT

The natural rhythm of expansive personal growth and rebirth begins with need, doubt, and disequilibrium invoking desire, selective interest, imagination, and creative inquiry. The cycle concludes with the aesthetic restoration of harmony. Dewey's theory of the context of inquiry allows us to understand the logic of the teachable moment. To illuminate this, let us look specifically at a context for reading Susan Cooper's (1973) novel *The Dark Is Rising*.

The "teachable moment" is perhaps the most sought-after pedagogical prize. All teachers know what it feels like even if they cannot name its characteristics. It is as wonderful as it is elusive. Teachers long for the moment when their class has that special quality of intimacy, openness, and creativity that provides the almost ineffable experience of getting through to our students, of connecting and of students learning and not just getting ready to take a test. All too often the moment slips away before we can seize it. The teachable moment comes so suddenly and departs so swiftly that many assume it is simply a gift of good fortune (tuchē).

The teachable moment is part of a larger event, and Dewey's ideas about the rhythms of life will help us understand it as such. The teachable moment arises in the natural rhythm of disequilibrium, practical deliberation, and the artistic restoration of harmony. It is a pause in a larger process. Leffers' (1993) reference to the idea of perchings and flight is helpful here. The teachable moment involves perchings and flight in a larger migration of thought. The migration of thought, like the migration of birds, has its seasons and rhythms. So do flights of fancy such as are found in *The Dark Is Rising*. Nature often gives us desirable goods, like a beautiful flock of Canadian geese landing on a lake where we are fishing. Nature is just as likely to inflict undesirable evils, such as a brutal spring storm. We may avoid the evils and enjoy the goods if we know the rhythms of nature's way.

It is no different with the rhythms of human nature. Every teacher knows that children are often as unpredictable as the weather. Comprehending the life rhythms of individual children and the rhythms of their relationships with other students and ourselves within the larger rhythm of the day and the seasons of the school year improves the possibility of sympathetically recognizing and intelligently responding to our students' unique needs, desires, and interests in ways that bestow value on us all. There is an art and science to recognizing, reproducing, and reconstructing the rhythms of human nature. There is a poetic technē of the teachable moment.

"The snow lay thin and apologetic over the world" (Cooper, 1973, p. 3). Without knowing anything more about this novel than this single sentence and the title, consider how snow can lay apologetically over the world. Why would the writer of this passage choose such a combination of words? What imaginative picture do you construct with this passage? What kind of feeling does this word choice convey to you? What do you think the author is trying to say here?

Questions are statements of problems that occur in the foreground of inquiry. Our task will be to return the reader to the background of an inquiring teacher, such as Linda Pacifici, that led her to ask such questions as those above. Cooper's passage is paradoxical. It is a statement that on the surface seems self-contradictory or absurd. Through inquiry, this paradoxical passage may prove well founded and insightful. This paradox appears to be a metaphor. Poetic tropes of all kinds—metaphor, metonymy, simile, synecdoche, and such—have a paradoxical quality. Paradoxes rip the pattern of ordinary thinking. Breaking habitual modes of interpretation, they confuse and entice. We feel the need to inquire into their meaning. Have you been subconsciously thinking about the title *The Dark Is Rising*? Paradoxes free us from the actual, ordinary, and everyday. Imagination allows us to create possibilities and explore their consequences.

For formal logicians, metaphors are category mistakes. Defying old, familiar, and habitual ways of interpreting the world, metaphors, say logicians, are simply false, or something to be explained away logically. Those who can live a time with the tensions occasioned by poetic tropes can initiate creative inquiries. These inquiries explore the primeval possibilities that flood through the opening in conventional thinking created by paradoxes. Released from the mind-forged manacles of conventional categories, identities, and essences, the inquirer enters the world of possibility. Personal need, desire, and interest internally motivate the exploration. Imagination facilitates the inquiry. The paradoxical passage, "The snow lay thin and apologetic over the world," provides the poetic space for exploration beyond old, familiar, and habitual categories or correct answers. Need, feeling, imagination, paradox, and possibility: These make up teachable moments. When students and teachers share paradoxes and inquire into them together, then they may, if fortunate, share teachable moments.

There are three dynamic and interactive movements to any teaching event: the student, the teacher, and the subject matter. In these movements the dance should be everywhere and the center nowhere for very long. There are, therefore, three movements within the paradoxical opening that converge to create the teachable moment. I began with the subject matter, or, in this case, a piece of text. It is time to turn to the teacher's perception.

Teachable moments involve shared inquiry into a matter (or subject matter) of common concern. The aesthetic elements of Dewey's theory of inquiry allow insight into the "logic" of creating and sustaining teachable moments. In the present case the teacher was seized by a text full of paradoxical passages that aroused in her animated feelings and imaginations. Linda thought that the text could also arouse intense, although distinct, passions, images, and ideas in her students. For Dewey, as previously discussed, there is no sharp separation between creative thought and rational thought.

The paradoxical snow passage particularly fascinated Linda.[8] She loved the implied contrast of the traditional image of snow as pure, fresh, soft, cushioning, and protective of the dormant winter earth with Cooper's image of a miserable, worn-out, thin blanket of snow unable to do its job sufficiently. Linda got a feeling of a well-worn landscape with patches of brown earth barely covered with snow: an untidy, almost unkempt, dysfunctional world, one not very aesthetically pleasing. The words in this passage created a forlorn feeling for her, a feeling of something's being not quite right, of something missing. Simultaneously, these words are setting up a tension, foreshadowing suspense, mystery, and danger in the novel. There was a tension and disequilibrium to Linda's feeling, an emotional sign of a conscious break actual or impending. Desire for restoration of union began to convert her emotion into interest in the objects or conditions that would restore harmony. Linda entered the creative rhythmic cycle of need–desire–inquiry–satisfaction. She was a motivated inquirer intent on resolving the tension created by the paradox.

For Linda the paradoxical passage, "The snow lay thin and apologetic over the world," felt forlorn and ominous. Linda's intuition of evil added to her uneasiness. She initiated her inquiry into this book against the background of her emotional intuition of the quality of a paradoxical passage at the beginning. The single poetic passage created doubt, disequilibrium, and uncertainty regarding her habitual interpretations of children's books. This disturbing mood accompanied not only a new-found doubt about the meaning of this individual text but also a disturbing awakening to the power, risks, and dangers of an entire genre. This is precisely the kind of all-pervasive mood that seizes us when we intuit a unique quality. Linda's mood set the context for her reading of the text. Her distinctions emerged as distinctions from the totality and massiveness of its unique, even if vague and undefined, quality. Dewey (1930/1984d) declared, "The immediate existence of quality, and of dominant and pervasive quality, is the background, the point of departure, and the regulative principle of all thinking" (p. 261). Subsequent selective discriminations depend on the feelings that direct selective attention and interests. These are matters of taste. Linda's desire to understand the text refined her taste and sustained her inquiry. What did it mean? Was it good for her? Was it a good book for fourth graders? Linda's initial intuitions created many tensions that required more than one course of inquiry to dissolve. Initial intuitions are not necessarily correct, but they are necessary to initiate inquiry. It is the consequences of the inquiry that determine its validity. Linda's inquiry eventually had hosts of classroom activities as its consequence. The quality of these activities allows us to evaluate the "quality" of her intuition and the intelligence of her inquiry.

The reasons why teachable moments, and how to study them, have remained hidden from research on teaching is that researchers do not acknowledge the existence of the precognitive qualitative background, insightfulness, teachers' (and students') intuitions, or the importance of mood and feeling to intuition. There is a tendency for even qualitative research to ignore the role of selective interest and imagination. Research that investigated the role of teachers' intuitions, interests, and imagination would help us create more teachable moments in schools with the joy and delight they bestow.

Linda imagined this snow personified as regretful because it cannot fulfill a perhaps universal wish to have an abundant white and pure covering of the earth in winter to soften and beautify any frozen ugliness in the landscape. Linda imagined that the author chose these words because of the paradoxical contrast this image presents to the reader; it plays on our desire for a cozy, blanketing picture of snow. It is imagination, of course, that creates possibilities for us to explore. It is imagination that suggests alternatives to our habitual ways of interpreting things. Linda imagined some of the possibilities in *The Dark Is Rising* and encouraged her students to imagine their own.

When reading a novel that tells a story of primeval powers carried forth into the present with ancient wise ones mysteriously guiding a young initiate; of a quest to fulfill moral visions in a battle of good versus evil; of a world where evil powers are aroused; a novel also abundant with symbolism and ominous foreshadowing that illustrates and reveals the depth and complexity of the see-saw motion of the battle raging in the text; a novel that plays back and forth between present and past, that sees time as a fluid, nonlinear entity—do you read, enjoy and dismiss, then place the novel as science fiction fantasy? Or do you allow yourself to imaginatively enter into this world and let the story feed your own imagination and stir your emotions? Linda was very aware of her love for literary genres that explore and bring to life quests, moral journeys, and soul-deepening experiences. She knew that she liked these stories because she loved possibilities. She did not accept the status quo as the only possibility for many things. Linda loved to consider the unthinkable and to imagine beyond our culturally determined notions of reality. She loved to challenge herself and her students' self-limiting beliefs, their habits of thought. She believed there are realities beyond and beside our everyday pressures and worries, and that breaking from ordinary everyday experience is essential and happens by looking, feeling, and experiencing the "misty gap between memory and imagining" (Cooper, 1973, p. 33). This novel *spoke* to her in the language of poetic possibility.

The paradoxical snow passage drew Linda into the imaginative world of the novel with her senses awakened. Alert and sensitized to the suspenseful, the mysterious, and the puzzling unexpected as well as amazed by the rich details and nuances as though hiking through the woods on a fresh, bright, sunny spring morning, Linda was compelled to read further, experiencing through the text a juxtaposition of ancient history interwoven with a modern setting, a tension of time and place, old and new. Her passion is reminiscent of Dewey's (1934/1987) observations:

> Impulsions are the beginnings of complete experience because they proceed from need . . . that belongs to the organism as a whole and that can be supplied only by instituting definite relations . . . with the environment. . . . It is the fate of a living creature . . . that it cannot secure what belongs to it without an adventure in a world that as a whole it does not own and to which it has no native title. . . . The impulsion also meets many things on its outbound course that deflect and oppose it. In the process of converting these obstacles and neutral conditions into favoring agencies, the live creature becomes aware. . . . The self, whether it succeed or fail, does not merely restore itself to its former state. . . . The attitudes of the self are informed with meaning. . . . Nor without resistance from surroundings would the self become aware of itself. (pp. 64–65)

For Dewey, the actions of the live creature striving to survive and enjoy living by carrying out erotic transactions with its world are the origins of art. Dewey speaks in this passage about organisms and environment. Substituting "Linda" for "organism" (or "live creature,") and "text" for "environment" (or "world") in the foregoing passage gives a remarkably apt description of how reading *The Dark Is Rising* was a moving experience for Linda. Reading a text that we feel we need to understand converts vague emotion into desire and interest; it induces reflection and we embark on an adventure. Inquiry into the meaning of the text becomes passionate. There is no question of motivation when learning is erotic.

The novel captivated Linda emotionally as a reader. It stimulated and enhanced relationships she enjoys creating with herself and her world. The novel stimulated her imagination; it drew on her emotions and nurtured the relationship she has with herself as a reader, a learner, a creative person able to make choices and explore possibilities. Linda's imagination and emotion created the relationship she had with the novel and all the possibilities there could be for her in exploring life and history through this novel. Linda also experienced anticipation through her emotional and imaginative connection to the novel. As a teacher, the novel let Linda submerge into emotional and imaginative spaces.

As with any relationship that offers resistance, just think about your relation to your students' or your own children; the resistance allows us to become aware of ourselves. In student–teacher relationships both can become increasingly self-aware and grow. Teachers may also grow vocationally as their abilities are called forth and refined. Participants in such creative activities bestow value on each other. As Dewey (1934, 1987) observed, "What might be or might have been stands always in contrast with what is and has been in a way only words are capable of conveying. . . . Words as media [daimōns] are not exhausted in their power to convey possibility. Nouns, verbs, adjectives express generalized conditions—that is to say *character*" (p. 247, emphasis in original). For Linda, the relationship with this complicated "children's" novel transformed her personal and professional character.

As her inquiry began to move from the background to the foreground the crucial point of transition for Linda was imagination. As Dewey (1932/1985b) indicated:

> Deliberation is actually an imaginative rehearsal of various courses of conduct. We give way, *in our mind*, to some impulse; we try, *in our mind*, some plan. Following its career through various steps, we find ourselves in imagination in the presence of the consequences that would follow: and as we then like and approve, or dislike and disapprove, these consequences, we find the original impulse or plan good or bad. Deliberation is dramatic and active; . . . it has the intuitive, the direct factor in it. (p. 275) [emphasis in original]

The capacity of novels to provide powerful vicarious experience makes them an ideal vehicle for educating erōs. Teachers educate their students' erōs by helping them reflect on the consequences of acting on their desires. By following out the consequences of acting on desires, students may learn the consequences of their actions. They may thereby come to distinguish the desirable from that which they merely desire, and by reading novels students may learn these distinctions without having to suffer the consequences in potentially enduring and damaging ways. Deliberation, inquiry, and practical reasoning allow all of us to grow. Deliberation has the power of genesis. It allows students to become different and, hopefully, better persons. The daimōns of practical reasoning (for instance, desire, interest, ideas, and imagination) mediate between students' actual present selves and their morally better possibilities. Relationships with literature can lead to expansive growth.

What does all of this have to do with imagination, emotion, being a fourth-grade teacher, and the teachable moment? I began by describing how Linda's imagination and emotion brought the novel alive for her; she let this happen for herself, even as a busy teacher. In this way Linda had an intuitive sense of how her students could discover for themselves a connection to the world of the novel. Linda's fourth-grade language arts class did not just read a novel, answer questions, and take a test. Students and teacher both "did" (as Linda put it) a novel in as many ways as possible, allowing for a direct experience with and around the novel. Linda's initial relationship with the novel served as a springboard for her to imagine possibilities for her students, ways they might use their own imaginations, emotions, and intuitions as they interacted with her and the text, thereby creating teachable moments.

I propose understanding teachable moments as the times when spaces open for the student and teacher to interact in a synchronistic and dynamic rhythm. It is like having a good dance partner. During these moments there is a special or enhanced quality of intimacy, openness, and creativity coupled with an experience of students or teachers having an "aha!" experience, a connection where there was none before, students realizing breakthroughs in learning or experiencing an effortless flow in learning. Good teachers know intuitively what teachable moments feel like and how these moments may come so suddenly and then so easily slip away, how sometimes these moments are very subtle, barely perceptible to even an experienced eye, and how at other times they are obvious to all involved.

Teachers develop relationships with themselves as literate persons by taking time to know themselves as they inquire into a novel (or any other curriculum-based activity). Relying on their intuition, emotion, and imagination is a key ingredient in the workings of teachers who desire to create teachable moments. Linda took the time to initially know herself, her own needs, intuitions, and interests regarding this novel before asking her students to know themselves with it. She struggled through some of the tensions and resistances that bring self-recognition and understanding before she asked her students to struggle through a similar inquiry. The novel, therefore, became an authentic experience for her that she hoped to share with her students. Linda's "doing" of the novel, as she likes to describe it, came from an important, personal place within herself. She built a relationship with her own imagination, emotion, and intuition: Linda knew how aesthetic experience through written and spoken text can enrich her life. She experienced the possibilities of literacy for herself and wanted to explore the possibilities for her students. The tension Linda felt and observed in *The Dark Is Rising* between the richness and aesthetics of old and new motivated her to see what her students would do with their own exploration. The snow quote was an opportunity because it presented possibilities free of our habitual ways of interpreting. As a paradox it creates a tension, a qualitative starting place.

Teachable moments occur when students and teachers share feelings of doubt, intuit qualities simultaneously, and initiate inquiries concurrently. What sustains the teachable moment is their creative exploration of imaginary possibilities together. Exploring possibilities is a further function of inquiry. Initiating the foreground cognitive phase of inquiry and then sustaining it requires even further use of imagination. The paradoxical passage, "The snow lay thin and apologetic over the world," provides the poetic space for exploration beyond old, familiar, and habitual categories, correct answers, or responses. Linda confided to me that *The Dark Is Rising* "is full of possibilities for myself and I wanted to find out the possibilities for my students." Having herself accepted the invitation to engage in paradoxical inquiry into possibilities propelled by her own interest, desires, and imaginings, Linda was well positioned to help her students initiate their own inquiries.

Linda sought to share the possibilities she saw in the novel with her students. Linda's desire to share her inquiry could have been destructive, especially if she fell victim to the fallacies of ignoring context. Fortunately, she did not confuse her own personal history and interests with those of her students, or assume that they participated in the same cultural tradition as herself. Teachers must strive not to project their own personal needs, desires, and so forth onto their students. That is domination, oppression, and part of the hidden meaning of colonialism. Teachers must remember that "the only general thought is the generous thought" and avoid the fallacy of unlimited universalization.

Teachers may use paradoxes such as the snow passage as occasions to help students, and themselves, reflect carefully and perhaps to create new meanings. Some teachers may consider the quote as a contradiction or interesting choice of words and nothing more. As a vehicle for generating teachable moments, the paradox in the passage creates a poetic context in which the teacher and students can suspend judgment, embrace the paradox, inquire into it together, and seek to create new dimensions of understanding. This requires that the teacher, through knowing herself, be completely present as she moves through the event with the students.

What about her students' experiences with the "doing" of this novel? How do teachers know that teachable moments are happening for the students? Are the students developing a relationship through their own sense of self with the novel in stimulating, creative ways? Linda intuited a sense of foreboding; others—for instance her students—may feel otherwise. They may react to or interpret the passage many different ways. As Dewey (1925/1981) saw it, "The same existential events are capable of an infinite number of meanings" (p. 241). Different people of different ages or different personal and cultural histories are likely to experience the same event differently.

The role of the students is the third dramatic movement that converges in the dance that creates teachable moments. Linda knew the power of "kidwatching" (Goodman, 1982) and used this knowledge to "read" her students and their learning. Through years of watching and observing children, she has developed an intuition about reading her students' emotional and physical comfort levels, their engagement with learning, and what bores them, excites them, and turns them off or on to the learning at hand. "Reading" students and the stories of their lives is a far more difficult duty than the already difficult task of reading a literary text.

Knowing our students and ourselves is a difficult process of inquiry in which the most relevant data are sympathetic data. It calls for courage, moral commitment, faith and faithfulness, creative inquiry, and, above all, wisdom to solve problems. It also requires care, moral respect, and moral perception of the needs, desires, and dreams of others and ourselves. I take up the logic of moral perception in Chapter 6.

Linda noted her students' sense of excitement as well as their degree of engagement and involvement with the activities in the framework she set up to "do" this novel. Linda created the teaching and learning framework for this novel several years ago. It was part of her transition from a direct, whole-class instruction, and textbook-based transmission model of teaching to a learning-centered, process-oriented, and inquiry-based system. Linda was just beginning the transition to what is now called literature circles, reading-response logs, dialogue journals, and student inquiry as curriculum and knowledge construction. Her habits of teaching were undergoing reconstruction. Activities such as these allow us to read our students better by disclosing to us who they are and whom they hope to become. Linda recalls reflecting on open-ended questions through writing in a reading-response log and in dialogue journals and using the written responses to prepare the students for small-group and then large-group discussions. She remembers the emotion, the feeling in the room of powerful teachable moments. Looks of awe and astonishment (and sometimes confusion and anxiety) flushed the faces of her students as they read, discussed, and worked with the novel's language. The inquiry unfolded as each student made sense of the rich symbolism, the abundant and mysterious metaphors, and the fluid time movement in the novel. These were daily occurrences, sometimes very fleeting small moments of perching, but often prolonged flights.

Students' projects and activities indicated to Linda a high level of interest and engagement. For one final project, the class imagined themselves moving back and forth between the present and the past just as in the novel. They put themselves in the main character's clothes and, at times, they felt the spine-tingling mystery of the novel as each student or group of students shared their creative writing. This writing extended into the students' producing a "sitcom." In their script a knight lands in New York City. Ideas from *The Dark Is Rising* fueled the language and ideas written in the sitcom. The class videotaped three sitcom sessions. This project required no prodding from the teacher. She just guided and facilitated using teachable moments in all the activities for more writing, reading, and inquiry. All sorts of affiliated learning came out of this project: characterization, concise plots with punch lines, script writing, costume design, set design, using a camcorder, writing for an audience, timing of sessions, and so on.

Linda and her students created a lived experience with the novel that served to bring out the literacy of each student. Her imagination and emotion served as a sympathetic bridge to the students' imagination and emotion. In conjunction with the novel, the personal worlds of the students found a literate voice appropriate for each of them. Linda did not dictate what they had to learn. She provided structure and presented possibilities from her experience. The novel supported this effort by providing material to create a poetic moment for creative inquiry.

I have shown how Linda plowed and made fertile the ground for teachable moments to occur, yet there is no one best way to teach. Every teacher has his or her own unique artistic style. Given your own personal experience and style, how do you think you would approach teaching *The Dark Is Rising*? Answering this question requires respect for the precognitive background from which it, like all other questions, emerges.

Shared inquiry in which students and teachers share feelings of tension and disequilibrium, needs, desire, interests, imaginations, and self-disclosing reflective thoughts is the teachable moment or, more exactly, the aesthetic event of good teaching and learning that modulates such moments. The rhythm of nature, human nature, and learning is the same. It is an endless process of growth and becoming through the creation of meaning.

CHAPTER 5

The Education of Erōs: Critical and Creative Value Appraisal

Philosophy is inherently criticism. . . . Criticism is discriminating judgment,
careful appraisal, and judgment is appropriately termed criticism
wherever . . . discrimination concerns goods or values.

—*Dewey, 1925/1981, p. 298*

There is a great deal of talk these days about values and education, yet almost nothing is said about erōs and education. Instead, contemporary talk about values education expresses itself in the exclusively intellectual language of information processing that emphasizes the passive and passionless memorization of rules and standards or cost-benefit calculation. Dewey (1925/1981) decried what he called ''intellectualism,'' that is, the idea that ''all experience is a mode of knowing'' (p. 28). His sense was that educators should cultivate the capacity of students to appraise, judge, and create values for themselves, not just memorize what the curriculum dictates to them. Ignoring the role of erōs in education is the most serious gap in the contemporary educational conversation. The gap may be closed by exploring the question: How should we educate the erōs of our students?

Teachers, including teacher educators, may educate erōs by teaching their students how to distinguish objects of mere desire from those that are truly desirable. Dewey (1939/1988) insisted, ''Every person in the degree in which he is capable of learning from experience draws a distinction between what is desired and what is desirable whenever he engages in formation and choice of competing desires and interests'' (p. 219).[1] Those who are wise are expert at making such discriminations. Teaching students to distinguish what they immediately and unreflectively desire from what they ought to desire after reflection is the ultimate goal of the education of erōs. It is an education that lies beyond knowledge alone.

How do we educate erōs? There are two parts to Dewey's answer to this question. For Dewey, the education of erōs requires both deliberate critical value appraisal and artistic value creation; value deliberation and artistic creation working together provide a complete theory of value appraisal. Call it a critical–creative theory of intelligent deliberation and the education of erōs. Remember that the precognitive aesthetic and imaginative background of inquiry remains influential in the cognitive foreground of all inquiry, including value inquiry. All intelligent inquiry is, therefore, potentially both critical *and* creative. One simple way of seeing how inquiry may become creative is if it becomes necessary to imaginatively create hypotheses to continue the inquiry.

Inquirers should not make the mistake, identified in the last chapter, of turning a useful distinction, such as that between the cognitive and imaginative functions of inquiry, into a false dualism between rational and creative thinking. Imagination plays a crucial role in both rational cognitive and creative value appraisals.

Critical value deliberation only concerns knowing and judging value alternatives. It is a mode of inquiry, a daimōn mediating between what we immediately desire and what is rationally desirable. Deliberation provides warranted assertions about values. Value inquiry for Dewey involved critical reflection on what we experience, directly or vicariously, as a *consequence* of our moral choices and actions.[2] Appraisal provides knowledge of things as they are. Recall that, for Singer (1984), "rational cognitive appraisal" is all there is to appraisal. In this chapter I will identify another sense of appraisal, as value creation or bestowal. I will also discuss Dewey's theory of deliberate and critical value appraisal. Since his theory of deliberation has already been extensively discussed, very little needs to be added to understand his theory of appraisal.

Traditional theories of value appraisal, like traditional theories of inquiry, consider the imagination and emotions as interfering with the proper employment of rational deliberation. This is not so for Dewey; creative imagination and desire are part of all deliberation, not just value deliberation: for Dewey (1922/1983):

> Deliberation is a dramatic rehearsal (in imagination) of various competing possible lines of action [ideas]. It starts from the blocking of efficient overt action, due to that conflict of prior habit and newly released impulse. . . . Then each habit, each impulse, involved in the temporary suspense of overt action takes its turn in being tried out. Deliberation is an experiment in finding out what the various lines of possible action are really like. . . . But the trial is in imagination, not in overt fact. . . . An act overtly tried out is irrevocable, its consequences cannot be blotted out. An act tried out in

imagination is not final or fatal. It is retrievable. (Dewey, 1922/1983, pp. 132–133)

Deliberation allows us to see into the future of our best possibilities. It is part of moral perception to see beyond what is immediately present. This refusal to separate imagination and emotion from rational deliberation allowed Dewey to defy one of the most devious threats to critical thinking. If our critical intelligence lacks imagination, emotion, and intuition, then we are only able to deliberate about preexisting alternatives. Value criticism would then be purely cognitive and dispassionately "rational," as described by Singer. Ironically, such a limited view of critical appraisal could be complicitous with oppression; for as we saw in our discussion of the metaphysics of Play-Doh, to be free we need to be able to imagine the possible beyond the actual, and to be moral we must distinguish those possibilities that ought to be (i.e., that are truly desirable) from those that ought not. Dewey understood that imagination could create new value alternatives for us to deliberate upon and, perhaps, pursue. That is why Dewey's complete theory of the education of erōs is imaginatively creative as well as analytically critical.

Because imagination allows us to determine consequences by exploring various possible lines of action while also creating alternative possibilities for us to explore, it is capable of what Singer calls "a new creation of value" or "loving bestowal." Dewey's complete critical-creative theory of intelligent appraisal and the education of erōs is compatible with Singer's (1984) intuition that "love is not primarily a way of knowing" but rather, as already intimated, a "means of bestowing value that would not exist otherwise" (p. 17). Awakening the young to their possibilities and the possibilities of the world around them often involves acts of loving bestowal appearing as acts of critical–creative appraisal. I will show that Dewey advocated a creative, poetic, and prophetic sense of appraisal as value bestowal that goes far beyond the common notion of appraisal as exclusively rational, cognitive, and unfeeling. Dewey would have viewed any sharp separation between appraisal and bestowal as an untenable dualism.

It is easy to see that those that use a critical–creative theory of value appraisal are far more intelligent than those confined to only critical deliberation. They are more intelligent because critical–creative theories bestow upon them a larger number of value alternatives to choose among. Recall the etymology of intelligence, *inter* ("among") and *legere* ("to choose"). Critical–creative value appraisal is more intelligent because it provides more authentic choices, more degrees of freedom for rational cognitive appraisal to pass judgment upon.

In the first part of this chapter I will develop Dewey's critical–creative theory of practical deliberation and value appraisal. Because value appraisal is a straightforward extension of Dewey's general theory of inquiry, I will spend most of my time investigating the more creative aspects of Dewey's theory of value appraisal. Next, I will develop an approach to educating erōs that teachers may use in the reading and writing workshop. The guiding idea is that life is like a story. The erōs of our students may be educated by teaching them to edit and emend the text of their lives. We will follow the adventures of a young woman, Gwyn, in Cynthia Voigt's novel *Jackaroo*. I will show how Gwyn first rejects and then rewrites the dominant cultural scripts for young women and peasants in her medieval world. The wise bestowal of value, I conclude, may not only require us to go beyond knowledge alone; it may also require us to go beyond conventional good and evil.

DEWEY'S CRITICAL THEORY OF MORAL DELIBERATION AND APPRAISAL

Dewey (1939/1988) explicitly connected personal desire and interest with means–ends reasoning, and both with value appraisal:

> The more overtly and emphatically the valuation of objects as ends is connected with desire and interest, the more evident it should be that, since desire and interest are ineffectual save as they cooperatively interact with environing conditions, valuation of desire and interest, as means correlated with other means, is the sole condition for valid appraisal of objects as ends. (p. 216)

In practical means–ends reasoning, practitioners reason for those values or ends-in-view they desire to obtain. In value appraisal, we bear the additional burden of discriminating ends that prove desirable after mediated reflection from those immediately desired. This discrimination ultimately involves something that, in the next chapter, I call moral perception. Moral perception allows us to see the needs, desires, and interests of unique individuals interacting in unique, one-time-only situations. It also allows us to imaginatively look into the future to see the best possibilities in the present.

Dewey (1916/1980a) understood reflection as a transactional process:

> When an activity is continued *into* the undergoing of consequences, when the change made by action is reflected back into a change made in us

[habits], the mere flux is loaded with significance. We learn something. . . . To "learn from experience" is to make a backward and forward connection between what we do to things and what we enjoy or suffer from things in consequence. . . . Two conclusions important for education follow. (1) Experience is primarily an active-passive affair; it is not primarily cognitive. But (2) the *measure of the value* of an experience lies in the perception of relationships or continuities to which it leads up. (pp. 146–147) [emphasis in original]

This passage echoes four familiar themes. First, there is the prominent role of consequences in reflective inquiry. People learn by reflecting on the consequence of their acts. Inducing such reflection is crucial for educating the passionate desire, the erōs of our students. Second, there is the idea that reflection originates in the precognitive quality of immediate experience—"it is not primarily cognitive." Third, reflection can lead to practical wisdom about the values by which it is best to live. Fourth, habits are learned responses that channel affective impulses; therefore, to learn something is to alter our dispositions to act in the future. Our habits of conduct are transformed. If reflective deliberation leads to the formation of better habits, then the result is moral growth.

Dewey (1939/1988) found that when we deliberate, we are always deliberating for the sake of some desired value or end-in-view:

For what is deliberation except weighing of various alternative desires (and hence end-values) in terms of the conditions that are the means of their execution, and which, as means, determine the consequences actually arrived at? There can be no control of the operation of foreseeing consequences (and hence of forming ends-in-view) save in terms of conditions that operate as the causal conditions of their attainment. Any survey of the experiences in which ends-in-view are formed, and in which earlier impulsive tendencies are shaped through deliberation into a *chosen* desire, reveals that the object finally valued as an end to be reached is determined in its concrete makeup by appraisal of existing conditions. (p. 213)

For Dewey, the means frequently constitute the ends that follow as their consequences; therefore, value deliberation is about coordinating means and ends to create the desired state of affairs. All deliberation, for Dewey, is about values. For him, all reasoning is practical reasoning. Recall that the major premise of practical deliberation states, "I desire some value."

As already established, for Dewey, reflective deliberation occurs when habitual modes of response fail and we are cast into a state of need and doubt about our future action. Moral deliberation occurs whenever there is a conflict of desired values in a given situation. When we find ourselves in such a conflict, our duties, obligations, and sense of the good life are in disarray and disharmony. We do not know what to do or how to act. These are value conflicts and we must choose between various perhaps incommensurable, hence incalculable, value alternatives. This is the state of disequilibrium when habitual patterns of recognition and response fail or when we must choose among the competing values or goods, the state that, as we saw in the last chapter, begins in need and doubt and demands inquiry to be transformed into a more desirable and harmonious state.

Opportunities to educate erōs occur in the context of value conflict. Dewey (1932/1985b) wrote:

> The office of reflection [deliberation] . . . [is] the formation of a judgment of value [appraisal] in which particular satisfactions are placed as integral [habitual] parts of conduct as a consistent harmonious whole. If values did not get in one anothers way, if, that is, the realization of one desire were not incompatible with that of another, there would be no need of reflection. . . . Wisdom . . . is the ability to foresee consequences in such a way that we form ends [values] which grow into one another and reinforce one another. Moral folly is the surrender of the greater good for the lesser. (pp. 210–211)

Linda Pacifici gives us a good idea about how to educate erōs, both the students' and her own, in situations of tension and conflict. Value conflict requires us to deliberate about which among a number of alternative values we ought most to desire.[3] This description of moral deliberation and appraisal of values is primarily intellectual in the familiar etymological sense of choosing among alternatives; let us call it critical appraisal. What Dewey described above concerns our choosing among already existing value alternatives that are in actual conflict. That is to say, we seek knowledge about the way things actually are so that we may act wisely in the existing situation. Such inquiry does not seek to go beyond knowledge of what is. The task of critical appraisal is to locate the best possibility in any given set of alternatives in a situation and then move to find the means to actualize the end desired. Poetic and prophetic criticism, in contrast, may perceive the need to go beyond existing value alternatives by creating new ones (see Garrison, 1995a).

A significant part of educating erōs is reflection on, deliberation about, and appraisal of the consequences of our actions. As Dewey (1939/1988) put it, "Nothing more contrary to common sense can be imagined than the notion that we are incapable of changing our desires and interests by means of learning what the consequences of acting upon them are, or, as it is sometimes put, of *indulging* them'' (p. 218, emphasis in original). Rational critical appraisal is one way to educate the human erōs by requiring students to reflect on consequences of their acts, actual or imaginary.

The critical appraisal of objects of desire, of values, is certainly a link among teaching, loving, and logic. There is, though, a sense of criticism other than purely rational appraisal located in Dewey's theory of value inquiry. Dewey's theory of inquiry respects the aesthetic aspects of moral inquiry and deliberation (especially the role of creative imagination) as well as the artistic con-struction of the artifacts of inquiry (such as warranted assertions). It is capable, therefore, not only of appraising already existing value alternatives but also of contributing to creating new value possibilities.

As we saw in the last chapter, we cannot separate the creative from the critically reflective in Dewey's theory of deliberation or inquiry. We can, therefore, not only locate a sense of criticism as appraisal of existing value alternatives in this theory; we can also locate a sense of criticism as bestowal through the creation of value alternatives. To understand the role of value creation in Dewey's theory of intelligent critical–creative evaluation, we need to return to the primacy of the aesthetic encounter in Dewey's philosophy. We are about to see that for Dewey, unlike for Plato, both prophecy, in the sense of Diotima's practice, and poetry, in Diotima's sense of ''calling into existence,'' are parts of the love of wisdom.

AESTHETIC ENCOUNTER IN CRITICAL
APPRAISAL: POETRY AND PROPHECY

Alexander (1992) recognizes the key role accorded to artistic imagination in Dewey's philosophical thought:

> Dewey asserts *the primacy of the aesthetic encounter as the paradigm for grasping the possibilities of existence.* Through the aesthetic, we grasp the significance of the imagination as the transformation of the world through action. The ontological dimensions of the creative are the intertwining of the actual with the possible and this is the context in which action makes sense. (p. 209) [emphasis in original]

Imaginative play, like modeling with Play-Doh, can open up and allow us to grasp the infinite transformational possibilities. Wisdom requires moral imagination. Imagination is what opens the doors of perception, including moral perception, and allows us to see the infinite possibilities hidden in the actual. It is the most powerful possession of poets and prophets. The poetic sense of life is a powerful paradigm for educating the human erōs. Such a poetic education is the most moral education possible and may even be prophetic.

Alexander's characterization is accurate. Recall Dewey's recognition of the similarity between the judgment of the good in conduct and the recognition of beauty. Recall, too, the Greek emphasis upon the good life (*kalokagathos*) as indicating grace, rhythm, and harmony in conduct. The good life is artistically created aesthetic harmony. The values that genuinely constitute kalokagathos can only be determined through cautious critical appraisal. It is an artifact of prudent portrayal, cautious composition, carefully constructed relationships, harmonious blending and balancing of diverse interests, well-designed social relations, and competently orchestrated interpersonal performances. Warranted assertions and judgments are also artifacts of careful deliberation. They allow us to distinguish objects of immediate desire from the desirable. Skill at artistically pro-ducing and aesthetically appreciating the good of moral conduct involves poiēsis and technē.

Because we cannot entirely separate the creative aesthetic background of Dewey's theory of inquiry from the cognitive rational foreground, we cannot entirely separate creative from critical value appraisal. Mark Johnson (1993) discusses creativity as one of the most important similarities between art and morality:

> In art we make things: physical objects, texts, tunes, events, or even conceptual entities. We mold, shape, give form to, compose, harmonize, balance, disrupt, organize, re-form, construct, delineate, portray, and use other forms of imaginative making. . . . This is exactly what we do in morality. We *portray* situations, *delineate* character, *formulate* problems, and *mold* events. When we act we engage in various forms of creative making: we *compose* situations, *build* relationships, *harmonize* diverse interests, *balance* competing values and goods, *design* institutional practices, and *orchestrate* interpersonal relations. (p. 212) [emphasis in original]

We grow in a rhythm that moves from harmonic unity, through disharmony, and back to harmony again. It is a moral and aesthetic as well as intellectual journey.

At the very end of *Art and Experience* (1934/1987), Dewey turned to the relation between art and morality, accepting the dictum that "poetry is criticism of life" (p. 349). He recognized that the poet calling into existence new things, meanings, and values did not need to intend her acts to be cultural criticism to critique society effectively. Still, Dewey

acknowledged the question remained: How is poetry a criticism of life?
His answer was:

> Not directly, but by disclosure, through imaginative vision addressed to
> imaginative experience (not to set judgment) of possibilities that contrast
> with actual conditions. A sense of possibilities that are unrealized and that
> might be realized are when they are put in contrast with actual conditions,
> the most penetrating "criticism" of the latter that can be made. It is by
> a sense of possibilities opening before us that we become aware of the
> constrictions that hem us in and of burdens that oppress. (Dewey, 1934/
> 1987, p. 349)

Dewey explicitly rejected criticism as mere rational cognitive judgment
and appraisal alone. Disclosure through imaginative vision yields truth
not as warranted assertions, but as unconcealment (alētheia). Unconcealment of what? The answer is unconcealment of the possibilities hidden by the actual. Imaginatively creating (or revealing) alternative possibilities is part of bestowal if those possibilities turn out, on appraisal, to
be truly desirable. It is also a part of intelligent criticism in the sense of
intellectus because it creates value alternatives from which to choose. For
Dewey, it is the most penetrating criticism. To bestow love we must
imagine intensely beyond knowledge of established fact or any actual
state of affairs. That is why Singer (1984) is right to say that "love is not
primarily a way of knowing," although knowing—for example, rationally appraising values—is part of loving and caring for others and oneself (p. 17). Singer (1984) suggests that love is creative in the strong
sense of Diotima's "calling something into existence that was not there
before, so that every kind of artistic creation is poetry, and every artist
is a poet" (*Symposium* 205b). Poetry and prophecy went together for
Dewey as much as they did for Diotima.

The most penetrating criticism involves a new creation of value. It is
an art of bestowal. Part of creative criticism, therefore, is to bestow the
possibilities of freedom. It is a way of standing in critical relation with
others so as to foster mutual growth. Possessing this disposition is extremely important to teachers who would be creative critics of their
students' work. Without an expansive imagination—one willing to go
beyond conventional limits—teachers cannot be free, nor can they free
their students. Moreover, without imagination they cannot be moral.
Morality means the capacity to choose as well as to assume responsibility for those values chosen. Creating value alternatives instead of just
evaluating already existing ones introduces expanded possibilities for
free moral choice. If teachers can see that the way conditions are now is
not how they should be, then they might decide that these present

conditions are not morally acceptable. They may, then, choose to act wisely by calling what *is* out of existence and calling what *ought to be* into existence. Nonetheless, it is important to appraise the values bestowed on us rationally. There are, after all, false prophets.

Society often creates false choices. During much of the last half century, for example, women wanting to work in the field of education could contemplate the consequences of becoming elementary, middle, or high school teachers. They could not very readily imagine becoming principals, superintendents, or state commissioners as real possibilities. With few exceptions, they were constrained to the lower rungs of the social hierarchy. Society offers many false choices like this. We are free, but only within well-defined social boundaries. We may not even be aware of the constrictions that "hem us in and of burdens that oppress" (p. 349). The mind-forged manacles take many forms. Feeling free does not make us free. We may feel free only because we lack imagination, passion, or hope. We may be in need and not even know it. In need we feel doubt and disharmony, where before we were sure and certain. It is in such needful times that we often require prophets to name what is missing for us. In responding to the needs of and in educating the desires of their students, teachers must often act practically as prophets and poets. They must be, and teach their students to be, intelligently critical–creative.

"Imagination is the chief instrument of the good," Dewey (1934/ 1987) stated, "Hence it is that art is more moral than moralities. . . . The moral prophets of humanity have always been poets even though they spoke in free verse or by parable" (p. 350). Dewey preferred poetic moral prophets to Plato's scientistic philosopher kings as inspirers of democratic social hope. The difference between them is that Plato's ideal was of a static society, one constructed according to timeless laws, while Dewey's vision was of a democracy constantly reconstructing itself to adapt to changing circumstances and—hopefully—progressing. Prophets are social critics, even when they do not intend to be so. Powerful agents of social manipulation, control, and domination easily recognize and fear them. Prophets have the capacity to penetrate the veneer of supposedly fixed and final actuality and name what constrains and oppresses us. They expose the aesthetic and moral possibilities that lie beneath knowledge and unalterable rules and laws. Their poetry is a criticism of life. Prophets may envision ethereal things, vague values, and ends-in-view that are capable of guiding humankind's future quest for more meaning.

Recall Rosen's (1968/1987) comment: "Philosophy, as the pursuit or love of knowledge, is ignorance [a *lack* of knowledge]. . . . Prophecy

. . . allows us to surmise what we seek to know. The disjunction between intuition and discursive reason is bridged by the mantic [prophetic] art'' (p. 207). Because the love of wisdom is beyond knowledge for Dewey, prophecy and poetry are both parts of philosophy. Prophets have the passionate capacity to recognize the needs and desires of people and places, name them, and respond imaginatively by naming and striving to create the needful values. Prophets are the finest poets and philosophers, for it is their task to call into existence the novel values that, if we truly desire them, will lead us toward a better destiny. Thus transformative teachers must serve as prophets if they are to respond fully to their students' need to become free authors of their own lives.

Prophets often speak in parables to prevent their creative insights and naming of healing possibilities from being captured and transformed into new instruments of oppression. Eventually prophets must go beyond good and evil as conventionally defined in the rules, laws, and regulations of tyrannical regimes. Recollect the passage in Chapter 3 where Dewey explained the sense of truth working in Keats' ''Ode on a Grecian Urn.'' In that tradition, Dewey (1934/1987) observed, truth ''never signifies correctness of intellectual statements about things, or truth as its meaning is now influenced by science. It denotes the wisdom by which men live, especially 'the lore of good and evil' '' as (p. 40).

Consider the following remark by regarding what becomes of the wisdom of the prophets:

> Uniformly, however, their vision of possibilities has soon been converted into a proclamation of facts that already exist and hardened into semi-political institutions. Their imaginative presentation of ideals that should command thought and desire have been treated as rules of policy. Art has been the means of keeping alive the sense of purposes that outrun evidence and of meanings that transcend indurated habit. . . . Mankind is divided into sheep and goats, the vicious and virtuous, the law-abiding and criminal, the good and bad. To be beyond good and evil is an impossibility for man, and yet as long as the good signifies only that which is lauded and rewarded, and the evil that which is currently condemned or outlawed, the ideal factors of morality are always and everywhere beyond good and evil. (Dewey, 1934/1987, pp. 350–351)

Not only are wisdom and bestowal beyond knowledge; they are sometimes beyond good and evil. At first, Dewey's position seems morally outrageous; yet often what we culturally condemn and outlaw are liberty and freedom. Often the actual state of affairs is as it is because oppressive power legislates what must be condemned or outlawed to suit its interests. In such circumstances, going beyond the actual to the possible is going beyond good and evil. Obeying a society's rules, laws, and regulations does not necessarily make us moral; it may just make us complicitous with oppression. Think about the Jim Crow laws in the old South, or the need for a constitutional amendment for women to obtain the vote. Schools are outstanding institutions for dividing sheep from goats. This system is called tracking. Some may interpret these rules of policy as contributing to a more efficient educational system. Others may see them as contributing to oppression by reproducing the existing power hierarchy. Similarly, we may see the "norms" of testing as fairly evaluating human potential and achievement, or as instruments of social injustice. The ethics of justice and the ethics of care are not always compatible. Caring for others, for instance, sometimes requires us to break the rules of justice to avoid breaking people.

A colleague, Kim Oliver, shared the following example with me from her days as an elementary school physical education teacher. The President's Physical Fitness test is widely used as a standard for assessing students' physical fitness. Envision now an overweight child struggling to do pull-ups. It is impossible for him to do the minimal number to demonstrate competency. Some of the other children are beginning to titter with almost cruel amusement. What is the wise practitioner to do? Kim held his bent legs so he could press on her arm as he struggled to do the minimal number necessary (one pull-up). Was this the right thing to do? What would you have done? The answer requires wisdom, and wisdom goes far beyond actual conditions, approved knowledge, or moral conventions. I believe this is a wonderful instance of caring and compassionate rule bending. It helped the child realize his best possibilities on the occasion and provided a powerful example as an alternative to cruel teasing. Some may disagree with me, and perhaps they are right. The example, though, does illustrate the sometimes difficult conflicts that can arise in teaching between caring and rule-governed response.

Philosophy, the love of wisdom, is a moral term not restricted to things already in existence. It refers not to accomplished reality, but to the most desirable of future possibilities. Indeed, Dewey (1925/1981) once declared that "philosophy is inherently criticism, having its distinctive position among various modes of criticism in its generality; a criticism of criticisms, as it were" (p. 298). Philosophy, so comprehended, has a much more modest task than that conceived by Plato. It is not a prerogative reserved for a few "philosopher kings," philosophy professors, or technocratic experts. Philosophy is something everyone does sometimes, and something we should all engage in more often than we do. Considered as "a criticism of criticisms," philosophy simply seeks a holistic, unified, and harmonious view among diverse values. This is Dewey's (1916/1980a) philosophy *"as the general theory of education"* (p. 338).

Philosophy concerns itself with critiquing the fundamental dispositions, the habits and beliefs that constitute the self. Ultimately a complete doctrine of intelligent critical–creative appraisal allies itself to creativity and poetry in Diotima's sense, and, eventually, to Diotima's prophetic calling, that is, the ability to foresee consequences and name what we need in needful times. Still, wisdom also refers to choice about what we should do and requires critical value appraisal to distinguish desire from the desirable. We especially require critical deliberation when we go beyond good and evil.

Some students desire to dominate classmates, while others dream of cruel teasing. Part of the education of the human erōs is redirecting desire, perhaps by helping students to imagine the full consequences of their acts, for instance, that cruel people are lonely because they have no real friends. The ability to imagine remote consequences is understandably absent among the young. Sometimes caring acts of bestowal require us to imagine for students and act creatively in the present to discipline student actions and desires. Reciprocally, practitioners must appraise their own desires and dreams. For example, in caring, are teachers too self-sacrificing or self-assertive? Do they expect too much or too little from their students or themselves? Further, teachers must be constantly critiquing their practice and its products. Are they really good? How could they be better? Further still, they must constantly reappraise their earlier appraisals.

Students, too, need to learn to appraise their own needs, desires, and dreams. They must learn to critique their classroom practice and its products. In language arts this may simply mean checking grammar and spelling and revising accordingly. It may mean appraising the consequences of their own creations. It may mean appraising the social consequences of students' creative writing and censoring them if students will not avoid cruelty. Censorship may sound terrible, but do we allow creation at the expense of humiliating someone else? If you are the teacher, then it is your tragic decision.[4] Either you must censor or contribute to cruelty. Philosopher kings with homogeneous value rulers can only follow the rules and calculate. If you are not a king, or do not have a ruler to consult, then the only way out of this either/or dilemma will require a great deal of practical wisdom and personal growth.

Things become very dangerous when we go beyond conventional good and evil. We must not forget that there are false prophets and the only way we can know them is by the consequences of following them.

Critical deliberation allows us to follow out the consequences imaginatively in ways that are revocable. Deliberation must be critical as well as creative.

THE EMERGENT NARRATIVE SELF

Dewey held a transactional and social constructivist theory that stressed the continuous emergence of the mind and self as a consequence of physical and cultural interaction (Garrison, 1995b). Dewey (1925/1981) wrote, "Personality, selfhood . . . are eventual functions that emerge with complexly organized interactions, organic and social" (p. 162). Dewey insisted that his work "be conceived as an attempt to contribute to what has come to be called an 'emergent' theory of mind" (p. 207). To assume that our minds and selves exist antecedent to any cultural context is to commit the philosophical fallacy. When we cultivate the emergent self properly, it will bring forth continuous expansive growth.

The discussion of habits in the preceding chapter took us to the heart of Dewey's theory of the self. Beliefs, for him, are habits. Habits are somatic dispositions to act. Dewey (1932/1985b) rejected any dualism between the mind and the body:

> Habit reaches . . . down into the very structure of the self; it signifies a building up and solidifying of certain desires; an increased sensitiveness and responsiveness . . . or an impaired capacity to attend to and think about certain things. Habit covers . . . the very makeup of desire, intent, choice, disposition which gives an act its voluntary quality. (p. 171)

We may understand "habits" as habits of interpretation and response to the roles we and others play in the contemporaneously enacted drama of culture. Educating students means improving their habits of conduct so that they may grow in good health to the greatest expanse possible, and that means altering their dispositions to act so that they may make better voluntary choices for themselves. Altering those beliefs that structure and express passion is the education of erōs. For Dewey, the education of erōs involves altering bodily habits and, thereby, desire.

Habits are social functions for Dewey. "Customs persist," wrote Dewey (1922/1983), "because individuals form their personal habits under conditions set by prior customs. An individual usually acquires the morality as he inherits the speech of his social group" (p. 43). The questions of customs, conduct, and habits are not in themselves moral ones. Dewey (1922/1983) concluded, "Conduct is always shared; this is the difference between it and a physiological process. It is not an ethical 'ought' that conduct *should* be social. It *is* social, whether bad or good" (p. 16, emphasis in original). To acknowledge oneself as controlled by habits and conditioned by social customs is simply to recognize that one's values, beliefs, interests, perceptions, and so on are largely predetermined by scripts and plot lines that comprise the social context, including dominant cultural texts, of a given historical epoch. Such self-awareness is the first step to conscious freedom. The second step consists in reflecting on the consequences of leading prescribed lives. Acquiring the habit of intelligent reflection is extremely difficult. It is so difficult because social conditioning has the power to control the development of emergent minds.

For Dewey, to have a mind means to be able to participate in some culture's social practices for making meaning by coordinating our behaviors with others; to have a self is to be able to assume the culturally assigned roles of the culture and to respond to others in their roles. Dewey (1925/1981) asserted, "Through speech a person dramatically identifies himself with potential acts and deeds; he plays many roles, not in successive stages of life but in a contemporaneously enacted drama. Thus mind emerges" (p. 135). Mark Johnson's (1993) neo-Deweyan narrative theory of the self and social action takes the notion of role playing and dramatic identification very seriously.[5] So will we.

Johnson (1993), following Dewey, argues that our selves and our minds are emergent, contingent, and socially constructed. In this Deweyan view, the self and mind emerge from a physical and biological basis through role playing and dramatic identification. Johnson (1993) proposes taking Dewey's analogy literally and develops a notion of "the narrative character of selfhood and agency" (p. 150). These cultural narratives answer the three fundamental existential questions of life for us: What is life? How should we live? What does life mean? Cultures and traditions have us before we have them. They provide canonical answers to our existential questions in advance. If we are ever to be free, if we are ever to re-create ourselves, we must provide our own answers to these questions. Doing so involves an endless process of growth and becoming through the creation of meaning, eventually creating ourselves by reconstructing our habits of interpretation and conduct in social contexts.

Sociocultural narratives preinterpret our own experience to us. They assign meaning to what we do and what we enjoy or suffer as a consequence, and they provide a predetermined assessment of value. Even the norms of critical deliberation are themselves social constructions. However private our experience, the predominant cultural narrative scripts structures and assigns meanings, values, and purposes to our actions and their consequences.

We inherit prescripted roles authored for us by our ancestors on a stage they designed. These scripts tell us how to act out the drama of our lives, and they take many forms, for example, storytelling, literature, music, the plastic arts, drama, and dance. The mass media have become the most influential source of deliberately designed narrative structure in our time. For example, popular music and the drama of MTV prescribe preferred social roles for young people. Saturday morning and after-school cartoons and adventure tales influences those who are younger. Advertisers in these media control the meanings and values they valorize. The commercials manipulate value choice in the marketplace by prescribing socially prized and popularly approved conduct. They sell us scripts about how to play approved social roles within the culture and seek to condition our habits of material consumption. They construct stereotypical identities of what it is to be members of a given gender, race, ethnic group, age cohort, or social class.

Schools are selling something, too. There are different scripts for boys and girls, jocks and nerds, and those on the college track versus those on the so-called vocational track. Schools are selling destinies, usually without any opportunity to reflect on them critically–creatively. Others have already made the choices for us. In American schools, these stories are told by the communities that contain them: principals, teachers, PTA members, and the students themselves. Oddly, the best-known and often most powerful stories created in schools have numbers as their moral resolution. They are the pencil-and-paper, machine-graded texts called examinations. These probably are just the climax of many other stories told elsewhere. The numbers are just summative appraisals confirming conformity to culturally prescribed roles and values within a social narrative called tracking.

We all live prescribed lives. Culture wrote the scripts for us in advance. They constrain our possibilities and control our thoughts, feelings, and actions. If we are ever to know ourselves, if we are ever to formulate our own answers to life's existential questions, if we are ever to be free, we must become reflectively aware of the cultural scripts that prescribe the roles we play. If we are ever to know, much less re-create, ourselves, then we must intelligently critique those scripts. What we need is the most penetrating criticism, poetry, and prophecy. Knowing how culture composes our scripts is the start of intelligent critique.

According to Johnson (1993), we compose narratives of human action from at least six functional components.[6] A well-constructed narrative will create and connect each part into an organic, continuous, and harmonious whole. First, human action is intentional and goal-directed.

We do things for a purpose. These purposes are ideal states that we desire to actualize. Goals are values. They function as ends-in-view.

Second, our actions are motivated. For Dewey, the term *motive* had a double function. To understand motivation requires properly conjoining both functions: (1) "Those *interests* [and desires] which form the core of the self and supply the principles by which conduct is to be understood" and (2) "the *objects*, whether perceived or thought of, which effect an alteration in the direction of activity" (Dewey, 1932/ 1985b, p. 290, emphasis in original). As long as we are living, we are motivated to obtain those objects that sustain life, such as food, water, and a mate, objects that allow us to maintain, enjoy, and enhance our existence.

Teachers often make the mistake of thinking they must motivate behavior. All impassioned beings have needs, desires, and interests that move them. Motivation is never a problem. The problem is how to educate the human erōs to take an interest in truly valuable things. Teachers could avoid a host of errors in motivation if they would realize the following: "The union of the self in action with an object and end is called an interest" (Dewey, 1932/1985b, p. 290). Interest is obviously an intermediary daimōn connecting the self to the valued objects or state of affairs it desires. There is no need to motivate the live creature. The education of erōs only involves modifying and redirecting already existing desires.

Dewey (1932/1985b) insisted, "An interest or motive is the union in action of a need, desire of a self, with a chosen object. . . . It is true enough when we take the whole situation into account that an object moves a person; for that object as a moving force *includes the self within it*" (p. 291, emphasis in original). Need, desire, selective attention, ideas, and the logic of the agents' interests are all part of inquiry for Dewey; therefore, it is usually possible in his view to provide an account of the students' conduct that discloses the underlying intelligence. This becomes especially important when trying to diagnose a student's pattern of error in order to improve performance. Instead of seeing students as stupid and uncomprehending, what we ought to do is strive to understand the logic of the interests that motivate them and use that logic to improve our teaching.

The third functional component of narrative is agency. The motivation and goals that figure into a given action are those of the agent of the action. Our students' identities emerge in and through their actions, although they are not identical with them. Dewey (1932/1985b) stressed "the *essential unity of the self and its acts*" (p. 288, emphasis in original). Through choice and action we not only express the intentions of the present self; through the consequences of the act we also form the future self. As Dewey (1932/1985b) put it:

> Now every such choice sustains a double relation to the self. It reveals the existing self and it forms the future self. That which is chosen is that which is found congenial to the desires and habits of the self as it already exists. Deliberation has an important function in this process, because each different possibility as it is presented to the imagination appeals to a different element in the constitution of the self. (pp. 286–287)

Emergence of a new self is possible through narrative action because of the double relation our choices and actions bear to our self-identity. Recognizing the consequences of our acts either imaginatively or in reality may lead us to reconsider and revise our future habits of conduct.

The fourth narrative component is context, which was discussed extensively in the last chapter. All that requires mentioning here is that, for Dewey, the self, its motives, and its goals connect holistically within some context. Separating students from those objects that interest them is an instance of the analytical contextual fallacy. It mangles internal motivation.

We all desire to live a more meaningful life. That striving is part of the character of human action and the fifth functional component of narrative existence. We attempt to live existentially meaningful and fulfilled lives and to tell stories that answer the three fundamental existential questions in hopeful ways. This means that any action, no matter how routine or trivial it may seem, is part of a larger existential project. Most of our choices are unconscious and unreflective, but if we want to create our own narratives and grow, we must reflect upon all our choices, however trivial or routine. Striving for full narrative consciousness is part of the hard logic of living and realizing that all beliefs are dispositions to act.

Temporality is part of life and the sixth functional component of narrative existence. Remember the rhythm of growth. There is harmonious equilibrium, disequilibrium, inquiry, and, if we are fortunate, the restoration of harmonious functioning. Temporality, as lived, has a narrative structure. We are born, mature, acquire an education, love, work, perhaps have children, grow old, and die. This temporality unfolds like a piece of music or a story. The narrative structure of life is not simple and linear. Events from the distant past return with meanings and values resignified, just as future ends-in-view serve as blueprints for present action. Memory and imagination are mediating daimōns that cooperate in aiding us in creatively authoring the text of our lives. We often strive to realize values that do not turn out to be very desirable, or obtain values we desire only to learn they are desirable in ways we had never thought. The values of the vocation of teaching and the rewards of creatively connecting to students sustain many teachers in ways that they had no idea existed when they first answered the call. The temporality of listening to a call, answering it responsibly by questioning it, and perhaps becoming it are experiences that every good teacher has lived through many times. If we can recall those moments now, we may reflect upon where they have taken us and where we might desire to go from here. Such reflection requires imaginative foresight.

As Dewey (1922/1983) understood it:

> The future situation involved in deliberation is of necessity marked by contingency. . . . But foresight which draws liberally upon the lessons of past experience reveals the tendency, the meaning of present action . . . it is this present meaning rather than the future outcome which counts. Imaginative forethought of the probable consequences of a proposed act keeps that act from sinking below consciousness into routine habit. (p. 145)

Lived time, the time of narrative, dance, and drama, is rhythmic, cyclic, and seasonal. Practical reasoning, that is, rational deliberation, seeks to recover the past into the present that imaginatively anticipates and creatively constructs the future. Intelligent sympathy—for instance, memory of what it is like to be a child with a child's needs, motivations, and dreams—calls into the present and alters understanding of self, students, and classroom circumstances.

THE NARRATIVE SELF, NARRATIVES, AND THE PEDAGOGICAL FRIENDSHIP OF POETRY

So, the reader might still wonder, what do the six functional components of the narrative self have to do with educating erōs to desire the good? The answer is startlingly direct and straightforward in language arts. Reading narratives and writing stories are a powerful way to teach. They are potent because narratives of all kinds *do* structure our very existence. By assigning meaning and value, narratives allow us to interpret and organize what we do and suffer. After we have experienced the consequences of obtaining some object of desire, we are in a much better position to appraise the genuine value of the object or circumstance. Dramatic narratives are excellent instances of vicarious experience, but not overt fact, wherein students may imaginatively indulge their desires. They may suffer the consequences of their imaginary actions, and learn from the experience. They can condense a lifetime of suffered consequences into an afternoon of exciting reading. In language arts the narratives of our lives, composed from the customs of our social habitat and our personal habits, meet with other student narratives. These narratives may conflict with the stories society tells and that we tell ourselves. Our habits of interpretation may be disrupted, needs may arise, and emotions may be created that establish a context for further inquiry.

To comprehend fully what it means to accept a certain scheme of values, we must follow out the consequences of acting on them over a long interval of time. We cannot know the consequences of accepting a value scheme until we have lived it out over an entire life cycle. This implies that we cannot know how to live well until we are dead. Through reading and writing we may live vicariously through an entire lifetime or a long rhythmic cycle of experience, thereby learning from the consequences. With a lively imagination and a sense of poetic analogy, we can apply the lessons learned to our own lives.

The expansive, experimental, and inquiring self is constantly reevaluating situations for further possibilities of healthy growth. Said differently, we are constantly seeking to unify the story of our lives aesthetically while adding more interesting characters, meaningful action, and life-affirming adventure. Johnson (1993) concludes: ''Making judgments of the morality of an intention, action, or character requires that we first understand the narratives that frame the situation. To sum up, *only within a narrative context can we fully understand moral personality (the self) and its actions. The unity of the self and its acts is, in the broadest context, a narrative unity*'' (p. 164, emphasis in original). It is the unity of the self and its acts in a given context that leads to the double relation that choice sustains to the self. We may therefore extend Johnson's notion of the narrative unity of the self and its acts to include the double relation choice sustains to itself. We may think of reading a text as a potentially transformative transaction between two narrative events, the reader and the text. We may just as easily think of reading a text as a transaction between two or more selves striving to render some meanings common between two or more centers of action, two or more people. If Johnson is right, then there is no difference. Readers may interpret the narrative of the text using the culturally customary habits of interpretation that constitute present selves; but what if the narrative of the text does not conform well to the interpretation? The result is a conflict of values. We meet with resistance that induces value deliberation.

To grow it is necessary to edit and emend the text of our lives. It requires critical reflection to recognize our selves by recognizing the roles our culture has prescribed for us as well as the unique stories we have begun to author for ourselves. Literary narratives often provide an alternative telling to culturally dominant narratives. These alternatives may create tension and cause resistance to habitual forms of interpretation. They allow us to look creatively at life from alternative perspectives as well as appraise the consequences of living out those alternatives over long periods of time. Since human beings exist in and through time, anything that allows us to gain command over the temporal constraints of the present empowers us as future creators. Reading novels and stories allows us imaginatively to envision alternative possibilities for acting and vicariously to experiment with those possibilities, especially if we sympathetically identify with a character. Exploring literary texts, conversing with other persons, and employing intelligent practical inquiry and imaginative deliberation allow us to make critical appraisals and form more discriminating judgments of value. They can also be the most potent form of criticism. That is why dialogue across gender, race, and ethnic diversity can be so rewarding. Deliberation helps us become responsible authors of our own unique narratives of self.

Exploring the consequences of the vicarious experience that arises from reading a book, watching or participating in a drama, or writing a story has many advantages. One, of course, is that we do not have to suffer the overt consequences. Another is that we may detach ourselves from the events and thereby gain reflective distance. That, for instance, is the powerful effect Eva Moore had by having her students write to Randy telling him not to misbehave in class. It provided an occasion for the students to reflect on their own patterns of misbehavior. Stories also have a stop-action quality. Students, and teachers, may return to the same scene of conflict repeatedly to think about it some more, experiment further, and deliberate better. In real life, unlike dramatic action in a play, we cannot go back and do it over until we get it right. Play has many such advantages. Students may rehearse roles just to see how they fit and how they look and feel in them. Imaginatively identifying with a character in a story has a similar effect. They may enter into an entire world of alternative possibilities.

Deliberating on the consequences of vicarious action is a relatively safe and secure way of educating erōs. In reading persons may dramatically identify with potential acts and deeds; they may play many roles contemporaneously. Trying out different roles in alternative narratives of all kinds allows students to reconstruct the narratives of their own lives. It is like trying on new clothes while shopping and discovering a new "look." Writing narratives allows students to explore their existing selves and creatively explore possibilities for their emergent selves.

I want to investigate the following Deweyan notion: *"Narrative explorations . . . are, in fact, what moral reasoning is all about"* (Johnson, 1993, p. 198, emphasis in original). Reading narratives provides an excellent opportunity to educate the human erōs intelligently through narrative exploration. It allows us to explore personal narratives while exploring the narratives of a story authored by another. By entering into a relationship with the text, either as friend or foe, we can simultaneously explore the narrative self and the text in a reciprocal transactional relationship that could lead to expansive growth. Such vicarious relationship requires a vivid imagination and sympathetic understanding.

Dewey (1934/1987) declared:

> It is by way of communication that art becomes the incomparable organ of instruction, but the way is so remote from that usually associated with the idea of education, it is a way that lifts art so far above what we are accustomed to think of as instruction, that we are repelled by any suggestion of teaching and learning in connection with art. But our revolt is in fact a reflection upon education that proceeds by methods so literal as to exclude the imagination and one not touching the desires and emotions of men. (pp. 349–350)

Language arts provide powerful instruments of education that include the imagination and touch the desires and emotions of young men and women. An education that includes the imagination and touches the desires and emotions of our students is the education of erōs. Such an education includes the discipline of devoted feeling, imagination, deeds, and thoughts.

Dewey (1934/1987) felt that "poetry teaches as friends and life teach, by being, and not by express intent" (p. 349). For young readers, books are often best friends. Books can open up worlds of possibility, satisfy needs and desires, and sustain hopes and dreams when all others—including teachers, parents, and peers—fail. Books are warm and caring friends, the kinds of friends that listen well, speak sincerely, and give a different perspective on things. Let us return to the functional components of narrative discussed above and see how they can operate in the critical construction of a personal narrative.

THE PROPHETIC ART OF FRIENDLY INSTRUCTION AND CRITICAL-CREATIVE APPRAISAL

I want to provide an example of a book that teaches by being a friend. The book is Cynthia Voigt's *Jackaroo*.[7] Voigt's story goes beyond the norms of conventional good and evil, and it is certainly full of "outlaw emotions.'' It is an instance of creative, imaginative criticism, that is, the most penetrating criticism. *Jackaroo* bestows remarkable value on its readers. If Johnson (1993) is correct, then when in a narrative context literature instructs as friends instruct, the reading must be aesthetic. I want to show that this is the most penetrating criticism that can be made and is more moral than moral codes alone.

Jackaroo is set sometime in the Middle Ages when the peasants, especially the women, are silenced by suspicion and fear. They often tell the old stories, especially of the legendary hero Jackaroo, although they do not quite believe what they say. Gwyn is different because she questions, imagines, and suffers different feelings than those around her. The book begins in the heart of a brutal winter with Gwyn in the ''Doling Room,'' where she has gone to receive a dole of food. Gwyn's basic conflict of values and context of choice is established early:

> Men didn't come to the Doling Room. The shame would be too great for a man to carry. So the women carried it, Gwyn thought. It was a hard thing to be a woman, her mother had often told her. . . . In the spring, then, she would have to say yes to some man, or let Da announce her intention never to marry. One or the other, because service in a Lord's house was unimaginable. One or the other was her choice, and she liked neither; but she could do nothing about the hardness of that. (Voigt, 1985, p. 4)

It is not difficult to intuit the quality of this passage. Gwyn's world is a man's world. It is also hierarchically organized according to social class. There are the lords and the peasants. Gwyn is a peasant, but a privileged one, as we will learn. In Gwyn's world, a woman's choices are limited. Some chose service in the Lord's house; Gwyn would not even consider it. She could choose to marry or not. No matter what she does, she will ultimately be governed by men. The roles women may dramatically identify themselves with as potential acts and deeds are few. Women in Gwyn's world are captured by exclusive either/ors. Her choices are false choices prescripted by the social customs of the culture into which she was born. Her life is tracked by the customs of her culture. There is also irony and paradox in this passage, especially in the second sentence where what it means to be strong is called into question. Paradox and ironic reversal prevail throughout this novel.

We soon learn that Gwyn's family is prosperous. Her father is a prudent innkeeper who has amassed considerable wealth. Indeed, Gwyn will learn that her father himself exploits the poor in bad times. Gwyn wonders, ''Why should she feel badly to have warm, dry feet? Or guilty—because she felt guilty too—that she had good fortune and did nothing to share it'' (p. 13). Gwyn, as it turns out, is not in the Doling Room for herself or her family; she is there for "old Megg" because her friend is too feeble to come herself. As she leaves the Doling Room she sees an old woman and offers to accompany her home to provide safety in numbers and help carry her load. Gwyn's character is already beginning to emerge. Gwyn is reflective, has emotional sympathy, and is perceptive. We can also see that there is ambiguity and tension in her and in the world in which she lives. We wonder what she will do.

At home we learn more of Gwyn's character. Her mother observes, "If it's not your imagination that gets you into trouble it'll be your soft heart" (Voigt, 1985, p. 40). Gwyn has an unconcealing imagination that is able to see beyond the actual: "Such snow, Gwyn thought, had a way of turning the world into what it was not and making it seem safe." (p. 41). In self-reflection Gwyn recognizes the difference between herself and her sister, Rose, who is so eager to marry: "Whatever Rose did, whatever gesture she used, there was something dainty to it. Gwyn had never seen herself, but she felt inside herself a strength that flowed down her arms and legs, she could feel it especially in her shoulders" (p. 44). Gwyn feels and knows that she possesses a physical strength that defies the customary gender construction in her culture.

On my reading, Deweyan excellencies of character, including discriminating judgment, emotional susceptibility, and effective execution, are all part of Gwyn's character. It is vital to the story that these virtues are all seen as deficiencies by her family and community. Docility, unquestioning conformity, and obedience to law are the virtues customarily associated with "good" members of her social class and her gender. To be free, to know and re-create her self, Gwyn will need to go beyond the social conventions of her culture.

Gwyn has many virtues, but she still needs to grow. Voigt's female protagonists frequently grow by learning through relationships with males, relationships that are almost always between equals and without romance, although with a great deal of earned respect. Voigt often displays patterns of warm, helpful friendship between males and females, sometimes with large differences in age. The relationships are typically between those whose differences are considerable, but wherein each has something that the other needs. In *Jackaroo* such a relationship is established between Gwyn and a young ("almost eleven") lordling when they become stranded in the dead of a very hard winter in an abandoned hut.

The young lordling, Gaderian, is ill prepared to care for himself in such hardship. He is also accustomed to aristocratic privilege. As Gwyn observes: "They would have to use the side of the house as a privy, until the snow ceased. But the lordling would require his privacy, she thought with a sigh, so when she made her way back to the door of the house she trudged on through the snow to the right, making a path that turned the corner to the side opposite that which she had used" (Voigt, 1985, p. 86). There are frank and matter-of-fact references to normal bodily functions throughout the novel including references to "soft cloths for Gwyn's time of the month" (pp. 274–275). In the case of the lordling's needs, Gwyn's responses are prefigured as much by her being accustomed to caring for her brother (who in many ways is even less able to care for himself than the lordling, although he is older) as by the necessity of serving the needs of the lords.

Whatever his deficiencies, the young lordling has inner strength and determination to care for himself. Further, Gwyn is forced to admit to herself, "For all that he was so much younger than she was, he had a much broader knowledge of the world" (p. 125). Gaderian, like all of the ruling class, knows how to read and write, and he teaches Gwyn.[8] Such instruction is strictly forbidden by the customs of the kingdom. Gaderian enlarges Gwyn's world. He and his father make maps; in fact, that is how they became stranded. Gwyn and Burl, a burly servant at the inn, had guided the lord and lordling to the frontiers of the land. The lord and his son had verified some of the topography and were on their way back when they were separated and stranded in a snowstorm. The young boy knows what is beyond the mountains; Gwyn does not. That knowledge is a metaphor for the power of the knowledge that the Lords use to rule the peasants and that, for all of her intuitiveness, Gwyn lacks.

Gaderian has other needs. Most of all Gwyn is able to comfort him over the recent death of his mother. If Gwyn has unusual physical strength, Gaderian displays remarkable emotional perceptiveness. As Gwyn strives to console Gaderian, their conversations come to have the quality of an inquiry into the meaning of life and death for both. Together they dare for the first time to address the fundamental existential questions. Gwyn teaches Gaderian to fight with a peasant's weapon, the staff, something at which she is surprisingly adept. In turn, he teaches her how to use a sword. Gaderian learns the virtues of hard work and being able to take care of himself. They each ask other questions they "had no right to ask" (p. 119), questions that transcend the norms of acceptable discourse between men and women as well as between lords and peasants. They both learn a great deal about the life of the other. Gwyn has to admit that she "was enjoying his idea of her" (p. 120). In this long interlude, separated by bitter winter from the rest of the world, both Gaderian and Gwyn learn a great deal from and about each other and their lives. The grand questions are addressed: What is life, how should we live, and what does it mean? The answers of a lordling and an innkeeper's daughter are quite different. At the end, both are changed. They have become friends and are transformed in the conversational transaction. It is important that much of this "conversation" involves learning to do what the other does and with caring for each other's needs. There is tension and conflict in this relationship, and it will never go away entirely. These two people are very different, but their tensions are creative and they bestow a great deal of value upon each other because they have the moral courage to live with the conflicts.

There are two brilliant moments of radiantly clear perception for Gwyn in the novel. Neither features rational cognitive appraisal. Rather, the reality of her situation is simply disclosed to her. Both of them occur on occasions of violent death or near-death. The first occurs when, at winter thaw, Gaderian and Gwyn make their way back to the inn, where Gaderian's father has been waiting in dread that he has lost his son. Demonstrating the skills Gwyn had taught him about covering his tracks in the snow, a lesson that resembles playing hide-and-seek, Gaderian rushes ahead by a different route that Gwyn cannot follow. When Gwyn arrives at the inn alone, the lord, thinking his son dead and blaming her, immediately draws his sword and places the blade to her throat, fully intending to have his revenge at the cost of her life. Her family is frozen with fear and can say or do nothing. Only Burl defends her by demanding that the lord "hear her" because, he avers, "I know her" (p. 129). He does. We do not find out what would have happened to Gwyn next, because it is at this moment that Gaderian breaks into the room. It is also at this moment that Gwyn sees through everything. It is a moment of truth, and alētheia can be ugly. In the same instant, she loses belief in both her family and the wisdom of those who rule the kingdom.[9]

The unconcealment is put into words only after Gwyn has left the room. The dialogue begins with the lord speaking:

"How was I to Know—" "Aye, the Lords know nothing of the people—" "—when you didn't say—" "—and care little for what they know or do not know," Gwyn finished. He warned her then: "You shall not speak to me so." So Gwyn stopped speaking. She held his eyes and held her tongue. But the anger burned in her. . . . At last the Lord broke their silence. "I would know how the Innkeeper got such a daughter, and such a servant" he said. "The irony of it is that now you will never trust me and now you can trust me for anything." (pp. 129–130)

There are many ironies and reversals in this exchange. The lord only knows what he hears stated. Gwyn knows that the lords have power over the people but lack knowledge of those they govern. She holds her tongue as she holds his eye. Her courage is tempered, as it should be, by prudence. There are no rules that govern such morally ambiguous situations as these, only wisdom. Power is real and dangerous for the perceptive and courageous as well as for the inattentive and timid.

The dialogue continues with Burl after the lord has left:

> "You cannot be angry at them, Gwyn," Burl's voice said behind her. "They thought of what they would have done in the same situation. Later, when they had thought more they—" "Later would have been too late, wouldn't it?" Gwyn asked, surprising herself by her calm. "The Lords don't stand under the law." "They are the law." "It's their own law." "Aye. They will not want you to have seen," he advised her. Gwyn knew which *they* he meant. She knew also how they must be feeling now, to know they had betrayed her so: sick at heart. She was the one betrayed and she felt a death in her heart. How would they feel, being the betrayers. "Well then," she said, "I will not have seen." What had been done could not be undone. What she had understood could not be forgotten. "It will be a small lie." (pp. 130–131)

The loss of belief in the depth of her family's love or in the wisdom of the law of the lords is paradoxically liberating for Gwyn. It will take her beyond good and evil. Her comfortable, habitual ways of responding to those she loves, to authority, to herself, to her personal identity—what she thought she knew—have all been destroyed. If love can be lost, then anything can die. That it is ambiguous at first who "they" (lords or family) are is itself revealing.

The last sentence of the first half of the novel reads: "The lie would be pretending that everything had not changed" (p. 131). Gwyn no longer believes in the necessity, much less the goodness, of the actual world she occupies. As yet, though, she lacks any vision of alternative possibilities. The irony of the last line for the remainder of the book is that the actual situation has been unmasked; it is an unmasking that will open up the possibilities that lie beyond the good and evil of the law and love Gwyn has "known." The last sentence in the opening paragraph of the next section reads: "She wore her face like a mask" (p. 135). Similar passages are found throughout the second half of the novel, where masks of all kinds play prominent roles. Such dramatic recognition and reversal are quite common to quality literature. It is a part of self-discovery and creation.

Loss is part of growth in a living world, and if love be for our growth, it is also for our pruning. The loss of love and loyalty is part of pruning. Although it may lead to growth, loss interrupts the wholeness and health of our organic and social functioning. Loss allows us to become consciously aware of what we unconsciously have, are, and need, and sometimes it frees us from emotional vines that block sunlight and strangle growth. Loss is real, and with its vulnerability comes incontestable risk. As with Gwyn, the reader experiences extreme vulnerability at the moment of nascent understanding. Those who want to live and grow will acknowledge the vulnerability and the need to live with it for a time. Gwyn's loss leaves her with a vague, unconscious feeling of actual or impending disequilibrium. She is in doubt about how to continue. It is here that her self-reflective inquiry may begin. Gwyn must intelligently and critically re-create herself.

Voigt divides her novel into halves. The first half is titled "The Innkeeper's Daughter," a characterization Gwyn herself acknowledges in the beginning of the novel. Ironically, at the end of the first half of the novel, Gwyn is no longer the innkeeper's daughter She is in the possession of no one, including herself. It is here, with the loss of integration, that her inquiry begins into self and into the social customs that create the roles she has played thus far. The desire for restoration will eventually convert her emotions into interests in objects as conditions of the restoration of harmony. The most notable object will turn out to be the mask of Jackaroo that she found while she and the lordling were stranded in old Megg's cottage. With this mask Gwyn forms ends-in-view and begins the quest to restore harmony and complete a cycle in the rhythm of her larger growth. By dramatically identifying with the values of the mask and the deeds, feelings, and thoughts associated with it, Gwyn eventually re-creates her self. We can see that Gwyn is morally perceptive and caring about the needs and desires of others and is becoming more perceptive and caring about her own interests.

We learn early in the second section, simply titled "Jackaroo," that Gwyn has decided not to marry, even though her father is prepared to bestow his inheritance on her. When she made the announcement "she understood herself. . . . She would not throw her days away caring for the comfort of some man who asked for a bag of twelve gold pieces, never mind the girl who came with it" (p. 141). The reference to gold is to the gift bestowed on Gwyn by the lord for saving his son. The gift, in conjunction with being the innkeeper's daughter, means that Gwyn is a highly attractive catch and that she can have her choice of available men. She might well imagine it a source of social security and independence, but significantly she does not. Gwyn's loss is complete. She is in a state of disharmony with herself. She no longer knows herself; indeed, she has lost her self-identity. What she does know is that the old harmony cannot be restored. She does not want to marry and she knows it, but she is in doubt about what to do with her life; her emotions are, as we saw in the last chapter, a conscious sign of a break:

> It was not that she wanted to change her mind. Far from it, although she understood her own reasons for that no better than she understood the reasons for the many other changes she felt taking place within herself. A few years earlier, when her body had so suddenly changed, she had felt awkward and uneasy, unsure; she recognized that same feeling now, but it was not her body that caused it, it was her self. Everybody seemed a stranger to her now, even the Innkeeper's daughter, Gwyn, herself. (p. 160)

The heart has its reasons that without reflection reason will never know. Since we reason for what we desire, this kind of ignorance is the most dangerous. It not only deceives many who are proud of their "rationality," it may even make monsters of them. Doubt for Dewey is a living, embodied, and impassioned condition. Gwyn does not even know herself, but she intuits her desires, and that is a beautiful and liberating beginning. In a Deweyan sense, we can say Gwyn's unconscious, habitual ways of functioning have been disrupted, but, as yet, she has no idea of what to do. Gwyn's analogy to profound bodily changes during an earlier life transition should help us understand Dewey's theory of inquiry better. Understanding such profound unconscious transformations requires sustained reflective inquiry. Remember, it is an idea that converts vague intuitions and feelings into focused emotions and interests that select for the sake of the end-in-view.

Gwyn's feelings of tension are yet to evolve and become more specific and namable. Her intuitions concerning the quality of her situation are acute, and at least she knows that what is conventionally lauded and rewarded is no longer possible for her, even if she has no vision of what the alternatives are. She does have an active imagination, though. Gwyn has yet to translate her situation into a statable problem to be solved or values to be actualized; she has not yet reached the point in her inquiry where she can clearly and imaginatively envision alternative possibilities, much less rationally appraise them. Still, we can see the intelligent workings of emergent erotic, "desireful," thought. Before she knows how to act, she will have to refine her intuitions further by attending to things in her world that seem horribly obvious, things that almost no one else notices. She has learned a lot, but her vulnerabilities have placed her at great risk. In order to figure things out, Gwyn is prepared to take the risk.

For Dewey, embodied habits do all the perceiving, recognizing, imagining, recalling, judging, conceiving, and reasoning that get done, although habits do not, of themselves, know. Sometimes to know who we are, we must act according to our intuitions and without reason. Beliefs are habits, and habits are dispositions to act. Dispositions to action must involve the passions. If we do something, then we have something to reflect on. We may also reflect on feelings or ideas. Often awareness of feeling comes first:

> No reason, Gwyn thought later, striding through the woods. How could she know the reasons for anything when she didn't even understand the reasons for which she was where she was, dressed as she was [as Jackaroo], and for what purpose. (p. 162)

Paradoxically, to become herself, to realize her potential given her context, Gwyn must don a mask and become an outlaw. Given the political institutions and rules of policy in her world, Gwyn can only find the ideal factors of morality, as Dewey indicated, beyond good and evil. There is prophetic wisdom and sympathetic perception in what Gwyn is about to do. She gives one of her gold pieces to a poor fiddler who had come to her father but who was unable to strike a deal to save his humble holdings. In the act of giving, acting behind a mask and as an outlaw, Gwyn begins to recognize herself. From precognitive origins, Gwyn's outlaw emotions lead to the acts of an outlaw and eventually to acts that lie beyond good and evil as conventionally defined by the oppressive laws of her time and social place.

Dewey concludes *Art as Experience* by once again affirming the primacy of the aesthetic encounter with these words from the poet Robert Browning:

> But Art, wherein man speaks in no wise to man,
> Only to mankind—Art may tell a truth
> Obliquely, do the deed shall breed the thought. (cited in Dewey, 1934/1987, p. 352)

The artifices of costume and theatrical masking are superficial clues to the disclosing and transformative power of the poetically transformative art Gwyn now pursues. Acquiring the skills of an outlaw and performing outlaw deeds eventually allow Gwyn to feel liberating emotions and perceive moral possibilities beyond the actual oppressive conditions dictated by the laws of right and wrong that govern her world. Gwyn is also beginning, for the first time, to tell the truth of the ugliness of her world to herself and to humankind in acting out the role of the outlaw hero Jackaroo. Because she has acted in the world, Gwyn can begin to see herself in the reflection of others. Doing the deeds of an outlaw begins to breed creative thoughts and feelings in Gwyn.

The excitement of the action is liberating and intoxicating to her, and so later, ''Gwyn allowed the laughter that had been building up to go free. She laughed aloud. The laughter flowed out into the trees and rose up into the blue sky, like a song'' (p. 164). These feelings and emotions, as well as the sense of release from oppressive social scripts, repeat themselves throughout the latter stages of this novel, although often with an ironic twist. I want to suggest that such emotions are especially important for prophetic and creative teaching and inquiry beyond the limits of conventional good and evil. New actions or new thoughts may lead to nascent feelings. The birth of new desires may breed the bestowal of new values and ideas. Unlike other creatures, people not only have feelings, they can also know them, and in knowing them, in making conscious what they have and are, they can better come to know their selves, their motives, and the social customs that created them. Through feeling, action, and reflection, individuals may come to know, create, and own their selves. Moreover, when they create the activity that defines the feelings, they may create novel meanings. In this way they create, or rather re-create, their selves and grow. Experiencing alternative emotional possibilities is as much a part of the quest for freedom as experiencing ideas or trying out new scripts for social action. Simultaneously reconstructing our thoughts, feelings, and actions allows us to cultivate a new identity and grow. Dangerous freedom is what Gwyn experiences when she dons the costume and dramatically identifies herself with the outlaw role of Jackaroo.

Feminist writer Alison M. Jagger holds a theory of emotion that closely resembles Dewey's. Jagger (1989), too, insists:

> Every emotion presupposes an evaluation of some aspect of the environment while, conversely, every evaluation or appraisal of the situation implies that those who share that evaluation will share, *ceteris paribus*, a predictable emotional response to the situation. . . . Human emotions are not simple instinctive responses to situations or events; instead they depend essentially on the ways that we perceive those situations and events, as well on the ways that we have learned or decided to respond to them. . . . Just as observation directs, shapes, and partially defines emotion, so too

> emotion directs, shapes, and even partially defines observation. . . . What is selected and how it is interpreted are influenced by emotional attitudes. (pp. 153–154)

As with Dewey, emotions, especially desire, help constitute values and are therefore always involved in any critical appraisal. Anything that we desire possesses value. Subsequently, through appraisals, we may reconstruct our scheme of values as we more accurately discriminate objects of immediate desire from the truly desirable. Jagger also recognizes that emotions depend on selective attention. We respond to the qualities of a situation and how we have discriminated objects within those qualities. That we can be taught how to feel is important for both Jagger and Dewey. For Jagger, as for Dewey, the meanings of emotions, like all meanings, are social and "like all social constructs, they are historical products, bearing the marks of the society that constructed them" (Jagger, 1989, p. 159).

So what would happen if someone like Gwyn were to challenge our contemporary prevailing social constructions? She would experience outlaw emotions and might even become an outlaw. Gwyn breaks the rules by learning the ways of the lords. She even learns to write. Doing those deeds seems to breed new thoughts. These arts are helping tell her the truth. Gwyn's erōs is educated by going beyond the bounds of conventional good and evil. Do we as teachers dare to go so far?

Jagger discusses "emotional hegemony and emotional subversion." Gwyn is an emotional subversive. Jagger (1989) asserts:

> People who experience conventionally unacceptable, or what I call "outlaw," emotions often are subordinated individuals who pay a disproportionately high price for maintaining the status quo. . . . When unconventional emotional responses are experienced by isolated individuals, those concerned may be confused, unable to name their experience; they may even doubt their own sanity. . . . Outlaw emotions may be politically because epistemologically subversive. . . . Outlaw emotions are distinguished by their incompatibility with the dominant perceptions and values. (p. 160)

Part of educating our students' erōs involves orchestrating unconventional conversations and confronting students with texts that occasion outlaw emotions. I do not mean forcing our thoughts, feelings, and values upon students. I mean providing occasions for them to experience *their* outlaw emotions, not the teacher's. Gwyn does not know the meaning of her outlaw emotions, and she seems even to doubt her own sanity until she acts on them and the world reflects back on her the mythological role of Jackaroo.

Jagger (1989) helps us understand one other thing about Dewey's theory of inquiry: "The most obvious way in which . . . outlaw emotions can help in developing alternatives to prevailing conceptions of reality is by motivating new investigations. . . . Theoretical investigation is always purposeful and observation is always selective" (p. 161). Dewey's theory of inquiry, with its aesthetic and creative background of intuitions, emotions, selective attention, and imagination, provides an ideal model for what it means to carry out the kinds of investigations that create new alternatives. Jagger continues:

> As well as motivating critical research, outlaw emotions may also enable us to perceive the world differently from its portrayal in conventional descriptions. They may provide the first indications that something is wrong with the way alleged facts have been constructed, with accepted understandings of how things are. . . . We may bring to consciousness our "gut-level" awareness that we are in a situation of coercion, cruelty, injustice, or danger. . . . We may make subversive observations that challenge dominant conceptions of the status quo. (p. 161)

Gwyn surely makes subversive observations as a result of her outlaw emotions, and she acts on them in ways whose consequences take her beyond conventional good and evil. In many cases it is her actions that give rise to the emotions and thoughts. For Dewey, what is described here is simply part of the critical–creative inquiry.

The fair is the second moment of radiantly clear perception for Gwyn. Again, the truth of the situation is immediately unconcealed, this time on the occasion of a violent death. In the midst of the festivities, Gwyn's gaze moves up the city wall:

> She caught her breath. There, at the top of the wall, a body hung from a scaffold, its head down, turning in the wind. Its hands were bound behind it, and it looked, at the distance, like a broken doll or a scarecrow. . . . It made Gwyn uneasy. Why would the Earl leave him up there, on this day? It was as if the hanged man were on display there, to warn, to cause fear. Who had he been? What had he done? (pp. 167–168)

A scare crow, or a scare *Homo sapiens*? The perception of the man on the scaffold is one that Gwyn returns to repeatedly during her day at the fair. It is not just that she cannot stop seeing him that disturbs her most, though; it is the thought that no one else sees him at all. Gwyn reflects:

Nobody else saw him, nobody else looked to him. Only Gwyn. And who would want such a girl for his wife, if he knew what she saw. If, Gwyn thought, there were one of these young men who also saw the hanged man, then that one she might take. But if they saw, they did not speak of it, as if by not speaking they could make it disappear; and such men Gwyn would not marry. (p. 181)

The irony, of which there are many in this book, is that there is a man she knows well who has seen, who has even told her why the man was hanged because he knew she would want to know. For all of her amazing moral perceptiveness, Gwyn cannot see the love that is closest to her and that has given her ample evidence that he understands and cares for her. Gwyn still has much to learn about her own needs, desires, interests, and possibilities.

Her brother Tad, in a successful effort to hurt Gwyn, blurts out, ''You're not a proper girl at all. You might as well be wearing trousers and a beard'' (p. 174). Gwyn is different. She is physically strong, strong enough to play Jackaroo and get away with it, but not coquettish enough to pander to men and procure a husband. In a day of reflective self-understanding, ''Gwyn realized that much as she might long to fit in, she was also glad she did not. Tad had said it to hurt her, but it was the truth just the same. . . . She fit into this world as the hanged man did, she thought. She could not see his form where she stood, but he dangled at the edge of the fair, and she did not forget that. Let others forget'' (pp. 175–176). Gwyn cannot help seeing, and she cannot help remembering. Having awakened from the common dream, she cannot go back to sleep. We appear strange and awkward to ourselves as well as others when we can no longer remain unaware and unresponsive. It is a conflicted, complicated, and clumsy way to be.

Gwyn continues to ride as Jackaroo, the one who rights wrongs. She finds it ''odd that dressed up as Jackaroo she felt much more like herself. . . . She liked herself. And in the disguise, she was free to do what she really wanted to do, much freer than was Gwyn, the Innkeeper's daughter. . . . Gwyn had never been so pleased with her life'' (p. 196). Gwyn is becoming her destiny, but the sense of exhilaration and freedom begins to fade as she begins to perceive the ironies and paradoxes of her role in this culture. The laughter of Jackaroo takes on a harsher tone. Gwyn begins reflecting on the paradoxes of freedom.

Acting according to the script for the role of the Jackaroo draws out of Gwyn actions for which she did not even know she had the potential. What the role begins to demand of her, however, leads Gwyn to a stunning and disturbing perception. As Jackaroo, Gwyn gains a broader

sense of what is truly good for people and acts accordingly to respond
to their needs. In some ways she is like a prophet. She also comes to
perceive that many of the people have internalized their own oppression. They will not even do what is good for themselves, much less
others, unless ordered to do so. Gwyn's perception allows us to distinguish positive from negative freedom; it leads to the paradoxical understanding that when we are free and committed to pursuing the good,
we often have no choice what course of action to take.

Riding as Jackaroo she comes across robbers who have killed a
woman and her husband. Upon her arrival they flee into the woods and
disappear. Nearby she finds the couple's child hidden in the bushes.
What is Gwyn, or Jackaroo, to do? The child needs a mother and
Gwyn's older sister Blithe had lost her son and spent the last year in
irreconcilable despair. Riding up to Blithe's cottage, Gwyn simply
places the child on the table and declares, "Woman, you will raise this
child." Blithe protests, "No . . . I will have none but my own son."
Jackaroo commands with the authority of a lord, "You will take this
child and he will be your son. . . . He has need of you, woman" (p.
200). Blithe obeys the command and soon becomes firmly attached to
the child. It gives her a reason to live again. Jackaroo sees the best
possibility in a needful situation for the child, Blithe, and Jackaroo, and
acts appropriately to ameliorate the situation and actualize the good.
What Gwyn does is necessary, but it is paradoxical that Blithe will only
do what is best when ordered to in a commanding masculine voice. The
irony, of course, is that Gwyn is a woman that has learned to be a "man
of action." The paradoxes and ironies in this novel multiply and become
increasingly complicated. The source of the paradoxes, and part of the
beauty of the novel, is that Gwyn becomes a mixture of the best virtues
of both genders as constructed in her world. We must be careful not to
turn historically contingent constructions of gender into timeless Platonic essences.

Unable to confront the three robbers physically, Gwyn, who suc-
ceeds by daring, deception, and cunning—not physical power—con-
trives a successful plan for having them captured and hanged. She also
helps Am, the pig herder, and his daughter, but Am is a fool and by
boasting about his windfall from Jackaroo he is robbed of it and everything else he owns. His situation, bad before, is now desperate. His best
hope is to find someone to take in his children. On this occasion,
"Gwyn had no pity for him. It was his own loose tongue that had done
this to him, and he felt only pity for himself. The man was spineless.
The two coins had been wasted on him. . . . It was little use to give him
gold. If she could find a fine, strong-tongued woman to drive him, that
might be of use to him" (p. 225). Ironically, the voice of Gwyn's father

may be heard in this passage. Da often refers to Gwyn as "strong-tongued" (p. 215). It becomes clear later that Tad will grow up sturdier than earlier thought, so Da asks Gwyn for her advice. She agrees that Tad could eventually learn to run the inn well but observes, "You must find him someone strong and steady to marry, someone who can govern him when he needs it" (p. 251).[10] Here we start becoming trapped in the paradoxes of freedom that embroider the second half of this novel. These paradoxes are part of the fact that human beings do need each other not only to live well, but to live at all. Da and Gwyn are both right, after a fashion, in what they say. The freedom gained by Gwyn by riding as the masculine hero Jackaroo and her use of the knowledge of the powerful lords gained from Gaderian have given her masculine traits, and power in her world, that she must reconcile with the virtues of the conventional gender construction in which she was raised. The oppressed can quickly become the oppressor, and Gwyn has felt the lure.

To be free for some desirable state of affairs, value, or end-in-view requires that we exercise practical reason and discipline ourselves to the inquiry. This is Gwyn's way, but she must avoid one of the pitfalls of freedom. Negative freedom, freedom *from* constraint, obsesses us. For many negative freedom is the only kind of freedom they know. Gwyn surely feels the thrill of negative freedom when she rides as Jackaroo. To be free *for* something, positive freedom, we must bind ourselves to it. If we answer a calling—say, to teach—we are bound by the virtues of the vocation; we have no choice. We must ask ourselves for what it is that we desire freedom. Playing the socially constructed dramatic role of Jackaroo is an exercise in both kinds of freedom. Once we enter paradoxical situations, the paradoxes begin mounting up, yet there is wisdom in Voigt's irony. Gwyn's situation is quickly becoming unpleasantly complicated. So, too, is the reader's.

Am the pig herder is certainly a fool. Nevertheless, his innocent daughter is in desperate need. Gwyn ponders this almost cruel irony:

> There were too many like Am among the people, too many who gave up the fight. But what could you expect, when all of life was so hard and hopeless? How could someone fight and know he never would win? And who was the enemy? Could a man fight off a long winter or a dry summer? No more than he could fight against the Lords. Aye, the people could not manage without the Lords, they were children unable to take care of themselves. . . . Why should Jackaroo take such risks, for such people. . . . She had no choice in the matter any more. (p. 226)

Commitment in thought and feeling along with free action in pursuit of the good sometimes leave us with no choice. That is one of the paradoxes of positive freedom. For those of you, like myself, who were expecting Jackaroo to be a simple young woman's romance, things are getting surprisingly difficult. If someone assumes a caring social role such as teaching, and if they play it well, then they must do what those they care for need done, including ordering them about and even punishing them. As with Gwyn, teachers must work themselves through many paradoxes and live with many ironies. If they advance the good of a calling, then they must accept not only that children are sometimes unable to take care of themselves but that many adults, including colleagues and supervisors, are sometimes unable to do so as well. Teachers, like Jackaroo, are bound by the needs of others and will have no choice. I am not talking about the self-sacrificing fixed self; I am talking about exercising positive freedom in a resistant and imperfect world according to our unique potential. Beyond conventional, rule-governed good and evil, there are no easy passageways.

The reversals of self and identity begin to accelerate as this novel moves toward its conclusion. When Gwyn next rides as the Jackaroo, it is with a double purpose. First, Gwyn disburses two more gold coins to the fool Am. Second, she rides to free her uncle, Win.[11] We are surprised to learn that Win is a captured highwayman. He had left many years earlier, and the family thought he was dead. Highwaymen are "journeyed" before their execution as a warning to the people, and they had been expecting the highwayman at Da's inn for days. It is not until Win and the escort of solders arrive at the inn that Gywn's family learns who he is. When Gwyn arrives to rescue Win in the costume of the Jackaroo, Win starts laughing uncontrollably and with genuine joy confesses, "I thought I had laughed my last. . . . Oh, but life always holds one more joke. I thank you, whoever you are" (p. 231). He means it. Win had himself once ridden as Jackaroo in his youth. It was too heavy a burden; the power and privilege of unconstrained negative freedom eventually corrupted him. Win wonders:

> "Did you know what it meant when you put on the mask?" Gwyn shook her head, no. "Aye, you'll find it out. Maybe, if we knew, we'd never dare to put it on, and maybe that's why nobody tells that hated truth. Think you?" Gwyn had nothing to say. "Except there is need now. That much, at least, is in your favor. You ride in need. It'll make no difference in the end. Things will turn out the same. . . . Aye, because what changes putting on the mask had begun, I had myself finished. So farewell to you, Jackaroo. I pity you, with all that's left of my heart—but that's not much. . . . I'm out of the trap that held me, and it's that same trap you're snared in." (pp. 232–233)

Sometimes what one comes to know beyond good and evil is not very lovely. Gwyn, though, is answering the call of authentic need; hers is a prophet's vision. Prophecy, true or false, is frequently a fatal calling. So how do we distinguish true from false prophets? By the consequences of their acts they will be known. Both Gwyn and Win have ridden as the outlaw Jackaroo. What is the difference when one is beyond good and evil? It does matter that Gwyn rides with a self-eclipsing sympathetic need and desire to perceive and respond to the genuine needs and desires of others and not for glory, although she feels the self-assertive exhilaration that entrapped Win. Being beyond good and evil is very dangerous. There are so many temptations. Gwyn's self-eclipsing need to be needed helps her evade the egotistic temptations of the power implicit in riding as an outlaw. She is able to grow expansively in caring for the needs of others. It also matters that Gwyn's acts deprive her of the twelve gold pieces given her by the Lord. Gwyn cares and is a kind, giving person who bestows her bounty on others in need. Still, the outlaw fate of Jackaroo begins to close in and the paradoxes mount.

The outlaw script for the dramatic role of Jackaroo involves real risks and places Gwyn in an extremely vulnerable position. Embracing a social role and responding to a calling, even responding responsibly as Gwyn does, have elements of fate about them. To perform any social role correctly it is necessary to do, feel, and think what the customs of the culture require of the costume. To be good teachers, we must embrace the virtues of the vocation and strive to become, each in our own unique way, what it is to be good practitioners, able to bestow value on our charges. The demands of being good teachers can often cause value conflicts. We must make difficult character-expressing and -forming choices.

When the values of good teaching and good practice, including the ethics of caring, conflict with the rules of policy in a bureaucratic community or with the ethics of justice, then good teachers must often go beyond good and evil as "currently condemned or outlawed." Whether to break the law or people is a tragic choice that arises because the rule-governed ethics of justice and the ethics of care are sometimes incommensurable. It requires moral perception to act morally beyond good and evil as defined by the rules of the ethics of justice. Good teachers are often outlaws who violate the intent if not the letter of institutional laws, regulations, and rules of policy to actualize the values of their vocation. Many teachers have lied, or at least bent the truth, to bestow value on their students. The more oppressive the law, the more imaginative must be the prophetic responses that create alternative values. The practical inquiry that calls these values into existence must be just as creative. On such occasions, the artful teacher is being more moral than the moralities. Wisdom not only goes beyond knowledge, it goes beyond an exclusively rule-driven ethics of justice as well.

Win's words require Gwyn to reflect on what she has become through her acts:

> He had been telling the truth, she understood that. . . . Knowing herself, she knew she could not . . . hide the masquerade away forever. She would ride as she was riding now, without any joy. . . . She would ride as she was riding now, in darkness, because she was an outlaw. Jackaroo rode outside of the law, and that was why the Lords wanted to take him. The law couldn't hold Jackaroo. He would do what he wanted and that made him an outlaw. Gwyn could never have chosen to be an outlaw. She hadn't chosen that, she had only chosen to do what good she could, for the people. It was just as Mother said, she had too much imagination, too soft a heart. She had not known what she was choosing. But even if she had known, Gwyn knew that she would have chosen the same. This knowledge was not sweet, not joyful. . . . Before the first dawn showed at the rim of the sky, Gwyn was back in her own room with nobody—except her—the wiser. (pp. 233–234)

Gwyn has chosen to become her destiny. There is only so much disharmony, only so much destruction of personal identity, that anyone can take at any one time. In losing herself she has grown wise, but Gwyn's losses are accumulating with her wisdom. I have heard teachers in my classes say to me that they know they are giving their students a better life. Better than what? How do they know? To embrace these "better" values students must deny those of their family and friends. To make a "good" living they will almost certainly have to leave, in our case, these lovely Blue Ridge Mountains that people come from all over the world to see. Educating our students' desire for a better life would lead to the same paradoxes in the inner city. As teachers we are asking our students to give up their "bad" habits. That means losing their personal identity and becoming someone else, perhaps someone other than the person their parents love and with whom their companions share friendship. It is hard to move agilely in the world when we are coming out of our skin or when we stumble moving between two worlds. Sometimes we forget what we are asking of students, or maybe we do not even know. Perhaps we were just lucky and the habits of privilege were the social customs we acquired in our childhood habitat. This is treacherous ground.

Part of Gwyn's fate, part of growing wise, is to understand the larger pattern and rhythms of life. Gwyn asks Burl, "Is there any reason . . . why any one man should serve another?" (p. 248). Burl finds no reason; he only observes that it is so. Gwyn ponders this:

"It's like a child's rhyme, Burl. The land serves the people, the people serve the Lords, the Lords serve the Earls, the Earls serve the King, and the King serves the land." . . . Even Jackaroo, Gwyn thought to herself, fit into that circle. He served the people. He served them outside of the law, but within the turning of the wheel. (pp. 248–249)

Even in oppressive regimes, everyone needs everyone else. That is part of what makes the master–slave dialectic so vicious and corrupting for all who participate. Without the hope provided by the almost mythical Jackaroo to relieve their suffering, the people might find it unbearable. They might either rebel or, lacking the energy to do so, just give up in despair and refuse to work. Besides, without outlaws there would be less need for soldiers, and without soldiers it would be harder to create the fear necessary to govern as the lords see fit. Like adolescent rebellion, simply negating oppressive laws is not real freedom. The transgressor remains bound by the laws he deliberately breaks. An antithesis remains tied to the thesis that still defines the situation. Authentic freedom requires intelligent creative criticism, and intelligent criticism requires prophetic and poetic creation.

Eventually, through her own fatuous daring, an innocent person is falsely accused of being Jackaroo. Events move quickly from here as identities begin to change so rapidly that this reader finds it difficult to follow the action. For my part, I felt a bit of the nausea experienced by Jackaroo in her, or his, confused identity. Only the appearance of the "real" Jackaroo will save the innocent individual, but Gwyn is caught unaware by the swiftness with which the lord will carry out the hanging. Just in time, someone appears as Jackaroo. She recognizes that it is Burl, although in a costume she does not recognize. Burl's getaway is dangerous and difficult, so Gwyn must intervene in her own masked costume. It is at this moment, when she cannot reason her course of action carefully, that Gwyn realizes "exactly how ill-prepared she was for the role she was playing" (p. 259). It is rather like that first day in one's own class all alone. Nearly fatally injured, Burl rescues her. We learn that Burl's costume for Jackaroo once belonged to Gwyn's "Granda." In another complicated turn, Gaderian's father, who in the aftermath of the southern revolution has become the Earl of Sutherland, appears himself as Jackaroo. This Jackaroo demands that the innkeeper convey to the Earl of Sutherland (that is, to himself) Jackaroo's desire that the innkeeper take "before his Lord [the Earl] the needs and requests of the people and any of their quarrels that the Lord must settle" (p. 271). These are glad tidings of better times. If we find all of these rapid changes of Jackaroo's identity a farce, then we may have some haunting sense of what Win found so frightfully funny. The tragic and comic masks can transpose quite quickly. These rapid and jarring reversals bestow on us a better idea of what it is like to be young and still growing, when emotional identity changes so rapidly that we can barely tell who we are, much less who those around us are.

Gwyn wonders about the lord, now the Earl of Sutherland, appearing as another Jackaroo:

> She had not thought that the Lords, too, would go outside their own laws to ride as Jackaroo. . . . What had Gaderian's father given up to ride as Jackaroo? Unless it was only the Lords who could ride outside of the law safely, and that was why any of the people who did must pay—for their high dreams, for taking a Lord's high place. (pp. 270–271)

It is significant that, according to the customary scripts of this culture, any lord or earl who would do good by the people would have to go beyond the law that they themselves make. What is to be made of all of these Jackaroos? Burl realizes that the costumes must be all over the kingdom and, in any case, easy to tailor to fit anyone who has the potential to answer the call. The role of Jackaroo, the role of the outlaw who lives beyond good and evil, seems to be a character that the land and times need.

I would like to suggest that any morality that recognizes the limits of hierarchically ordered rules and laws and whose values are, at least sometimes, incommensurable with them will have need of a Jackaroo to ride beyond the laws of conventional logic as well as jurisprudence. Eventually the ethics of care will take us beyond the good and evil of rule-governed morality. Most teachers know this intuitively.

The novel ends with an irony that captures well some of the paradoxes of freedom. The lord has seen through Gwyn's mask; so, too, have Burl and even her younger brother, Tad. In the convoluted ending of the novel, Gwyn must disappear. The lord orders her to the edge of her world. The people assume that she ran off with one of her suitors. That is their script for the vanishing of healthy, headstrong young women possessing gold pieces. Gwyn hides behind this one last lie and obeys the lord's command that she live happily ever after. The lord commands Gwyn and Burl to live in and restore, at his expense, a hunting lodge at the frontiers of his lands. She starts to object, but when she looks into the lord's eyes she reflects:

> This was the man . . . who had fled the intrigues of his father's court to put himself under the protection of the King, letting his brothers slaughter one another in their greed. Now he gathered up their inheritance for his own.

He was also the man . . . who had ridden as Jackaroo, for the sake of the people. He was a man to respect and fear and trust. (p. 284)

Reluctantly Gwyn obeys, like a student obeying a respected teacher. The last order the lord gives requires that Gwyn marry Burl. This is a romance novel, after all. You have probably already guessed it. I did not until almost the very end. Yet I should have remembered that Burl stood up for Gwyn when her family would not because he knew her, and Gwyn overlooked the plain fact that Burl also saw the hanging man. Indeed, it was Burl who volunteered to her why he was hanged without being asked, because he knew she would want to know. The lord must command this extraordinarily perceptive young woman to see what is closest and most dear to her, the man who by her own remarkable rules of policy she had said to herself she would marry if he could be found. Gwyn completes one rhythmic pulse upon her life's journey only to return to someone already well-known to her, seeing him for the first time.

THE IRONIES AND PARADOXES OF EDUCATING THE ERŌS OF UNIQUE INDIVIDUALS

In disciplining her to her own greatest good, the lord is Gwyn's friend. It is crucial, of course, that Gwyn see this for herself. If friendly teachers discipline their students in any other way, then they have fallen short of realizing the best possibility in the situation. *Jackaroo* is an ironic, paradoxical novel in many ways. One paradox is that Gwyn learns that if she seeks to ameliorate suffering, she is bound to the best possibility that can be secured in any given situation. Moral freedom is right action and the greatest weight to bear. Moral action leaves us with no choice at all. Once intelligent, critical–creative inquiry has revealed the best possibility, then, expressing our positive freedom as moral agents concerned with ameliorating the situation, we must do the right thing. There is no choice. In expressing the virtues of their vocation, teachers frequently come across this paradox.

Another ironic paradox is that the role of teacher, like the costume of Jackaroo, is there in our culture for anyone who hears the calling. Each of us, however, must wear the costume in our own unique way. That is something that we need to remember when we teach our students, including our student-teachers.[12] Understanding the meaning of this ironic paradox will return us one last time to the theme of daimōns.

The same truth, the same social role, does not mean the same thing to each unique individual with her own unique potential. Plato's teacher

Socrates was famous for his irony, and many have criticized him over the millennia for not just coming right out and saying what it was he knew. Socrates, though, was a prophetic teacher whose preferred poetic form was irony. Perhaps that was because what made him a great teacher was itself ironic. The oracle at Delphi had pronounced Socrates the wisest Greek. Socrates himself did not believe it, but in time he came to see that he "knew" that he did not know, unlike all the other "wise" men who thought they knew but did not. Socrates was empty and in lack and need, so he actively sought learning. He was open-minded, while others in their false wisdom were not. Gwyn, too, was empty. For much of this novel she does not know who she is; she has no identity, but she actively seeks to know herself. In many religious and philosophical traditions, we must be in a state of emptiness before we can receive enlightenment.

Recall the Greeks who thought that at birth a daimōn that determines our unique individual potential and possible destiny seizes us. If each of us has our own unique daimōn and our own unique style, then the meaning of any teaching is unique for every one of us. At some important level we must work out the mystery of life on our own. We must always ask: What does it mean for me and for those I love? For Plato, as for any ancient Greek, the personal daimōn was an innate supernatural presence. Dewey held an emergent naturalistic theory of the mind and self that might seem to disallow any idea of a personal daimōn. Craig Cunningham (1994) has, however, convincingly argued that Dewey held an ideal similar to that of Plato and the ancient Greeks. The following passage is a significant one for understanding Dewey's (1934/1987) theory of the unique self:

> Individuality itself is originally a potentiality and is realized only in interaction with surrounding conditions. In this process of intercourse, native capacities, which contain an element of uniqueness, are transformed and become a self. Moreover, through resistances encountered, the nature of the self is discovered. The self is both formed and brought to consciousness through interaction with environment. . . . The self is created in the creation of objects, a creation that demands active adaptation to external materials, including a modification of the self so as to utilize and thereby overcome external necessities by incorporating them in an individual vision and expression. (pp. 286–287)

Let us examine this passage carefully. I begin by noting that initially "individuality itself" is a unique potential that may only be realized by carrying out transactions with the external environment. The sociolinguistic community in which we participate is the most important part of our environment with which we conduct transactions. Dewey, as learned while playing with the Play-Doh, held a transactional metaphysic in which all natural events are a mixture of the actual and the possible. Human beings on their journey through life are just such natural events. We are born with a unique natural biological inheritance encoded in our DNA, one small expression of which is our fingerprints. No one has, or ever will have, our exact biological structure. Furthermore, no one can ever have our same personal history, our own unique pattern of experience. The nascent self has a unique potential at birth, although that potential will itself continue to evolve as a person grows. As certain potentials are actualized in our transactions with our environment, others are excluded. That is why choice is so hard and heavy and often tragic. Most of us recognize that the event of our own individual lives will end. That adds to the burden of choice and makes wise deliberation even more important. Every one of us is a unique, one-time-only event. No matter how similar our socialization, each of us has unique needs, desires, interests, dreams, and involvements. Our unique potential assures the permanent possibility of freedom. Even in an oppressive medieval society, Gwyn can become free.

Every one of us is fated to tell a story never told before and never to be repeated. We can find freedom by becoming the authors of our own lives. It is significant that in the passage above Dewey insists that we create ourselves. We create ourselves in and through the making of meanings that help us react to the environmental resistances we come across and must respond to, especially the social resistances. The self strives to transform the world creatively according to its emerging vision of values, and in actualizing its vision it actualizes itself, as Gwyn does by riding as Jackaroo. We transform the world and it transforms us. That is the basic rule of Dewey's transactional realism. Other persons in our social world are the most important "objects" we create, and they are most important to the kind of selves we become. We cannot become free alone. Expansive personalities embark on an unending journey of growth. Part of the journey is a quest for self-knowledge and self-creation through transformative transactional relationship.

Freedom, I want to suggest, is freedom to grow in healthy relationships with others to the greatest, most integrated expanse we can attain without despair: We are freest when bound by the greatest good that is within our unique potential to obtain. As teachers, we are free if we can perceive the best possibility for our students' and ourselves in any given situation, and if we act intelligently to obtain it. Freedom *is* right action. In the next chapter we will contemplate the appropriateness of a teacher's appraisal, her prophetic power to perceive a student's best possibility, and her poetic action in a context that carries her beyond good and evil.

CHAPTER 6

Teaching and the Logic of Moral Perception

> To perceive *is to acknowledge unattained possibilities; it is to refer the present to consequences, apparition to issue, and thereby to behave in deference to the* connections *of events.*
> —*Dewey, 1925/1981, p. 143 [emphasis in original]*

Moral perception is the capacity to comprehend particular contexts and the uniqueness of persons. It is especially important when we need to grasp mutable, indeterminate, and vague situations in which rules and clear criteria for their application are difficult to determine. It also allows us to see not just who our students are here and now, but to see into the future and imagine their best possibilities. Moral perception allows us to see the unique needs, desires, and interests hidden in the words and deeds of our students. Thus moral perception is an indispensable part of practical rationality. Moral perception is crucial to exercising the ethics of care. Surprisingly, almost everyone overlooks its significance. Perhaps this is because it occurs at the intersection of practical rationality and caring, a region thus far ignored by devotees of both the ethics of care and the ethics of justice.

Teaching is a caring profession, and good care requires personal connection. Perception and sympathetic connection depend on emotion and imagination. Moral perception is about recognizing and responding thoughtfully to the needs, desires, beliefs, values, and behaviors of others. It allows interpretation and understanding of what is going on in our classrooms so we can respond appropriately. Using our moral perception, we must strive to vividly imagine the contents of our students' character, recognize their unique potential, and foresee their future. For better or worse, we often imagine who our students will become based on their personal habits, social class, and test scores. In the case of test scores, we even track them in ways that help realize our predictions. Perceptions become a self-fulfilling prophecy (Rosenthal &

Rubin, 1980). What we *should* always do morally is strive to perceive our students' best possibilities. Assessing our students' best possibilities is difficult, however; it requires a great deal of imagination. Imagination is the greatest instrument of the good. It is the most important component in the art of prophecy. Prophecy requires poetry to bestow value on our students by calling into existence their best possibilities.

This chapter[1] is about the logic of perception and assessment. It asks how we come to know our students and their unique capacities and potentials. Adequate assessment should be caring and creative assessment, and not just rational cognitive appraisal. It must involve moral perception of the individual student. To be complete and competent, assessment must include the role of emotions, imaginings, and sympathetic insights. Moral perception is too important to exclude from any good assessment of those for whom we care.

THE ROLE OF MORAL PERCEPTION IN PRACTICAL REASONING: OUTLAW LOGIC

Before the beginning of the 1993–94 school year, fourth-grade teacher Judith Samuelson walked down the hall of Thurber Intermediate School and into Ann McMann's fifth-grade classroom. Amid their conversations about summer vacation and the new school year, Judith told Ann about Tony Mitchell. "He does not know how to read or write," Judith said as she gave Ann the phonics and math workbooks Tony had used in fourth grade the previous year. Judith described Tony's math skills as weak and explained that he needed "lots of individual help and adult assistance."

Before telling Tony's story and exploring the place of perception in assessing his ability and achievement, I would like to alleviate the reader's impression that talking about moral perception is muddle-headed or romantic. Moral perception is a necessary part of the logic of practical reasoning. Practical reasoning is always contextual, as we have seen. It deals with the difficulties of doing the right thing in the right way and at the right time in response to problems posed by particular people, in particular places, on particular occasions. Moral perception is an indispensable part of practical reasoning because such perception is necessary for grasping the uniqueness of a practical context and the particularity of those participating in it.

Intelligent action requires more than the abstract, universal rules of pure logic or of the rule-governed ethics of justice. Applying universal rules alone cannot realize the unique purposes of practical reasoning. If it did, how would we know which universal rule to apply in a particular, unique, and one-time-only context, or with this particular student who is like no other? We would need more specific rules, but then how would we know when to apply these more specific rules? We would need still more specific rules, and so on forever. We have started an infinite and vicious regress. It is precisely this kind of regress that led the first authority on practical reasoning, Aristotle, to conclude over 2,300 years ago that "these are matters of perception. If we are to be always deliberating, we shall have to go on to infinity" (Ross, trans., 1941, p. 970). Eventually we must rely on our perceptions to recognize that something, someone, or some situation is an instance of a given rule. Either we see it or we do not. Moral perception allows us to see what we can and should do here and now. It has a place in the formal schema of practical reasoning. So much for practical reasoning's being guided exclusively by totally abstract, universal, and rational rules. Practical reasoning lies beyond the rules and laws of traditional pure theoretical logic. Dewey rejected the possibility of pure logic; for him all reasoning is means–ends reasoning. That is why conventional logicians tend to see him as something of an outlaw, that is, as operating outside the laws of logic. This chapter examines what happens if we look at Tony only with abstract laws, rules, and norms. What happens to Pam Simpson during her practical inquiry will make her, like Gwyn, an outlaw. Caring teachers must sometimes break the rules.

LOVE'S KNOWLEDGE

Martha Nussbaum (1990), relying on the thinking of Aristotle in her book *Love's Knowledge*, defends "the rationality of emotions and imagination" (especially pp. 75–82). She wants to refute the notion that emotions either have nothing to do with cognition or that they distort cognition, making it unintelligent. We have seen that the way we think about a situation alters how we feel about it. Knowing that a violent, disruptive child is abused at home affects not only how we feel about the child but also how we cognitively respond to the child's behavior. Emotions can also alter our beliefs. In spite of what tests indicate, psychological assessments assert, and sociological evaluations claim, in the case of particular children who we know have abilities unaddressed in their evaluations, we tend to withhold complete concurrence to the other claims.

Beliefs are, if we follow Dewey, passionate dispositions to act, not just statements of cognitive judgment. Nussbaum (1990) concludes,

"Belief is sufficient for emotion, emotion necessary for full belief" (p. 41). This statement is a good way of expressing Dewey's and Jagger's (1989) insights into the relationship between emotions and belief; all that is missing is the profound sense of embodiment.

Reasons can be self-deceptive rationalizations that prevent us from seeing the truth. It is easier to accept the assessment that particularly troublesome students cannot learn than to carry out the difficult and time-consuming practical actions of trying to teach them. We will meet with this kind of self-deception on an institutional scale when telling Tony's story. Moral perception involves the vicissitudes of human intentions and, as with the tragedies and comedies that portray these vicissitudes, we can never be absolutely certain of anything.

Recall that according to Clark and Peterson (1986), "On the average teachers make one interactive decision every two minutes" (p. 274). The quality of teachers' choices determines the quality of their classrooms, and good choice requires good practical deliberation. Aristotle wrote that "choice is deliberate desire, therefore both the reasoning must be true and the desire right. . . . This kind of intellect and truth is practical" (Ross, trans., 1941, p. 1023). Practical reasoning is reasoning for a purpose, and it involves emotion and imagination as well as cognition. If the reasoning is to be good, then what we reason for—the goal, the value, the end of reasoning—must itself be good. We require moral perception to see what is most desirable, what our students' best possibilities are, what should be the goal of a given lesson, or what kind of class structure is most desirable for these particular students. Such perception depends in part on having a vivid imagination that is able to see beyond the actual.

Recall Dewey's (1934/1987) observation, cited earlier:

No "reasoning," that is, as excluding imagination and sense, can reach truth. Even "the greatest philosopher" exercises an animal-like preference to guide his thinking to its conclusions. He selects and puts aside as his imaginative sentiments move. "Reason" at its height cannot attain complete grasp and a self-contained assurance. It must fall back upon imagination—upon the embodiment of ideas in emotionally charged sense. (p. 40)

Once we implement action in practice, we must suffer the overt consequences. Good teachers must be good practical reasoners or suffer undesirable consequences. That involves using not only rational rules, such as effective instructional strategies and management techniques, but also imaginative problem solving. Good teachers imagine noble ideals. They conceive the best of the various possibilities within the classroom context. These best possibilities then become objects of deliberate

desire, that is, practical reason. Moral perception involves many different uses of imagination. It is a part of practical reasoning, and it contributes to poetry, prophecy, and the education of erōs.

MORAL IMAGINATION AND
SYMPATHY IN MORAL PERCEPTION

Imagination is perhaps the most important daimōn in transformative
moral inquiry. However needful our situation, creative imagination is
our single greatest requirement. Johnson (1993) insists:

> What we need more than anything else in such cases [of moral conflict] is
> moral imagination in its various manifestations, as a means to both knowl-
> edge and criticism. We need self-knowledge about the imaginative structure
> of our moral understanding, including its values, limitations, and blind
> spots. We need a similar knowledge of other people, both those who share
> our moral tradition and those who inhabit other traditions. . . . We need an
> *imaginative rationality* that is at once insightful, critical, exploratory, and
> transformative. . . . Moral imagination would provide the means for under-
> standing (of self, others, institutions, cultures), for reflective criticism, and
> for modest transformation, which together are the basis for moral growth.
> (p. 187) [emphasis in original]

It is easy to recognize the Deweyan influences on Johnson's thinking
here, influences he acknowledges repeatedly. Johnson connects criticism with wisdom about transformational possibilities for improvement,
self-understanding, understanding others, and, eventually, expansive
moral growth.

Johnson (1993) identifies three interrelated functions that make up
moral imagination. They are "empathetic [sympathetic] imagination,"
"imaginative envisioning of possibilities for acting," and "imaginative
moral reasoning." The Deweyan influences on Johnson are easy to
identify. Dewey (1932/1985b) expresses the requirement for moral imagination this way: "The emotion of sympathy is morally invaluable. But it
functions properly when used as a principle of reflection and insight,
rather than of direct action. Intelligent sympathy widens and deepens
concern for consequences" (p. 251). Johnson, like Dewey, insists that
intelligent sympathy is a part of rationality that goes beyond mere calculation or rule following and contributes to expansive growth. Johnson
(1993) writes:

> It is not sufficient merely to manipulate a cool, detached "objective" reason
> toward the situation of others. We must, instead, go out toward people to

inhabit their worlds, not just by rational calculations, but also in imagination, feeling, and expression. Reflecting in this way involves an imaginative rationality through which we can participate empathetically. . . . I would describe this imaginative rationality as *passionate*. . . . It takes us beyond fixed character, social roles, and institutional arrangements. (p. 200) [emphasis in original]

Unless we can passionately and imaginatively grasp the "data" of moral inquiry and produce compassionate, creative response, rational moral thought is deficient. Creative imagination and caring are simply parts of moral agency, and moral agency directs us toward the best possibilities for expansive growth. Only imagination can grasp those possibilities that lie concealed within the current situation or the condition of the people in it. Johnson's (1993) pragmatism, like Dewey's, refuses to allow the idea of moral imagination to be captured by escapist romanticism: "Such a romantic view of empathy [or sympathy], as a kind of flowing-into-the-other by giving oneself up to strong fellow-feeling, is an artifact of an erroneous traditional separation of reason, imagination, and feeling" (pp. 200–201). Sympathetic understanding is a poetic achievement. It is something called into existence when we bestow value on one another.

Imaginings and emotions combine in particularly important ways in sympathetic recognition and response. Recall Dewey's (1932/1985b) observation:

The only truly *general* thought is the *generous* thought. It is sympathy which carries thought out beyond the self and which extends its scope till it approaches the universal as its limit. It is sympathy which saves consideration of consequences from degenerating into mere calculation, by rendering vivid the interests of others. (p. 270)

Sympathy and visionary imagination allow us to perceive the needs, desires, cares, concerns, and interests of our students. Such perception is absolutely necessary for everyday intelligent action and response in the classroom. Sympathy carries us beyond our selfish interests and directs our selective attention outward toward others. Such self-transcendence is typical of the caring professions. Sympathy, however, relies on seeing others as like ourselves in the sense that they, too, have needs, purposes, and interests. Seeing others sympathetically is an important part of moral perception.

There is, however, a danger in sympathy that we must acknowledge. When we imaginatively participate in another's experience, it is all too easy to interpret that experience using our own categories and habits of interpretation. Sympathy can invite us to interpret another in our own terms, without reflecting on our own habitual prejudgments in the process. Sympathy as mere sentimentality may often just be an unconsciously clever way of exercising dominion while assuaging moral guilt.[2] As Dewey (1922/1983) put it, "There is a sense in which to set up social welfare as an end of action only promotes an offensive condescension, a harsh interference, or an oleaginous display of complacent kindliness. . . . To foster conditions that widen the horizon of others and give them command of their powers, so that they can find their own happiness in their own fashion, is the way of 'social' action" (p. 203). Empathy may inspire a self-righteousness and self-assurance in do-gooders that they know all they need to know about themselves and others.

Wisdom is beyond knowledge, even sympathetic knowledge. Imaginatively envisioning possibilities is that part of wisdom that permits those that possess it to go beyond the bounds of the actual current situation. Johnson (1993) observes:

> Beyond knowledge of our own and others' cognitive and moral capacities and perspectives, beyond an abiding fellow-feeling, beyond the ability to inhabit imaginatively the world of another, something more is yet required. That . . . is an ability to imaginatively discern various possibilities for acting within a given situation . . . and to envision the potential help and harm that are likely to result from a given action. (p. 202)

Moral imagination allows us to create and dramatically explore possible alternatives beyond knowledge of the actual. Without alternatives freedom is impossible, because there can be no choice, much less intelligent free choice. Once we choose the most desirable alternative, it becomes a hypothesis for action, an end-in-view, a guide to inquiry. Then imagination will need to strive vividly to clarify the image of the end so that it may serve as a better blueprint of action. To grasp possible means to the end desired also requires imagination.

Johnson (1993) also connects moral imagination to value criticism and growth: "Our ability to criticize a moral view depends on our capacity for imagining alternative viewpoints on, and solutions to, a particular moral problem. In order to adapt and to grow, we must be able to see beyond our present vantage point and to grow beyond our present selves" (p. 203). To grow we must perceive the possibilities of growth. We must imaginatively unconceal the possibilities hidden in the actual. Critical deliberation is crucial to intelligent growth. For teachers, uncon-cealment means striving to see the best possibilities for moral, aesthetic, and intellectual growth for our children.

The third use of imagination for Johnson is imaginative moral reasoning. Imaginative moral reasoning is vicarious deliberation in the sense we saw in the last chapter, that is, ''a dramatic rehearsal (in imagination) of various competing possible lines of action. It starts from the blocking of efficient overt action, due to that conflict of prior habit and newly released impulse. . . . Deliberation is an experiment. . . . But the trial is in imagination, not in overt fact'' (pp. 132–133). Artistic practice, ''dramatic rehearsal,'' is exactly what we need to intelligently connect our personal narrative with the narratives found in language arts teaching. The experimental self can deliberate about competing possible (plot) lines of action.

The advantage of vicarious experience is that we can feel the emotional tension of deliberation, we can feel the tempting desire, we can deliberate, and we can remember what we felt and thought later. For instance, when we experience the evil consequences that befall characters whom we identify with, and when they yield to the tempting action, the consequences of the acts of vicarious experience are revocable. We can vicariously experience the educational consequences of their action without suffering the consequences overtly. That is the advantage of vicarious experience. There is an old saying that goes something like this: Smart people learn from their mistakes while wise people learn from the mistakes of others. It is a good saying. We might say that wise people learn a great deal vicariously.

As we have seen, imagination allows us to unconceal future possibilities in present actualities. When Martin Luther King, Jr., declared that he had ''a dream'' of a racially harmonious nation, he was not reporting the results of an exercise in pure reason. Reason alone will not provide prophetic moral values, nor was King reporting an empirical fact. Dreams can be perceptions of how things morally *ought* to be, visions of our best possibilities. Seeing that the United States *should* be racially harmonious, in spite of the manifest fact that it is really not, requires prophetic moral perception, and such perception requires poetic imagination. Prophetic leaders of all kinds, including visionary teachers, must vividly imagine the ideals and values that they seek to realize through the exercise of practical reasoning. Teachers, too, must be practical reasoners, poets, and prophets.

Moral perception provides insight into the needs of students that is very different from cognitive critical judgments or mere calculations alone. We will see that sad things begin to happen to students when we classify them according to the calculations of norm-referenced tests and provide resources to them according to cost-benefit equations. A moral response that relies on care, concern, and compassion based on moral perception focuses the classroom camera from a very different angle than that of educational technocrats and philosopher kings. It requires educators to perceive things from the perspective of the students' needs, interests, and involvements. It is absolutely necessary for learning-centered teaching (Rogoff, 1994) and for caring response generally. Poetry, prophecy, and practical reasoning are necessary to secure love's knowledge.

WHO IS TONY MITCHELL?
FOUR PERCEPTIONS AND APPRAISALS

We will examine four perceptions of Tony. They are those of his fourth-grade teacher, Judith; his special education evaluation; and his fifth-grade adult contacts, his teacher Ann, and Pam, a participant researcher in Judith's and Ann's classrooms. Pam worked with Tony in different settings and over an extended time. There is not much room to present Tony's story here to enable readers to see him distinctly, and like any story it expresses the passions and prejudices of the person telling it. I will construct Tony's story in such a way as to give preference to certain kinds of readings rather than others. Multiple interpretations and perspectives are characteristic of unique, one-time-only teaching situations, fraught as they are with the elusiveness of human intention. To see clearly in such complicated situations requires more than meets the eye. It involves emotional sympathy, a caring attitude, and creative imagination. These are the ingredients of moral perception.

Tony had spent much of his life traveling with a small carnival-type circus and very little of his life in school. He had enrolled in Thurber in February of the 1991–92 school year, attended two weeks, and was then withdrawn with no explanation. Those two weeks represented the entirety of Tony's formal education. When he enrolled again at Thurber at the beginning of the 1992–93 school year, eleven-year-old Tony was placed in Judith Samuelson's self-contained fourth-grade class. Meeting Tony's instructional needs created a problem for Judith and other school personnel. Peter Johnston (1992) suggests that the "failure" of a child must be situated in classroom interactions and learners' perceptions of them. We therefore begin by situating the assessment of Tony as a nonreader and nonwriter in the context of Judith's classroom. Let us look specifically at the overall structure of Judith's class, concentrating on curriculum and instruction, her interactions with students, and the institutional constraints imposed by standardized testing.

Language arts in Judith's classroom included reading, writing, grammar, and spelling. All four subjects were incorporated into activities and skill lessons that related to novels the class read. Skills were an important part of the curriculum and, along with standardized testing, influenced Judith's interactions with students. Each morning Judith began with an activity called the early bird special. Students were asked, for example, to write sentences for their spelling words. The early bird special provided a focus for students' attention at the beginning of the day, reviewed previously taught skills, or provided additional practice with new skills. As students finished the early bird special, they often brought their papers to Judith. She looked at their work, asked questions, encouraged their efforts, or praised their accomplishments. She did not document how much of the task students completed, their individual level of understanding, or any questions pertaining to the activity. The early bird special focused on fourth-grade math and language skills. "The skills he [Tony] needed," Judith concluded, "were not the skills we worked on in the fourth grade." Judith did not require or expect Tony to complete the early bird special.

Throughout the year, as Judith's class read novels, Tony was included in class discussions, expected to listen as others read aloud, and asked to complete related instructional and assessment activities. Although he was immersed in that aspect of the fourth-grade curriculum, other parts of Tony's instructional program were individualized. He was asked to memorize flashcards stacked on his desk and complete pages in a phonics workbook called *Explode the Code* (Hall & Price, 1986). "He needs the skills to make up for what he missed by not being in school," Judith mentioned to Pam on several occasions.

During fourth grade Tony finished three levels of the phonics workbook. He worked his way through beginning sounds, ending sounds, blends, and vowels. On almost every page of his *Explode the Code* workbook, Tony corrected his own handwriting. He often spoke about his progress in school in terms of his handwriting. He mentioned to Pam, "The only thing that's improving of me is my [hand]writing." Tony measured improvement in his handwriting by looking at samples of his work over time and comparing his letter formation to a standard. He defined needed corrections and evaluated his success. Handwriting was an area in which Tony had control over his own learning and could assess his own progress.

In most cases Judith assumed responsibility for Tony's learning and assessed his progress, which was measured solely in terms of answers that were either right or wrong. For example, Judith corrected Tony's answers in *Explode the Code* when he wrote *jog* instead of *hop* (see Figure 6.1). The picture could be interpreted as involving either activity. The

FIGURE 6.1. *From Tony's* Explode the Code. (*Reprinted with permission of* Teachers College Record.)

word Tony wrote matched the meaning of the picture and was spelled correctly. Tony's answers were considered incorrect because he did not use the words listed at the top of the page. Mike Rose (1989) writes of such students, ''Even when they're misunderstanding the test and selecting wrong answers, their reasoning is not distorted and pathological'' (p. 218). Tony's answer was logical, not pathological. It is just that he was not following the logic of the test publisher. Instead, he was following, as I call it in the pages to follow, the logic of his artistic interests in creating his own interpretation. We could see him as incapable of following instructions; we could just as easily see him as too creative to be constrained by predetermined choices. It requires wisdom to know the difference. Systematic errors such as the misunderstanding illustrated in Figure 6.1 are often intelligent, even creative. It is part of the teacher's own practical reasoning to perceive the logic of the error, when there is one, so that she may develop the best strategies for correcting it. Recall that for Dewey it is sympathy that ''carries thought out beyond the self.'' A sympathetic response to Tony's mistake would suspend judgment and strive to perceive the situation with regard to the student's personal history, needs, interests, and abilities. Generous thought would try to imagine the logic of Tony's mistake. If successful, generous thought would provide the most efficacious *intellectual* standpoint for responding to Tony's error and helping him learn.

Judith's assessment of Tony's efforts implied that selecting the right answer was more important than creating a viable meaning for the sentence. Completing pages in *Explode the Code* did not necessarily help Tony connect words and texts as a meaningful form of communication, given his needs, desires, and interests. Pictures in the workbook were ambiguous and the text was unconnected to his everyday literate needs.

Focused on decontextualized skills that were introduced and practiced in isolation, exercises in *Explode the Code* could not adequately challenge or assess Tony's literate abilities. *Explode the Code* defined Tony's reading and writing experiences in terms of simple sentences that had little connection to the everyday world of reading and writing (Taylor, 1990, 1993; Taylor & Dorsey-Gaines, 1988).

If moral perception allows us to grasp particular contexts, contexts facilitate moral perception. The speech and actions of our students in active relation with their environment, especially classroom environments that we as teachers partially create and control, reveal a great deal to the perceptive eye and ear about what our students need and value. Tony's assignments focused on the mechanics of literacy learning, rather than the use of print to communicate in meaningful ways, and assumed that skills taught in isolation were transferable to real-life situations (Lave, 1988). Relationships are mechanical when means are separated from ends. In a living, vibrant reading experience the means that facilitate reading help constitute the end of learning to read better. For example, words, letters, and punctuation marks are the author's means for constructing a text, the author's end. Their meaning depends on the context within which they are placed respective to each other (e.g., *tip* vs. *pit*). Students who desire to understand a text as a whole need to understand the means by which it was constructed, at least in their own terms if not the author's. A living interest in something internally motivates students. Perceptive teachers look for each student's unique interests and desires to internally motivate their students or, more accurately, to educate their erōs. When means are separated from ends, teachers must use external carrot-and-stick motivation. Ironically, such a mechanical curriculum sparks no intrinsic interest in the student that the teacher can observe.

By the end of the fourth grade, Tony's sentences became mechanical in construction. What Rose (1989) has to say about a student he was tutoring, Suzette, could be said of Tony: "Many people respond to sentence fragments of the kind Suzette was making as though the writer had some little hole in that part of her brain where sentences are generated. They repeat a rule: 'A sentence has to have a subject and a verb and express a complete thought.'" (p. 172). We require moral perception precisely when the application of rules breaks down. Tony knew the rule but could not always see how to apply it, nor could Judith see how to help him see how to use the rule. Sentences written by Tony later in the year lacked transactional dialogue, followed a simple subject–verb pattern, and did not demonstrate the variations in content exhibited initially. Teachers and school systems that rely more on abstract rules and norms than moral perception of unique individuals discourage creativity and unique self-expression. Instead, they prefer conformity to predetermined academic "norms." Students are seen as distributed somewhere on the "normal" bell-shaped curve and responded to accordingly. Having failed to render students' interests vividly, we should not be surprised that all consideration of consequences degenerates into "mere calculation."

Judith used novels as the basis for her reading and writing instruction. Tony was included in one reading group. Given a copy of the book, he was asked to listen as other students read the text and encouraged to participate in discussions. Whole-class discussions and small-group tasks allowed Judith to assess students' comprehension. Focusing attention on particular passages, Judith assessed students' understanding of figures of speech or vocabulary and their ability to use reading strategies. Through oral and written questioning, she ascertained students' ability to recall specific details or retell the story sequentially. Tony would sometimes not even attempt to answer. At other times, he would start an answer but not complete it. Judith might then help him, but not by continuing the development of his own answer. Instead, she would begin by restating the question, allow Tony to dictate an answer, and then write it down for him. By rephrasing Tony's answers, Judith modeled an appropriate structure for answering questions and perhaps provided scaffolding for Tony as he formulated his ideas (see Palincsar & Brown, 1984; Wood, Bruner & Ross, 1976). Ignoring or drastically restructuring Tony's initial thought, however, implied that there was but one correct answer, the one that Judith was looking for; therefore Tony's own response was assumed to be inadequate.

Judith's interests, beliefs, and values entirely determined the one right interpretation of the text. Rather than encouraging Tony to explain the connections he had made, Judith's rephrasing thwarted his own efforts to understand the story and formulate an answer to the question. Judith could not see beyond Tony's failure. Rose (1989) wonders what happens when we "view literacy problems from a medical-remedial perspective" (p. 210). The medical-remedial model requires teachers to perceive students pathologically. If they fail to get the right answer, teachers must try to diagnose their deficiencies, defects, and deficits using preconstructed categories. Teachers are then expected to strive to remedy them by prescribing proper pedagogical treatments. With Rose (1989), we must also worry about "how much we don't see when we look only for deficiency, when we tally up all that people can't do" (p. 222). Viewing students pathologically does not allow us to perceive their best possibilities. For Rose, moral perception means looking for hidden intelligence, for what he calls the "logic of error."

The pathological medical-remedial model blinds us so that we tend to look for what our students *cannot* do rather than for what they can (Taylor, 1990, 1991, 1993). Failing to properly perceive our students' real abilities, we respond poorly. Judith's perceptions of Tony framed her expectations for him (cf. Rosenthal & Rubin, 1980). As Rose (1989) puts it, "We won't understand the logic of error unless we also understand the institutional expectations that students face" (p. 171). The logic of error resembles the logic of interests. The structure of Judith's class was a barrier for Tony. In fairness to Judith, though, she, too, was constrained by institutional expectations, her experiences as a student, and her training as a teacher. Perhaps the most severe of these were the constraints imposed by standardized testing. It is possible that the constraint of standardized testing kept Judith from seeing her own best possibilities as a teacher. Self-perception is an important part of perceiving others properly. Judith tended to see good teaching as defined by the laws and rules of policy of the bureaucratic institution.

Fourth-grade students in Judith's class were required to take two state-mandated tests, the Literacy Passport Test (LPT) in February, the Iowa Test of Basic Skills (IOWA) in March, and the district-mandated Survey of Basic Skills achievement test (SBS) in early May. Judith felt responsible for "teaching students what they needed to know for the tests." The perception of the needs of all fourth-grade students at Thurber Intermediate School were filtered through mandated standardized testing. Many educators, including Pam, are dubious about the ability of standardized testing to perceive the unique abilities of particular individuals, much less their best possibilities, and such testing was extraordinarily damaging for Tony's individual needs.

As dates for administrating the IOWA and SBS achievement tests approached, Judith assigned worksheets during language arts and spelling rotations. To familiarize students with the content and multiple-choice format of the standardized tests, Judith copied pages from *Test Best*, a test preparation program published by Steck-Vaugn (cf. Smith, Edelsky, Draper, Rottenberg, & Cherland, 1991). Tony was given copies of the worksheets but did not complete the assignment. He listened but did not participate as the class discussed the questions and answers. He did not take the three standardized assessments administered during the spring of the 1992–93 school year with the rest of Judith's class. Judith consulted with principal, Aaron Jones, and together they determined that the testing situation would be too difficult and too frustrating for Tony. Just before the LPT in February, Pam asked what happened to students like Tony during testing situations. "I think students like Tony just disappear from our rolls on test days," Judith suggested. Another teacher in the conversation suggested "they would bring our scores down" (cf. Darling-Hammond, 1991).

Judith was in a difficult situation concerning Tony, and she had to operate within severe institutional constraints. Later, though, in the fifth grade Ann, operating with the similar constraints, came much closer to seeing Tony's best possibilities and responding to them creatively within her classroom context. Judith tended to see Tony for what he could not do, while Ann saw him for what he could. The difference in the two perceptions made a profound difference in how they responded to Tony in their classrooms.

Judith believed special education placement was one way Tony would be able to get additional assistance in school. By referring Tony, Judith initiated the special education evaluation cycle (Anderson, Chitwood, & Hayden, 1990). Ironically, although Tony did not take the LPT, IOWA, or SBS with his class, the SBS as well as eight other assessments were administered to him individually as part of his special education evaluation during the last three weeks of the 1992–93 school year. Typically, at Thurber and other schools in the district, the LPT, IOWA, and SBS were given in different months and the subtests were spread out over several days. Results of the tests were recorded on the Student Multi-Reference Report and included in Tony's confidential Category II file. These tests provided the narrative that permanently defined Tony's institutional identity and the way the institution was to perceive and respond to Tony in the future.

Rose (1989) observes, "Through all my experiences with people struggling to learn, the one thing that strikes me most is the ease with which we misperceive failed performance" (p. 205). Moral perception involves participating in the social practices of the classroom or other learning contexts *with* the student. It involves intimate connection. The misperception of failed performance is due, in part, to a misplaced confidence in pseudo-scientific techniques that emphasize detachment from the students evaluated and from the context in which the student is working. Further, the observation instruments developed according to this scientistic perspective to detect and assess learning distort our perception. Typically, such instruments ignore context, and their dependence on norm-referencing does not allow us to see the unique abilities and potentials of our students. Finally, these instruments are constructed to conform to the medical-remedial model.

Formal evaluation of Tony for special education placement began in mid-May 1993 with an observation completed by the school's guidance counselor. The guidance counselor used the Classroom Observation Checklist required by the district's special education office to identify a list of behaviors as occurring seldom, frequently, or not observed. Relying on her 20-minute observation in Judith's class, the counselor summarized Tony's behavior. She concluded:

> During instruction Tony never copied down the problems while Ms. Samuelson worked them out on the board. He did not have a book and was just sitting when students were working independently. Ms. Samuelson asked, "Where is your spelling book?" Tony got it out and within seconds he was interacting with peers and playing with a pencil sharpener.

At the end of the 1992–93 school year the Classroom Observational Checklist and the guidance counselor's summary became part of Tony's confidential Category II file.

Neither the "observational" checklist nor the summary reflected Tony's behavior in the context of Judith's classroom or his instructional and curricular program. The guidance counselor described Tony as inattentive to the math lesson Judith was teaching. The observer either did not know or did not document Tony's placement in second-grade math rather than in the fourth-grade book used by the rest of his class. Tony's math assignments corresponded not to what Judith taught the rest of the class but to work he was to do independently in his second-grade workbook. Tony was not participating in the class because his unique needs were not being addressed at the moment the guidance counselor happened to be looking at him. Just as importantly, the guidance counselor was not looking at Tony; she was just aiming an optical instrument at him. Like any instrument, the Classroom Observation Checklist filters out a great deal in order to focus on its target. It saw what it was designed to see, and ignored the rest. In particular, it ignored Tony's unique needs and desires and the context of his actions.

The Classroom Observation Checklist focused on what Tony could not do in a particular situation. Separating Tony's behavior from his personal history and instructional experiences and interactions in his fourth-grade classroom, the checklist and narrative summary implied that the behaviors seen during a brief observation were representative of Tony's actions over time. Such exclusively cognitive categories cannot detect passion, imagination, or creative activities. The limited view of Tony's strengths and abilities presented in the Classroom Observational Checklist and narrative summary reinforced other pathological assessments of Tony.

FIGURE 6.2. *Confidential report.*

Results and Impressions. Cognitively, Tony appears to be functioning
within the borderline range of overall ability according to WISC-III. His
Full Scale IQ of 75 reflects the fifth percentile by normative comparison.
According to this assessment, Tony demonstrates a mental age of
approximately 9 years.

Another measure of intelligence was administered. The TONI is a
language-free measure of mental ability. The TONI relies on nonverbal
problem-solving skill. Tony's responses earned him a quotient of 74, which
reflects the fourth percentile and the borderline range. This estimate is quite
consistent with the scores of the WISC-III.

Tony's responses to the PPVT-R suggest repetitive language skills in the
borderline range. His standard score of 78 reflects the seventh percentile by
normative comparison. this indicates an understanding of the spoken word
at an 8-year, 11-month level.

Summary and Recommendations. At this, the conclusion of Tony's one year
of formal education, he is achieving at a first to second grade level.

In late May 1993, seven tests were administered by the school psychologist, Paula Fletcher, to evaluate Tony's ability level and identify
any psychological factors that might interfere with his learning. This
battery of tests included the Wechsler Intelligence Scale for Children–
Third Edition (WISC-III), Test of Nonverbal Intelligence (TONI), and the
Peabody Picture Vocabulary Test–Revised (PPVT). Paula's report summarizing the test results and her recommendations were added to Tony's
Confidential Category II file (See Figure 6.2).

The psychologist's confidential report did not examine the effects of
the testing context during the time the tests were administered. The
report did not acknowledge that Tony had not met the psychologist
before the first day of the testing, nor did the psychologist note that
Tony had no experience with standardized tests of any kind before the
special education evaluation process began. None of the assessments
examined how Tony approached a problem or how he made sense of
new information and discrepant events. What Tony could do with the
support of human or technological resources was not assessed.

Besides concerns about the testing environment, the period of the evaluation procedure precipitated several questions. While other students focused on end-of-the-year activities, Tony was removed from his classroom context, placed in an unfamiliar setting, given tests by individuals he had not met before, and expected to perform (cf. Taylor 1990, 1991, 1993). Neither the possible adverse effects of the testing environment nor the impact of extensive testing in a relatively short time were addressed in the psychologist's report. The report did not address the lack of authentic activities or measures of skills in real-world tasks used in assessing Tony's ability. The assessments ignored the contextual and aesthetic background of Tony's intelligent efforts. The assessment of Tony's ability as "borderline" ignored his achievement in personally meaningful settings and evaluated instead how well he performed on the kind of tests given (Kornhaber, Krechevsky, & Gardner, 1990; Nespor & Barber, n.d.). Tony's capabilities were assessed according to his ability to reproduce *the* right answers to decontextualized questions. Instead of providing examples of what Tony could do, the psychologist suggested that Tony and school personnel should lower their expectations to be more consistent with his limited, or "borderline," abilities.

Scribner (1984) notes that students' literacy skills and problem-solving abilities are far more complex than present educational systems indicate. Too often the capabilities of children are underestimated and their skills devalued (Taylor, 1990, 1991, 1993). Educators are systematically blinded from seeing students' strengths and potential by the superficial and decontextualized instruments and means used to measure intelligence and ability (Mehan, 1992). Tony was a victim of assault by a battery of tests that, once they became a part of his permanent record, turned the unique self that was Tony into ciphers (75, 74, and 78). This is the kind of Platonism that can conceal cruelty. Recall that for Dewey (1932/1985b), "It is sympathy which saves consideration of consequences from degenerating into mere calculation, by rendering vivid the interests of others" (p. 270). A more sympathetic assessment of Tony's interests and abilities would yield a clearer perception of his best possibilities.

Pam had been an observer at Thurber Intermediate School for several weeks as part of a collaborative research project before she met Tony Mitchell. One Wednesday she offered to teach his fourth-grade class while Judith Samuelson conferenced with individual students. Pam was to have the class read and discuss a chapter in the novel *Guns for General Washington* (Reit, 1990). The book describes Colonel Henry Knox's efforts to move 183 cannons plus ammunition 300 miles over mountainous terrain from Fort Ticonderoga to Boston. When asked to explain Knox's strategy, several students described elements of the plan, but most could not demonstrate how it worked. When Tony raised his hand, Pam called on him. Tony explained how ropes attached to large trees had been used as pulleys to move the cannon up and down the mountains. "Coming down . . . they put these tree trunks in front of the cannon. Sort of like wedges. They kept it [the cannon] from going too fast." Tony had listened to other students read the chapter, processed the author's explanation, and accurately described the complicated procedure for his peers.

"The cannon story," wrote Pam, "was my 'aha!' experience." It was a moment of moral perception. Judith's description of Tony had painted a picture of a nonreader and a nonwriter. Yet what Pam had seen and heard suggested a wide range of literate ability. The discrepancies puzzled Pam and raised questions that she could not ignore. Our neo-Aristotelian and Deweyan perspective on moral perception supports such intuitive recognition and questioning inquiry. Situations like the cannon story have an inherently vague, indeterminate, and mutable "quality." Initially, as we saw, we feel a situation and in our inarticulateness we may utter "aha!" Dewey (1930/1984d) wrote: "When it is said that I have a feeling, or impression, or 'hunch,' that things are thus and so, what is actually designated is primarily the presence of a dominating quality in a situation as a whole" (p. 248). The perception of such vague, indeterminate, and mutable quality can only be intuited.

Pam's intuition occurred in the background of inquiry. We should not ignore an intuition just because we cannot articulate it as a stateable problem. Intuition precedes conception and goes deeper. What is required is what Pam did: She continued the inquiry. Because the precognitive, affective, and imaginative background of inquiry continues to influence the foreground of cognitive inquiry, the latter can only be as good as the background intuited. If Pam, or anyone else, makes a mistake in that intuition, the cognitive component of inquiry that follows, including the rigorous quantification that we derive from tests, may also include mistakes. We must compare Judith's intuition that led to the kind of inquiry into Tony's possibilities identified by standardized testing with the intuitions of Pam and Ann that led to an alternative assessment.

The cannon incident marked the beginning of Pam's ongoing relationship with Tony. Beginning in December 1992 and continuing through December 1993, her interactions with Tony bridged his fourth- and fifth-grade years. When Pam asked Judith at lunch in November 1992 if she could work with Tony, Judith replied, "That would be great! He could use the individual attention." Thereafter Tony and Pam met for an hour once or twice a week and sometimes even more frequently. As Pam worked with Tony, she documented how he used reading and writing to construct autobiographical stories to gain information to meet the practical and re-creational need of his everyday life. We will see how those stories provided a better perception of Tony's literate possibilities.

At a conference in February 1993, Pam told a colleague who had worked extensively with writers of all ages about Tony and asked if she had any ideas. "Why don't you let him make a book?" the colleague suggested. "It would give you a chance to talk about the way books are set up and let him write about things that are important to him. He could dictate or write himself or even some of both." The book provided opportunities for Tony to use reading and writing to express himself in the autobiographical stories he created. It also allowed Pam to learn more about Tony's unique experiences and better perceive and respond to his needs.

When Pam returned from the conference, she bought Tony a blank book and took it with her to Thurber. "I brought something for you today," Pam said as she and Tony cleared a space in the teachers' workroom to sit.

"Oh, yeah, what?" Tony asked.

"It's a book, but it's empty," Pam said. "I thought over the next few weeks, between now and the end of the year, this could be a place for you to dictate or write things you wanted to share."

Pam also brought a copy of Scott O'Dell's *Island of the Blue Dolphins* so Tony would have a model to look at as he began his book. Opening O'Dell's book and flipping through the first several pages, Tony said, "[There's] sort of like a nothing page and then a title."

"You're right. One thing you could do is leave those pages blank so you could think about what you want to name it. You may not want to think of a name today," Pam replied.

"I was thinking. I was thinking about *Tony's Dreams,*" Tony responded.

Pam said, "Ooo, that's a neat idea. You could put *anything* in a book like that, couldn't you?"

Tony wrote the title *Tony's Dreams* across the middle of the page of the book, identified himself as the author and illustrator, and that added information to the title page. Thurber was the name he wanted for a publishing company, and 1993 would be the copyright date.

Tony did not hesitate when Pam asked what he would like to write about first. "I can write about when I was traveling [with the carnival], about people throwing their self in cannonballs—human cannonballs," he said. The story of the human cannonball Tony dictated that day was the first of many stories recorded in *Tony's Dreams*. Tony added a draw-ing to the story. He labeled the cannon, hay bales, and mattress without assistance. Tony and Pam talked about his narrative, the picture, and the dangers of being a human cannonball. Questions reflecting Pam's lack of familiarity with the topic of launching a human cannonball vali-dated Tony's out-of-school interests and experiences and encouraged him to provide a more detailed description (Cazden, 1988; Gallimore & Tharp, 1990; Wells & Chang-Wells, 1992).

While Tony talked and Pam recorded his thoughts in *Tony's Dreams*, she noticed how animated and articulate he became as he created a narrative based on his out-of-school experiences. He was the expert; Pam, the learner. As Pam learned about being a human cannonball, she also learned about Tony. Pam began to understand the uniqueness of his experiences with the carnival and the wealth of knowledge his travel brought to the learning environment (Moll & Greenberg, 1990). "The Human Cannonball" and all the other stories in *Tony's Dreams* provided an opportunity for him to organize his thoughts and relate them in his own words.

Later, Tony began to write down his own stories rather than dictate them to Pam. Inventive spelling served Tony well as he authored his own stories, and later it became a useful device for improving Tony's spelling. For instance, Tony once observed, "Sometimes when I don't really write things right it sounds like it." The right sound of words was a device Tony used to improve his spelling. Using inventive spelling also helped Tony expand his vocabulary. The stories in *Tony's Dreams* demonstrated his ability to use print to share personally meaningful stories about himself, his family, and his out-of-school experiences.

Because it involves creative self-expression, how a student, or any-one else, interprets a story sustains a double relation to himself. If we are perceptive, it reveals the needs, desires, interests, and habits of the existing self and forms possibilities for the future self. The interpreta-tions we choose to construct are those most congenial to our existing self. The perceptive teacher in such moments can see not only who her students are, but who they may become. The imaginative perception of a student's best future possibility is extremely important to prophetic teaching. It allows us to respond in ways that form the future self of the student. It involves sympathetic feeling and generous thought. The perceptive teacher will help students critique their stories without dog-matically authoring the students' stories for them. It is a difficult and dangerous task, dangerous because we can make serious mistakes and, as teachers, we are partially responsible for the consequences for whom the students become.

Teachers also reveal their selves in how they perceive and interpret students' stories. A double relation obtains regarding the existing self and forming the future self of the teacher. Her deliberations shape both herself and her students. We have entered an infinite transactional and transformative hall of mirrors in which students and teachers interpret their own stories as well as those of others. Good transactions lead to expansive growth. Similarly, both students and teachers are deliberating constantly about how to shape their own conduct and that of others, including the teacher, in the classroom context. We could easily become lost in trying to follow theoretically the infinite complexities and sudden dialectical reversals in this hyperreflective space, just as we become lost in practice every day.

Pam followed Tony's interests and questioned and encouraged connections between his in-school experiences and his out-of-school world. She emphasized fluency first and mechanics only to provide clarity. His writing and dictating often and for a variety of reasons were more important than his having spelled or punctuated correctly. Pam understands that we care about our own creative self-expressions and are motivated to perfect them once we have produced them.

When they met, Tony decided what to read and how to structure the reading. Sometimes they took turns, alternating paragraphs or pages. Pam established the parameters (that they would spend some time reading each time they met) and Tony defined the rest. In their interactions they focused on what Tony could do both independently and with Pam's support (cf. Garrison, 1995b; Newman, Griffin, & Cole, 1989; Palincsar & Brown, 1984; Vygotsky, 1935/1978). These various moves allowed Pam to follow the logic of Tony's interests, his selective bent.

As we saw earlier, for Dewey (1934/1987), ''An artist is ruthless, when he selects, in following the logic of his interests while he adds to his selective bent an efflorescence . . . in the sense or direction in which he is drawn'' (pp. 100–101). The ''selective bent'' here refers to the idea of selective attention. From the limitless possibilities within our environment, we select according to our interests and for our purposes, that is, the direction in which we are drawn. For example, a literary and pictorial artist like Tony selects from his personal experience those events and their details that interest him just as surely as did William Blake or Shakespeare.

What Dewey has to say about aesthetic perception helps us understand moral perception and why autobiography is so powerful for allowing us to understand our students' needs, emotions, desires, interests, and purposes. ''For to perceive,'' wrote Dewey (1934/1987), ''a beholder must *create* his own experience. And his creation must include relations comparable to those which the original producer underwent" (p. 60, emphasis in original). Works of art work on the sensitive and thoughtful perceiver, and part of the work of understanding the work of art is carrying out one's own re-creative production. Moral perception is as creative and careful as aesthetic perception. Both must follow, at least by analogy, the logic of the creator's interest. Moral perception allows us to respond to our students' unique individual needs, interests, and purposes. Following the logic of our students' creative interests allows us to see the logic of their errors, or even that a student's answer, the artifact of thought, was not mistaken or poorly constructed. Perhaps the answer was an instance of creative self-expression, a perfectly logical expression of the student's purpose. Following and responding to our students' interests means that the students will be internally motivated to learn and that learning is genuinely creative for all concerned; otherwise we cannot follow the logic of *their* interests. Pam learned from Tony, and together they created their own private world.[3]

When Judith referred Tony for special education evaluation, Pam's role began to change. Following Tony's referral in March 1993, Pam began to see herself as an advocate rather than simply an outside resource person interested in supporting Tony's learning. Special education evaluation and possible placement, Pam believed, could inaccurately label Tony and limit his educational opportunities. Dewey's comments on aesthetic perception allow us to better comprehend moral perception and what Pam felt was wrong with Tony's standardized assessment. Dewey (1934/1987) wrote:

> But receptivity is not passivity. It, too, is a process consisting of a series of responsive acts that accumulate toward objective fulfillment. Otherwise, there is not perception but recognition. . . . Recognition is perception arrested before it has a chance to develop freely. . . . In recognition we fall back, upon a stereotype, upon some previously formed scheme. Some detail or arrangement of details serves as cue for bare identification. . . . Perception replaces bare recognition. There is an act of reconstructive consciousness becomes fresh and alive. Bare recognition is satisfied when a proper tag or label is attached. (pp. 58–59)

Pam participated in a lively, responsive, and intimate relationship with Tony in many real-world contexts, seeing what he could do and actively watching his creative processes over time. She was unable to reconcile her perception of Tony with the mere recognition, stereotyping, and labeling of the test. Recognition can never perceive the abilities and potential of the unique, one-time-only individual in today's never-recurring context; all it can do is re-cognize what it has already cognized before. That is why it must use stereotypes. The medical model treats children as so many museum pieces that we may deal with by labeling them as baroque, romantic, or impressionistic instead of trying to realize the unique genius of each masterpiece.

Advocating for Tony did not change the way Pam worked with him, but it did lead her to begin to systematically observe and record Tony's literate abilities. Pam prepared a document based on her work with Tony to counter Judith's assessment of him and the psychologist's report. Pam believed that continuing to define Tony's instructional and curricular program through individualized and decontextualized drills on skills limited his opportunities to read and write (Edelsky, 1991). She felt that Ann's fifth-grade class offered an environment in which Tony could learn through the type of social interaction and engagement of individual interests that, she had seen, allowed him to learn outside the classroom. Pam talked to Aaron Jones, the principal of Thurber, requesting that Tony be placed in Ann's class. She enlisted the aid of Tony's parents in her efforts to secure Tony's placement for the 1993–94 school year. Although Pam had documented literate abilities obscured by the structure of Judith's classroom and standardized testing, it remained to be shown that Tony could demonstrate his abilities in the classroom context. The situation required critical as well as creative appraisal. The role of advocacy and the desire to bestow value had, however, already pushed Pam beyond the good and evil of rules of school policy and the calculations of placement tests, and it did lead to value conflicts within herself and within the school community.

In the fall of the 1993–94 school year, Pam continued in the role of participant observer in Ann's classroom. Pam and Ann often discussed Tony's progress. Believing "Tony should be part of the class and to do what the rest of the class was doing," Ann put the *Explode the Code* and math workbooks from fourth grade in the closet. "We'll work on his skills in the context of whatever the class is doing," Ann explained at lunch during the first week of school. Ann believed that Tony's literacy learning could be supported most effectively in the give-and-take of classroom activities rather than through individualized skill-oriented instruction. Tony would not be treated any differently from the rest of the class. The structure of Ann's fifth-grade classroom invited and encouraged Tony to participate actively in a literate community of readers and writers. Beginning the first day of the 1993–94 school year, Tony's experiences were part of the seamless continuity of classroom life.

Ann recognized the central role of language as a medium through which literacy learning can occur. She encouraged the purposeful use of linguistic resources, both spoken and written, as tools for thinking, cooperating, and communicating about the task (cf. Taylor & Dorsey-Gaines, 1988). Ann shared her thoughts with Pam in a follow-up interview in March 1994. Ann stated:

> What I want to do is to have the child steeped in opportunities to develop literacy. I don't mind the noise because I know that's the social development and they are learning from one another. I expose them to so many different types of things to broaden and stretch them. . . . I want them to be able to function anywhere. I provide a lot of print for my kids. I ask them to do a lot of impromptu writing.

Ann recognized that students learn best when encouraged to make personally meaningful connections between new knowledge and their prior experiences and to assume responsibility for their own learning, so she removed many of the artificial constraints associated with the transmission model of traditional schooling (Goodman & Goodman, 1990). "Being a facilitator frees you," she commented to Pam during an interview in mid-September. Facilitating creates more possibilities for perceptive and caring responses.

Ann frequently introduced new topics with "brainstorming" sessions. These sessions could run for quite some time as students shared what they knew about a topic. Ann occasionally added her thoughts to those of the group. Participating allowed her to insert ideas and build on concepts she believed to be important (Cazden, 1988). Occasionally the information students provided was inaccurate. In such instances Ann reminded students that all answers are acceptable in a brainstorming session. "We don't say that's wrong or that information is not right. As you do your research . . . you may find information that disagrees," Pam heard her say. Each suggestion allowed Ann to perceptively assess the nature of students' understanding and prior knowledge and respond appropriately. Ann was not looking for predetermined right answers. Instead, she encouraged students to identify questions that were interesting or important to them. The discussion of what they knew and what they wanted to know served as a starting point for future learning. Ann's willingness to follow students' interests illustrated her commitment to sharing some of the responsibility for learning with her class. "I like to think of the kids as our partners in education," Ann told her colleagues during an inservice meeting in the fall of 1993. Following the logic of our students is part of the moral perception of our students' feelings, needs, desires, and purposes. Without intrinsic interest, motivation to learn must be extrinsic and moral responsibility can only be enforced by external rules and laws such as ''don't cheat.'' Virtues such as intellectual honesty, integrity, and sincerity can only apply fairly to those students who are following the logic of their interests.

Ann began the year by imaginatively creating choices for Tony about whether he used cursive or manuscript writing, what subjects he wanted to learn more about, whom he wanted to work with, how he presented his work, and where his group wanted to work. During an interview in mid-September 1993, Ann explained: ''At the beginning of the year I don't . . . say 'What would you like to learn?' It's a gradual process. And as you continue on, [you're] increasing the choices. My real goal . . . is that they have total choice in what they learn.'' Sharing control and allowing choices gave Tony a sense of purpose and self-expression in the classroom and in what happened there. He used reading and writing to communicate with real audiences for meaningful purposes. Ann created authentic contexts for Tony's learning and participated with him in identifying and satisfying his needs. She encouraged Tony to incorporate personal meaning into the reading and writing experience. Tony's sense of ownership and personal meaning enhanced his learning. Journal writing provided an opportunity for him to share his personal triumphs, thoughts, and experiences (cf. McLane, 1990). Through his journal entries, Ann discovered Tony's interests and desires and connected with his out-of-school life. She discovered what he liked to do, what was important to him, and how he felt about people or events. In all cases Ann responded in a personal way, linking what the students had written to her own experiences or asking questions to show her interest. Ann educated Tony's erōs, his desire to learn and participate, not just his cognitive centers of information processing.

In a series of entries in mid-December 1993, Tony talked about his girlfriend, Peaches. He wrote:

> If I koad [could] kiss Peaches 1 mor time i wood be a very hapy boy [.] [A]nd if I mare Peaches i wood be a good hasben and a hood fathr to my cids [.] I wood take my cids to the zoo and th partk [.] i wood tacke to chrj [church] evey day [.]

> I wont 2 cids a boy and grls [,] 1 dog and a cat [.] for my haemoon I'll go to hawaii and swiming and the beaches git a nise tan [.]

> Wat if peaches was't her [.] I wood be very sad [.] I wood be a flour with out watr and I love her very much [.]

Each entry offered Ann insight into Tony as a person with unique strengths, dreams, and feelings.

There is a logic to Tony's spelling errors. Perhaps you have already begun to intuit it as you attempted to translate his prose. Rather than requiring students to learn a list of words she determined were important, Ann validated students' uniqueness as their ability to address their own instructional needs. "Look at your . . . learning log and journal," she told students. "They can help you decide which words you want to learn how to spell. Pick words you know you have misspelled or had trouble with in your writing." Identifying words he would like to use in his writing brought meaning and purpose to Tony's spelling-vocabulary activities. Because the words were drawn from his own writing, Tony had ownership and an interest in improving. His spelling steadily improved. Ann created a context in which students had imaginative opportunities to control their own learning in many ways. Being able to use invented spelling provided the freedom and security necessary for Tony to take risks and become a fluent writer. Allowing students to use invented spelling involves recognizing a student's individual particularity, suspending judgment, and allowing the students to show what they can learn when they are personally involved. It requires emotional insight into students' needs and desires. Emotional reactions do indeed form the chief materials of our knowledge of ourselves and others.

By responding to Tony's entries in a personal way, Ann solidified their relationship of respect and caring (Atwell, 1987). Tony's entries about learning kung fu and Ann's responses provide an excellent example of the ongoing dialogue they had through the journal.

I lrnd a lot of thins in cong foow like in zapl a pote stans, a hroes stans and a soow

Dear Tony,
I'm interested in your taking karate. I took it for a while and learned self-defense and what to do if someone grabbed my purse or attacked me from the back. Keep it up and teach me some moves.

Love,
Mrs. McMann

I lrnd som neew steps in cong foow too day [,] like the elgo [.] [T]hat is ol [all] I'm going to tel you becos Devet my tegyr [teacher] told me to not to tel jenebote [anybody].

Dear Tony,
I'm interested in the reason David won't allow you to tell about kung fu. Will you ask him?

Love,
Mrs. McMann

Ann sympathetically linked Tony's kung fu lessons with her experiences in a self-defense class. She validated Tony's expertise by saying "Teach me some moves" and by asking questions to which she did not know the answers. Ann's questions and comments linked Tony's out-of-school experiences with the classroom and positioned Tony in the role of expert.

Ann mediated Tony's learning by asking questions, listening to his explanations, responding to his ideas, and introducing skills in the context of his reading and writing. "You can tell when you're talking to a child whether he understands or not," Ann explained. "And [if he doesn't] you're going back, . . . regroup and start over. I have Tony in my class . . . [and] I'm sensitive to his needs." Assessment for Ann was a continuous, ongoing, and emergent formative process that involved being sensitive to Tony's needs and responding thoughtfully to his desires and interests. Though she shared her knowledge, Ann also recognized the importance of Tony's relating new knowledge to what he already knew and developing his own strategies. She provided enough support to assist and extend his learning, but not to program or control it. During a follow-up interview in March 1994, Ann talked about Tony and the progress he had made in her class. "Tony's a reader and a writer. He's not afraid [to try]. I hope I've created a classroom where he can take risks." Ann created an environment in which Tony was willing and able to become an active participant in a transactional and transformative community of readers and writers. It allowed him to grow.

Who is Tony? What is he capable of learning? What about Judith's, Ann's, and Pam's styles of teaching and the perceptions to which their teaching leads? Are the standardized tests correct? We do not know with certainty. Why? We are dealing with the vicissitudes of human intentions, and intentions are always mutable, vague, and indeterminate. There is no science, no certain, universal, and necessary proof of the variable, indeterminate, and vague. We cannot complete the theoretical quest for certainty; there is only practical reason. The "real" world is vague, inexact, and indeterminate. Tough-minded practitioners know that. Practical reason does not hesitate to call on moral perception. We do know this much, though: There is only one Tony, he has unique potential, and only moral perception recognizes the unique, irreplaceable, and one-time-only characteristics of persons and contexts. In the end, only moral perception can see beyond the actual into Tony's best possibilities. It is a prophetic art.

Now we can see what is most especially and precisely moral about moral perception, particularly the capacity to see the best possibility of someone and some situation. Surprisingly, this insight will allow us to dismiss one of the most common misinterpretations of Deweyan thought, the widely held belief that Dewey was naively optimistic.

In "The Good of Activity," Chapter 23 of *Human Nature and Conduct*, Dewey (1922/1983) began by affirming, "The foremost conclusion is that morals has to do with all activity into which alternative possibilities enter. For wherever they enter a difference between better and worse arises. . . . Only deliberate action, conduct into which reflective choice enters, is distinctively moral, for only then does there enter the question of better and worse" (p. 193). Deliberation, the dramatic rehearsal of possible consequences in imagination, seeks the best transformative possibilities given the constraints of the actual situation. The best possibility within a concrete, lived context is what Dewey meant by "the Good." It is very different from the eternal fixed version of "the Good" of Plato and his modern emulators. Dewey's notion of the Good is what undergirds his often misunderstood ideal of social meliorism and progress. For Dewey (1922/1983), "Morals means growth of conduct in meaning. . . . It is all one with growing." (p. 194). Growth of meaning is, for Dewey, *the* aim of education for both individuals and society.

As Dewey saw it, progress is not movement toward some eternal fixed ideal, good, or value. Instead, progress means reconstruction, transforming a situation from worse to better. Dewey (1922/1983) wrote, "Progress is present reconstruction adding fullness and distinctness of meaning. . . . Unless progress is a present reconstructing, it is nothing. . . . Progress means increase of present meaning, which involves multiplication of sensed distinctions as well as harmony, unification" (pp. 195–196). For Dewey there are no cosmic purposes fulfilling themselves in history that guarantee progress in advance; there are only people like teachers trying to make things better. It is an endless task, as teachers know. Dewey (1922/1983) reflected:

> There is something pitifully juvenile in the idea that "evolution," progress, means a definite sum of accomplishment which will forever stay done, and which by an exact amount lessens the amount still to be done, disposing once and for all of just so many perplexities and advancing us just so far on our road to a final stable and unperplexed goal. (p. 197)

We do not need to think things are getting better to do our best, or that there is some cosmic backup story that guarantees success. That is part of maturity. It is the attitude of the meliorist in contrast to the optimist.

Dewey (1920/1982b) himself distinguished the meliorist from the optimist:

> Meliorism is the belief that the specific conditions which exist at one moment, be they comparatively bad or comparatively good, in any event may be bettered. It encourages intelligence to study the positive means of good . . . and to put forth endeavor for improvement of conditions. It arouses confidence and a reasonable hopefulness as optimism does not. . . . Too readily optimism makes the men who hold it callous and blind to the sufferings of the less fortunate, or ready to find the cause of troubles of others in their personal viciousness. (pp. 181–182)

We may be meliorists even at moments when we know that our world is in decay. We can seek to ameliorate a situation even when we recognize that we are living in a disintegrating world. Such situations often confront caregivers. Nurses ameliorate suffering even when they know the patient is going to die. Look into your children's eyes. Some of them were cursed at conception by a society that made large quantities of drugs readily available to mothers and a desired, although not desirable, alternative for them in a desperate life. The senselessness of genetic birth defects seriously constrains possibility. Others will be physically and emotionally abused in ways that will almost assuredly condemn them to much misery. They live, they dance, they play. They want to grow. Can you see what they need, what they desire, and what they dream? Can you make it better? It is a matter of moral perception, and practical reason.

The meaning of life for Dewey is expansive growth, that is, to make more meaning. Said differently, "Since in reality there is nothing to which growth is relative save more growth, there is nothing to which education is subordinate save more education" (Dewey, 1916/1980a, p. 56). The ultimate aim of education is more education. That is the Deweyan answer to the question: What is the meaning of life? For Dewey (1922/1983), the good, value, or ends-in-view could only be grasped by reflecting on purely human needs and the rhythm of life:

> From the standpoint of attainment of good that stays put . . . the ultimate goal of final good, progress *is* an illusion. . . . [We] have been compelled to recognize the truth that in fact we envisage the good in specific terms that are relative to existing needs, and the attainment of every specific good

merges insensibly into a new condition of maladjustment with its need of a new end and a renewed effort. (p. 198)

We may pause to rest and enjoy the aesthetic moments in life and sigh, but the moving rhythm continues to write. There are more possibilities to be perceived, inquired into, and actualized. The live creature must act in every moment. It breathes, listens, relaxes, sighs, tenses, and moves again. Every living creature wants to live and grow. Tony is a live creature. So, too, are his teachers.

Instead of revealing predetermined ends, prophets critique present conditions and poetically create new ends-in-view to guide their melio- ristic projects. The wisdom of prophets is a social hope for expansive growth reduced to a working program. Practical prophecy, though, may require that we reason far beyond good and evil as conventionally de- fined. Said differently, as a good educator, a teacher may need to violate the letter of school rules or otherwise, like Pam (or Gwyn), become an outlaw who ''bucks the system.''

Epilogue

When philosophy shall have cooperated with the course of events and made clear and coherent the meaning of the daily detail, science and emotion will interpenetrate, practice and imagination will embrace. Poetry and religious feeling will be the unforced flowers of life.

—Dewey, 1920/1982b, p. 201

Using the formal schema of practical deliberation as our roadmap, and trusting our intuitions along the way, we have arrived at our destination. We have unconcealed the hidden relation among teaching, loving, and logic. Reflecting on the major premise of practical reasoning, "I desire V" (see Figure I.1), we started by recovering and reconstructing ancient Greek wisdom regarding the education of the human erōs to passionately desire the good. In Chapter 2 we saw how an individual, the "I" of the major premise, grows expansively by needing to be needed and by bestowing value on others while allowing others to bestow value on him. We uncovered the paradox that those in the caring professions, such as teachers can care for others only if they care for themselves. Next we examined the creation of ethereal things. This allowed us to explore the aesthetic and ethical dimensions of creating values, the "V" of practical deliberation. This allowed us to better understand loving acts of bestowal. The paradoxes multiplied when we realized that teachers can bestow value on their students only if they bestow value on themselves. In Chapter 4 we learned that means–ends deliberation begins in the hidden aesthetic background of inquiry and that intuition precedes cognition and goes deeper. It became clear that we cannot completely separate creative thinking from rational thinking. This allowed us to better understand the magic of the teachable moment. Chapter 5 developed a critical–creative theory of value appraisal that eventually took us beyond good and evil. We ended by discussing moral perception, or the ability to see the particular needs, desires, and interests of unique individuals in one-time-only situations and to look into the future of their best possibilities. Eventually, we saw that to bestow value on their students, teachers, too, must sometimes go beyond good and evil.

Our pursuit of philosophy, our love of practical wisdom, and the erōs in the logic of practical deliberation seem to have taken us far from the classroom. We have journeyed beyond knowledge and beyond good and evil. We departed from the ordinary and everyday and disembarked in the province of poetry and prophecy. Prophets disclosed themselves to be poets. But we have not gone very far at all.

My deepest desire in writing this book was to transform our perception of our classrooms and our teaching so that we could see them for the miracle they are. Every day in every classroom choice we make, we answer life's most momentous questions: What is life (or teaching)? How should I live (or teach)? What does it mean? Dewey answered: Whatever life is, it is a miracle and the live creature must act to maintain its existence and grow. The human erōs desires growth and grows only if it desires what is truly good, if it needs to be needed, and if it bestows the goods it comes to possess upon others. Finally, the meaning of life is to make more meaning, and so the aim of education is growth. This is philosophy *as* education.

Moment to moment, as teachers move among their students, they are touching lives. Teachers, too, are poets and prophets. If they are wise, then they and their students will learn to care for each other, bestow value, and grow together. If teachers are foolish, no one will flourish. Of this, though, we may be sure: We become what we love.

Notes

INTRODUCTION

1. This scholarship includes important philosophical investigations such as Raymond D. Boisvert's (1988) *Dewey's Metaphysics*, Tom Burke's (1994) *Dewey's New Logic: A Reply to Russell*, Larry A. Hickman's (1990) *John Dewey's Pragmatic Technology*, R. W. Sleeper's (1986) *The Necessity of Pragmatism: John Dewey's Conception of Philosophy*, and J. E. Tiles' (1988) *Dewey*. The historian Robert B. Westbrook's (1991) *John Dewey and American Democracy* provides fresh insights into Dewey's extraordinary public life and private passions. So, too, does Steven C. Rockefeller (1991) in his sensitive theological study *John Dewey: Religious Faith and Democratic Humanism*. Other philosophers, such as Thomas A. Alexander (1987) in *John Dewey's Theory of Art, Experience, and Nature: The Horizons of Feeling* and Richard Shusterman (1992) in *Pragmatist Aesthetics: Living Beauty, Rethinking Art*, concentrate their attention on Dewey's aesthetics.

2. Many of the scholars mentioned in note 2 recently contributed directly to the philosophy of education for the first time in *The New Scholarship on Dewey* (Garrison, 1995c). Educators familiar with the new scholarship, such as Philip W. Jackson and Siebren Miedema, joined them. Significantly, almost half of the contributors to *The New Scholarship on Dewey* chose to write on some aspect of Dewey's aesthetics and education. Two of the contributors, Susan Laird and Mary Leach, critiqued Dewey's thinking before pointing to possibilities for ''(Re)searching Dewey,'' as Leach aptly put it, for feminist projects.

3. See especially the papers in the special issue on ''Feminism and Pragmatism'' in *Hypatia* edited by Charlene Haddock Seigfried (1993). Given the preponderance of the papers that discuss and praise John Dewey, this special issue could have been titled ''Feminism and Dewey.''

CHAPTER 1

1. This passage speaks of ''*men's* most passionate desires and hopes.'' Dewey was of his times and spoke as men of his time spoke. There is no point in constantly noting this. Dewey himself acknowledged that the disruption of habitual ways of speaking is one way of initiating reflective inquiry. He would have approved of reconstructing our habits of discourse in the service of democratic dialogue. We, too, are of our times and should strive to speak in more

inclusive ways. That can be hard to do, so we continue the conversation and do our best.

CHAPTER 2

1. Elsewhere Dewey (1939/1988) observes, "Any experience is miseducative that has the effect of arresting or distorting the growth of further experience" (p. 11).

2. Empirical studies have shown that prospective teachers enter teaching to obtain "creative autonomy" and the "psychic rewards" of teaching (see Lortie, 1975). The exact meaning of the phrase "psychic rewards" is elusive, but it means something like connecting to students and helping them learn. If teachers' institutions or colleagues cannot contribute to creative autonomy, then it is unlikely that they can obtain the psychic rewards of teaching. If teachers cannot create, then they cannot readily bestow care. The loss of creative expression and the opportunity to care and connect are the flint and steel of teacher burnout.

3. Pappas (1993), who cites part of this passage, remarks, "It is worth mentioning that moral sensitivity for Dewey is akin to aesthetic sensitivity" (p. 79).

4. Not every means constitutes the end; some means may be purely instrumental. As Dewey (1932/1985b) put it, "There are means which are constituent parts of the consequences they bring into being, as tones are integral constituents of music as well as means to its production, and as food is an indispensable ingredient with the organism which it serves" (pp. 249–250). The scaffolding that is removed while the building remains was merely an instrumental means, while the pillars and I-beams that remain until the building collapses or is torn down are constituent means. We should not let the distinction between instrumental and constituent means harden into a dualism. It is all a matter of functional relations in some context.

5. Dewey (1916/1980b) earlier observed: "Such words as interests, affection, concern, motivation, emphasize the bearing of what is foreseen upon the individual's fortunes, and his active desire to act to secure a possible result. . . . The difference imaginatively foreseen makes a present difference" (pp. 131–132).

6. Dewey (1938/1986) wrote, "In Plato change . . . has a direct ontological status. It is a sign of the defective ontological character of that which changes, its lack of full Being" (p. 189).

7. Dewey contrasted vocational education *for* some socially predetermined role with education *through* the occupations. He rejected the former entirely in his debate with Snedden and Prosser. Dewey eventually lost his debate with the passage of the Smith-Hartley act in 1917 that led to the establishment of tracking in American schools. It is clear, though, that education through the occupations is crucial to Dewey's educational philosophy (see Garrison, 1990).

8. Dewey did not ignore the caring perspective entirely. Indeed, he illustrated what he meant by "mind" using the parent and child relationship. Dewey (1934/1987) wrote:

Mind also signifies attention. We not only keep things in mind, but we bring mind to bear on our problems and perplexities. Mind also signifies purpose; we have a mind to do this and that. Nor is mind in these operations something purely intellectual. The mother minds her baby; she cares for it with affection. Mind is care in the sense of solicitude, anxiety, as well as of active looking after things that need to be tended; we mind our step, our course of action, emotionally as well as thoughtfully. From giving heed to acts and objects, mind comes also to signify, to obey—as children are told to mind their parents. In short "to mind" denotes an activity that is intellectual, to *note* something; affectional, as caring and liking, and volitional, practical, acting in a purposive way. . . . Mind is primarily a verb. (p. 268)

Dewey seems aware of the importance of caring in relationships. Still, this is at best an aside. Dewey should have made much more of the ethics of care; nor does he, at least here, seem to appreciate the need of the mother to care for herself, much less to recognize caring for oneself as part of caring for those that depend on one. Martin is correct: Dewey does needs reconstructing.

9. In a footnote Leffers (1993) observes, "Addams does not mean self-assertion in the same way that we would use that term today, because the residents of Hull-House certainly did assert themselves regularly. . . . I think that what she means is a kind of self-assertion made at the expense of others, which includes a certain amount of self-aggrandizement" (p. 76). It was the self-assertion of the fixed self that offended Addams.

10. In *Art as Experience*, Dewey (1934/1987) makes a very similar statement that explicitly connects aesthetics to practical activity:

The Greek identification of good conduct with conduct having proportion, grace, and harmony, the *kalon-agathon*, is a more obvious example of distinctive esthetic quality in moral action. One great defect in what passes as morality is its anesthetic quality. . . . Any practical activity will, provided that it is integrated and moves by its own urge to fulfillment, have esthetic quality. (p. 46)

As for Plato, for Dewey the beautiful, the good, and the harmonious are one, although Dewey's naturalistic understanding of this unity is much different from Plato's supernaturalistic understanding. For Dewey aesthetic harmony practically intervenes in the world of everyday affairs, whereas for Plato it merely supervenes theoretically.

CHAPTER 3

1. This idea is borrowed from Hansen (1995). I wish to acknowledge many helpful discussions with David.

2. It indicates how much we moderns have lost of the ancient wisdom that

we can only comprehend the word *erotic* as having a sexual connotation. It is even sadder that we seem to forget that human sexual relations *are* creative. Sexual relations call into existence joyous feelings, wonderful thoughts, and the greatest miracle, new human beings. They can also bring on anger, cruelty, and AIDS. If our relations are not good, beautiful, and harmonious, it is because we lack wisdom.

3. See Dewey (1934/1987, p. 40). The lines are from Keats's famous "Ode on a Grecian Urn."

CHAPTER 4

1. The first part of this chapter relies on Garrison (in press).

2. What all forms of the functionalist/positivist position share to some extent are these assumptions: (1) They are largely limited to problems of knowing and assume that our primary relation to reality is one of knowledge. (2) Thinking and knowing are assumed to involve the manipulation of abstract mental representations such as schemas, scripts, concepts, and categories. (3) These mentalistic entities are assumed to be distinct from any kind of naturalistic embodiment. (4) Thinking, construed to be founded on the canons of formal logic and information processing, is deductive, inductive, or computational. (5) It is assumed that thinking is an exclusively cognitive process unadulterated by noncognitive components. (6) No role is explicitly provided for noncognitive structures and activities. (7) Thought and knowledge are entirely decontextualized. Dewey's theory of inquiry rejects these assumptions.

3. Cognitive "ideas" emerge developmentally from less to more exact. Dewey (1938/1986) stated, "An idea is first of all an anticipation of something that may happen; it marks a *possibility*. . . . Because inquiry is a progressive determination of a problem and its possible solution, ideas differ in grade according to the stage of inquiry reached. At first, save in highly familiar matters, they are vague" (p. 113, emphasis in original).

4. The work of Carol Gilligan (1982) and Nel Noddings (1984) has demonstrated the need for caring in the conduct of moral inquiry. I urge that we follow Dewey in rejecting the positivists' fact/value dualism and recognizing that caring plays a crucial role in all inquiry from the beginning. Dewey (1949/1989) believed:

> "The words 'concern,' 'affair,' 'care,' 'matter,' 'thing,' etc., fuse in indissoluble unity senses which when discriminated are called *emotional, intellectual, practical*, the first two being moreover marked traits of the last named. Apart from a given context, it is not even possible to tell which one is uppermost; and when a context of use is present, it is always a question of emphasis, never of separation." (p. 247, emphasis in original)

5. Given the context of this quote, we can be confident that Dewey had the following passage from William James (1890/1950) in mind: "The *great* snare of

the psychologist is the *confusion of his own standpoint with that of the mental fact about which he is making his report*. I shall hereafter call this the 'psychologist's fallacy' *par excellence*" (p. 196).

6. Dewey (1931/1985a) also rejected the view from nowhere: "Bias for impartiality is as much a bias as is partisan prejudice. . . . One can only see from a certain standpoint, but this fact does not make all standpoints of equal value. A standpoint which is nowhere in particular and from which things are not seen at a special angle is an absurdity. But one may have affection for a standpoint which gives a rich and ordered landscape rather than for one from which things are seen confusedly and meagerly" (pp. 14–15). Thus Dewey held a standpoint, pluralistic, and perspectival, epistemology. We can only know the world from the different places we have stood to gaze upon it.

7. Significantly, Dewey (1931/1985a) begins "Context and Thought" with a discussion of "ethnographic field-work" (p. 3).

8. This observation, like all the rest reporting Linda Pacifici's feelings and thoughts about "doing" *The Dark Is Rising*, are borrowed from Linda's own composition taken from a joint paper (see Pacifici & Garrison, 1995).

CHAPTER 5

1. See the chapter in *The Theory of Valuation* titled "Propositions of Appraisal" (Dewey, 1939/1988).

2. The attention to consequences is crucial for the pragmatist. Consequentialism is the *sine qua non* of any pragmatism, including Dewey's. Charles Sanders Peirce (1878/1965a) first formulated pragmatism as follows: "Consider what effects, that might conceivably have practical bearing, we conceive the object of our conception to have. Then, our conception of these effects is the whole of our conception of the object" (p. 258). All that pragmatism can be is located in the alternative possible interpretations of Peirce's original formulation. The pragmatic maxim refers all determinations of meaning to their consequences. As Peirce (1878/1965a) put it, "there is no distinction of meaning so fine as to consist in anything but a possible difference of practice" (p. 257). There is no difference that does not make a difference.

3. Dewey (1939/1988) wrote: "Valuation takes place only when there is something the matter; when there is some trouble to be done away with, some need, lack or privation to be made good, some conflict of tendencies to be resolved by means of changing existing conditions. This fact in turn proves that there is present an intellectual factor—a factor of inquiry—whenever there is valuation, for the end-in-view is formed and projected as that which, if acted upon, will supply the existing need or lack and resolve the existing conflict" (p. 221).

4. For a good account of the ambivalence, vagueness, and complexity of making such decisions in the reading and writing workshop, see Timothy J. Lensmire's (1994) *When Children Write*. I would also like to take this occasion to thank Tim for sharing his tribulations with my classes in the spring of 1995.

5. Mark Johnson (1993) concedes that his book is a "Deweyan conception of morality" (p. xiv).

6. The following components are an attempt to summarize Chapter 7, "The Narrative Context of Self and Action," of Johnson's (1993) book.

7. The first part of this section is largely drawn from Garrison (1996).

8. Suzanne Reid (1993, 1995) suggests that many of Voigt's female protagonists are possessed of considerable intuitive insight and understanding. She places them at the level of "subjective knowledge" in the stages of development described by Belenky, Clinchy, Goldberger, and Tarule (1986) in *Women's Ways of Knowing*. At this stage knowledge is viewed as personal, private, and subjectively known or intuited. These people trust themselves and are skeptical of official knowledge. Reid shows that Voigt's characters typically do not succeed until they arrive at the stages of "procedural knowledge," involving the use of objective procedures for obtaining knowledge, and "constructed knowledge," wherein women experience knowledge as contextual and themselves as creators of knowledge, and value both subjective and objective strategies for knowing (see Belenky et al., 1986, p. 15). Whatever the case, the formal lessons involved in learning how to read are important to Gwyn's personal development. I would like to acknowledge a debt of gratitude to Suzanne not only for her valuable dissertation (Reid, 1993; see also Reid, 1995) but also for many helpful conversations over the years.

9. Reid (1993) notes, "In Voigt's stories, adults often prove inadequate and unresponsive to their children's needs" (p. 156).

10. Significantly, there are several mentions in the novel of another definition of husband: "to manage prudently and economically." One such mention occurs as Gwyn reflects on her father's offer to make her the heir of the inn. Gwyn realizes that "she would husband the holdings and take care of her family; she would do it well, she knew that, and she could do it easily" (p. 216). There are many paradoxical layers of meaning here.

11. Incidentally, have you been wondering where a simple innkeeper's daughter gets the horse to ride when peasants are forbidden any such? Well, for one thing, the mighty Jackaroo often walks. When she does ride it is on a horse "borrowed" from the stable at the inn where soldiers are often quartered in the troubled times in which this novel is set.

12. The hyphen in the odd location "student-teacher" tells us that it is an identity that cannot be captured in the usual logic of exclusive either/ors. It is a peculiar identity. Its logic is both/and. It is more exact to say it is an identity in the making.

CHAPTER 6

1. This chapter relies heavily upon Simpson and Garrison (1995). Pam contributed equally to this chapter and was the lead author of the published paper. She was a participant researcher in Judith's and Ann's classes from October 1992 to December 1993.

2. Dewey (1934/1987) observed, 'Charity' may even be used as a means for administering a sop to one's social conscience while at the same time it buys off the resentment which might otherwise grow up in those who suffer from social injustice. Magnificent philanthropy may be employed to cover up brutal economic exploitation'' (p. 301).

3. To grasp what is meant by creating your own private world, just think about how you sometimes talk to your lover, or your children, or other close family member. Anyone less intimately connected to you would not understand some things, especially because some of the words refer to things and events absolutely unique to your relationship.

References

All citations of the works of John Dewey are from the series *The Collected Works of John Dewey*, edited by J. A. Boydston and published by Southern Illinois University Press in Carbondale. In each Dewey reference, the following letter codes are used to identify the corresponding volume:

EW   *The Early Works, 1882–1898*
MW   *The Middle Works, 1899–1924*
LW   *The Later Works, 1925–1953*

Addams, J. (1981). *Twenty years at Hull-House*. New York: Penguin. (Original work published 1910)

Alexander, T. (1987). *John Dewey's theory of art, experience, and nature: The horizons of feeling*. Albany: State University of New York Press.

Alexander, T. (1992). Dewey and the Metaphysical Imagination. *Transactions of the Charles S. Peirce Society, 28*(2), 203–215.

Alexander, T. (1993). The human erōs. In John J. Stuhr (Ed.), *Philosophy and the reconstruction of culture* (pp. 203–222). Albany: State University of New York Press.

Anderson, W., Chitwood, S., & Hayden, D. (1990). *Negotiating the special education maze: A guide for parents and teachers*. Woodbine House.

Atwell, N. (1987). *In the middle*. Portsmouth, NH: Heinemann.

Belenky, M., Clinchy, B., Goldberger, N., & Tarule, J. (1986). *Women's ways of knowing: The development of self, voice, and mind*. New York: Basic Books.

Boisvert, R. (1985). John Dewey's reconstruction of philosophy. *Educational Studies, 16*(4), 343–353.

Boisvert, R. (1988). *Dewey's metaphysics*. New York: Fordham University Press.

Boisvert, R. (1995). John Dewey: An old-fashioned reformer. In J. Garrison (Ed.), *The new scholarship on John Dewey* (pp. 157–173). Dordrecht: Kluwer Academic Publishers.

Burke, T. (1994). *Dewey's new logic: a reply to Russell*. Chicago: University of Chicago Press.

Cazden, C. (1988). *Classroom discourse: The language of teaching and learning*. Portsmouth, NH: Heinemann.

Clark, C., & Peterson, P. (1986). Teachers' thought processes. In M. Wittrock (Ed.), *Handbook of research on teaching* (3rd ed.) (pp. 255–296). New York: Macmillan.

The Compact Edition of The Oxford English Dictionary. (1971). Oxford: Oxford University Press.

Cooper, S. (1973). *The dark is rising*. New York: Collier.

Cunningham, C. (1994). Unique potential: A metaphor for John Dewey's later conception of the self. *Educational Theory, 44*(2), 211–224.

Darling-Hammond, L. (1991). The implications of testing policy for quality and equality. *Phi Delta Kappan, 73*(3), 220–225.

Darwin, C. (1901). *The expression of the emotions in man and animals* (2nd ed.). London: John Murray. (Original work published 1873)

Dewey, J. (1971). The theory of emotion. EW, Vol. 4, pp. 152–188. (Original work published 1895)

Dewey, J. (1972). The Reflex arc concept in psychology. EW, Vol. 5, pp. 96–109. (Original work published 1896)

Dewey, J. (1976a). Emerson—The philosopher of democracy. MW, Vol. 3, pp. 184–192. (Original work published 1903)

Dewey, J. (1976b). *The school and society.* MW, Vol. 1, pp. 1–237. (Original work published 1899)

Dewey, J. (1978). Contributions to *A cyclopedia of education.* MW, Vol. 6, pp. 357–467. (Original work published 1911)

Dewey, J. (1979). The existence of the world as a logical problem. MW, Vol. 8, pp. 83–97. (Original work published 1915)

Dewey, J. (1980a). *Democracy and education.* MW, Vol. 9. (Original work published 1916)

Dewey, J. (1980b). Introduction to *Essays in Experimental Logic.* MW, Vol. 10, pp. 131–132. (Original work published 1916)

Dewey, J. (1981). *Experience and nature.* LW, Vol. 1. (Original work published 1925)

Dewey, J. (1982a). Philosophy and democracy. MW, Vol. 11, pp. 41–53. (Original work published 1919)

Dewey, J. (1982b). *Reconstruction in philosophy.* MW, Vol. 12. (Original work published 1920)

Dewey, J. (1983). *Human nature and conduct.* MW, Vol. 14. (Original work published 1922)

Dewey, J. (1984a). Affective thought. LW, Vol. 2, pp. 104–115. (Original work published 1926)

Dewey, J. (1984b). Conduct and experience. LW, Vol. 5, pp. 218–235. (Original work published 1929)

Dewey, J. (1984d). Qualitative thought. LW, Vol. 5, pp. 243–262. (Original work published 1930)

Dewey, J. (1984e). *The quest for certainty.* LW, Vol. 4. (Original work published 1929)

Dewey, J. (1984f). What I believe. LW, Vol. 5, pp. 267–288. (Original work published 1930)

Dewey, J. (1985a). Context and thought. LW, Vol. 6, pp. 3–21. (Original work published 1931)

Dewey, J. (1985b). *Ethics.* LW, Vol. 7. (Original work published 1932)

Dewey, J. (1986). *Logic: The theory of inquiry.* LW, Vol. 12. (Original work published 1938)

Dewey, J. (1987). *Art as experience.* LW, Vol. 10. (Original work published 1934)

Dewey, J. (1988). *Theory of valuation.* LW, Vol. 13, pp. 191–251. (Original work published 1939)

Dewey, J., & Bentley, A. (1989). *Knowing and the known.* LW, Vol. 16, pp. 1–279. (Original work published 1949)

Edelsky, C. (1991). *With literacy and justice for all: Rethinking the social in language and education.* London: Falmer.

Engestrom, Y. (1987). *Learning by expanding: An activity-theoretical approach to developmental research.* Helsinki: Orienta-Konsultit Oy.

Gallimore, R., & Tharp, R. (1990). Teaching mind in society: Teaching, schooling, and literate discourse. In L. Moll (Ed.), *Vygotsky and education: Instructional implications and applications of sociohistorical psychology* (pp. 175–205). New York: Cambridge University Press.

Gardner, H. (1985). *The mind's new science.* New York: Basic Books.

Garrison, J. (1990). Philosophy as (vocational) education. *Educational Theory, 40*(3), 391–406.

Garrison, J. (1994a). Realism, Deweyan pragmatism, and educational research. *Educational Researcher, 23*(1), 5–14.

Garrison, J. (1994b). Dewey, contexts, and texts. *Educational Researcher, 23*(1), 19–20.

Garrison, J. (1995a). Deweyan prophetic pragmatism, poetry, and the education of erōs. *American Journal of Education, 103*(4), 406–431.

Garrison, J. (1995b). Deweyan pragmatism and the epistemology of contemporary social constructivism. *American Educational Research Journal, 32*(4), 716–740.

Garrison, J. (1995c). *The new scholarship on Dewey.* Dordrecht: Kluwer Academic Publishers.

Garrison, J. (1996). A transactional reading of Cynthia Voigt's *Jackaroo:* The prophetic art of friendly instruction. *Alan Review, 23*(4), 12–21.

Garrison, J. (in press). Dewey, qualitative thought, and context. *Journal of Qualitative Studies.*

Gilligan, C. (1982). *In a different voice: Psychological theory and women's development.* Cambridge, MA: Harvard University Press.

Goodman, Y. (1982). Kidwatching: Evaluating written language development. *Australian Journal of Reading, 5*(3), 120–128.

Goodman, Y., & Goodman, K. (1990). Vygotsky in a whole-language perspective. In L. Moll (Ed.), *Vygotsky and education: Instructional implications and applications of sociohistorical psychology* (pp. 223–250). New York: Cambridge University Press.

Hall, N., & Price, R. (1986). *Explode the code.* Cambridge, MA: Educators Publishing Service, Inc.

Hansen, D. (1995). *The call to teach.* New York: Teachers College Press.

Hickman, L. (1992). *John Dewey's pragmatic technology.* Bloomington: Indiana University Press.

Jagger, A. (1989). Love and knowledge: Emotion in feminist epistemology. In

A. M. Jagger & S. R. Bordo (Eds.), *Gender/body/knowledge* (pp. 145–171). New Brunswick, NJ: Rutgers University Press.

James, W. (1950). *The principles of psychology* (Vol. 1). New York: Dover. (Original work published 1890)

Johnson, M. (1993). *Moral imagination: Implications of cognitive science for ethics.* Chicago: University of Chicago Press.

Johnston, P. (1992). *Constructive evaluation of literate activity.* New York: Longman.

Kornhaber, M., Krechevsky, M., & Gardner, H. (1990). Engaging intelligence. *Educational Psychologist, 25*(3/4), 177–199.

Lave, J. (1988). *Cognition in practice.* Cambridge, U.K.: Cambridge University Press.

Leffers, M. (1993). Pragmatists Jane Addams and John Dewey inform the ethic of care. *Hypatia, 8*(2), 64–77.

Lensmire, T. (1994). *When children write: Critical re-vision of the writing workshop.* New York: Teachers College Press.

Lortie, D. (1975). *Schoolteacher: a sociological study.* Chicago: University of Chicago Press.

Martin, J. (1985). *Reclaiming a conversation: The ideal of the educated woman.* New Haven, CT: Yale University Press.

Martin, J. (1992). *The Schoolhome: Rethinking Schools for Changing Families.* Cambridge, MA: Harvard University Press.

McCarthey, S. (1994). Opportunities and risks of writing from personal experiences. *Language Arts, 71*(3), 182–191.

McLane, J. (1990). Writing as a social process. In L. Moll (Ed.), *Vygotsky and education: Instructional implications and applications of sociohistorical psychology* (pp. 304–318). New York: Cambridge University Press.

Mehan, H. (1992). Beneath the skin and between the ears: A case study in the politics of representation. In J. Lave & S. Chaiklen (Eds.), *Understanding practice: Perspectives on activity and context* (pp. 41–66). Cambridge, MA: Harvard University Press.

Moll, L., & Greenberg, J. (1990). Creating zones of possibility. In L. Moll (Ed.), *Vygotsky and education: Instructional implications and applications of sociohistorical psychology* (pp. 319–348). New York: Cambridge University Press.

Nespor, J., & Barber, E. (n.d.). *Community expertise and inclusion: Parents' stories of the politics of special education.* Unpublished manuscript.

Nespor, J., & Garrison, J. (1992). Constructing relevance. *Educational Researcher, 21*(3), 26–27.

Newman, D., Griffin, P., & Cole, M. (1989). *The construction zone.* Cambridge, U.K.: Cambridge University Press.

Noddings, N. (1984). *Caring: A feminine approach to ethics and moral education.* Berkeley: University of California Press.

Noddings, N. (1992). *The challenge to care in schools.* New York: Teachers College Press.

Nussbaum, M. (1990). *Love's knowledge.* Oxford: Oxford University Press.

Pacifici, L., & Garrison, J. (1995, April). *Imagination, emotion and inquiry: The teachable moment*. Paper presented at the annual meeting of the American Educational Research Association, San Francisco.

Palincsar, A., & Brown, A. (1984). Reciprocal teaching of comprehension-fostering and comprehension-monitoring activities. *Cognition and Instruction, 1*(2), 117–175.

Pappas, G. F. (1993). Dewey and feminism: The affective and relationships in Dewey's ethics. *Hypatia, 8*(2), 78–95.

Parker, S. P. (Ed.). (1992). Extinction (biology). In *McGraw-Hill encyclopedia of science & technology* (7th ed.) (Vol. 6) (pp. 570–572). New York: McGraw-Hill.

Peirce, C. S. (1965a). How to make our ideas clear. In C. Hartshorne & P. Weiss (Eds.), *Collected papers of Charles Sanders Peirce* (Vol. V) (pp. 248–271). Cambridge, MA: Belknap Press of Harvard University Press. (Original work published 1878)

Peirce, C. S. (1965b). Pragmatism and pragmaticism. In C. Hartshorne & P. Weiss (Eds.), *Collected papers of Charles Sanders Peirce* (Vol. V) (pp. 13–131). Cambridge, MA: Belknap Press of Harvard University Press. (Original work published 1903)

Reichenbach, H. (1938). *Experience and prediction*. Chicago: University of Chicago Press.

Reid, S. (1993). *Becoming a modern hero: The search for identity in Cynthia Voigt's novels*. Unpublished doctoral dissertation, Virginia Tech, Blacksburg, VA.

Reid, S. (1995). *Presenting Cynthia Voigt*. New York: Twayne.

Reit, S. (1990). *Guns for General Washington*. San Diego, CA: Harcourt Brace Jovanovich.

Rockefeller, S. (1991). *John Dewey: Religious faith and democratic humanism*. New York: Columbia University Press.

Rogoff, B. (1994, April). *Models of teaching and learning: Development through participation*. Paper presented at the Annual Meeting of the American Educational Research Association, New Orleans, LA.

Rorty, R. (1979). *Philosophy and the mirror of nature*. Princeton, NJ: Princeton University Press.

Rorty, R. (1989). *Contingency, irony, and solidarity*. Cambridge, U.K.: Cambridge University Press.

Rose, M. (1989). *Lives on the boundary*. New York: Penguin.

Rosen, S. (1987). *Plato's symposium*. New Haven: Yale University Press. (Original work published 1968)

Rosenthal, R., & Rubin, D. (1980). Summarizing 345 studies of interpersonal expectancy effects. In R. Rosenthal (Ed.), *Qualitative assessment of research domains: New directions for methodology of social and behavioral sciences* (Vol. 5). San Francisco: Jossey-Bass.

Ross, W. D. (Trans.). (1941). *Aristotle: Nicomachean ethics*. New York: Random House.

Ross, W. D. (1971). *Aristotle*. London: Methuen & Co Ltd.

Ruddick, S. (1984). Maternal thinking. In J. Trebilcot (Ed.), *Mothering: Essays in feminist theory* (pp. 213–230). Totowa, NJ: Rowman & Allanheld.

Russell, B. (1977). Professor Dewey's "Essays in Experimental Logic." In S. Morgenbesser (Ed.), *Dewey and his critics* (pp. 231–252). New York: Journal of Philosophy, Inc. (Original work published 1919)

Schadewaldt, W. (1979). The concepts of *nature* and *technique* according to the Greeks. In P. T. Durbin (Ed.), *Research in philosophy and technology* (Vol. 2) (pp. 159–171). Greenwich, CT: JAI Press.

Scribner, S. (1984). *Studying working intelligence.* In B. Rogoff & J. Lave (Eds.), *Everyday cognition* (pp. 9–40). Cambridge, MA: Harvard University Press.

Seigfried, C. H. (1991). Where are all the pragmatist feminists? *Hypatia, 6*(2), 1–20.

Seigfried, C. H. (Ed.). (1993). Shared communities of interest: Feminism and pragmatism. *Hypatia, 8*(2), pp. 1–14.

Shusterman, R. (1992). *Pragmatist aesthetics: Living beauty, rethinking art.* Oxford: Blackwell.

Simpson, P., & Garrison, J. (1995). Teaching and moral perception. *Teachers College Record, 97*(2), 252–278.

Singer, I. (1984). *The nature of love: Plato to Luther.* Chicago: University of Chicago Press.

Sleeper, R. (1986). *The necessity of pragmatism: John Dewey's conception of philosophy.* New Haven, CT: Yale University Press.

Smith, M., Edelsky, C., Draper, K., Rottenberg, C., & Cherland, M. (1991). *The role of testing in elementary schools.* Los Angeles: Arizona State University and UCLA Center for Research on Evaluation, Standards, and Student Testing.

Taylor, D. (1990). Teaching without testing. *English Education, 22*(1), 4–74.

Taylor, D. (1991). *Learning denied.* Portsmouth, NH: Heinemann.

Taylor, D. (1993). *From the child's point of view.* Portsmouth, NH: Heinemann.

Taylor, D., & Dorsey-Gaines, C. (1988). *Growing up literate: Learning from inner-city families.* Portsmouth, NH: Heinemann.

Tiles, J. E. (1988). *Dewey.* New York: Routledge.

Voigt, C. (1985). *Jackaroo.* New York: Ballantine.

Vygotsky, L. S. (1978). *Mind in society.* Cambridge, MA: Harvard University Press. (Original work published 1935)

Wells, G., & Chang-Wells, G. (1992). *Constructing knowledge together: Classrooms as centers of inquiry and literacy.* Portsmouth, NH: Heinemann.

Westbrook, R. B. (1991). *John Dewey and American democracy.* Ithaca, NY: Cornell University Press.

Wood, P., Bruner, J., & Ross, G. (1976). The role of tutoring in problem solving. *Journal of Child Psychology and Psychiatry, 17*(1), 60–66.

Index

About the Author

Jim Garrison is professor of philosophy of education at Virginia Tech in Blacksburg, Virginia. His specialty is the philosophy of John Dewey. Jim has recently edited a collection of essays on Dewey's philosophy of education (*The New Scholarship on Dewey*, 1995) and is a member of the Board of Directors of the John Dewey Society. His interests include a large number of specialties in the field of education and in the last two years has published articles in journals of physical education, instructional technology, educational administration, secondary English education, and science education. Jim continues to spend time in schools and particularly enjoys the elementary school reading and writing workshop, even though the children no longer trust his spelling and grammar.